a **LIVING** | **FREE** guide

Disaster Preparedness

Rod Brouhard, EMT-P, and Crystal Kline, MEP

ALPHA

A member of Penguin Group (USA) Inc.

ALPHA BOOKS

Published by Penguin Group (USA) Inc.

Penguin Group (USA) Inc., 375 Hudson Street, New York, New York 10014, USA • Penguin Group (Canada), 90 Eglinton Avenue East, Suite 700, Toronto, Ontario M4P 2Y3, Canada (a division of Pearson Penguin Canada Inc.) • Penguin Books Ltd., 80 Strand, London WC2R 0RL, England • Penguin Ireland, 25 St. Stephen's Green, Dublin 2, Ireland (a division of Penguin Books Ltd.) • Penguin Group (Australia), 250 Camberwell Road, Camberwell, Victoria 3124, Australia (a division of Pearson Australia Group Pty. Ltd.) • Penguin Books India Pvt. Ltd., 11 Community Centre, Panchsheel Park, New Delhi—110 017, India • Penguin Group (NZ), 67 Apollo Drive, Rosedale, North Shore, Auckland 1311, New Zealand (a division of Pearson New Zealand Ltd.) • Penguin Books (South Africa) (Pty.) Ltd., 24 Sturdee Avenue, Rosebank, Johannesburg 2196, South Africa • Penguin Books Ltd., Registered Offices: 80 Strand, London WC2R 0RL, England

International Standard Book Number: 978-1-61564-302-8
Library of Congress Catalog Card Number: 2013945259

16   15   14   8   7   6   5   4   3   2

Interpretation of the printing code: The rightmost number of the first series of numbers is the year of the book's printing; the rightmost number of the second series of numbers is the number of the book's printing. For example, a printing code of 14-1 shows that the first printing occurred in 2014.

Printed in the United States of America

Note: This publication contains the opinions and ideas of its authors. It is intended to provide helpful and informative material on the subject matter covered. It is sold with the understanding that the authors and publisher are not engaged in rendering professional services in the book. If the reader requires personal assistance or advice, a competent professional should be consulted.

The authors and publisher specifically disclaim any responsibility for any liability, loss, or risk, personal or otherwise, which is incurred as a consequence, directly or indirectly, of the use and application of any of the contents of this book.

Trademarks: All terms mentioned in this book that are known to be or are suspected of being trademarks or service marks have been appropriately capitalized. Alpha Books and Penguin Group (USA) Inc. cannot attest to the accuracy of this information. Use of a term in this book should not be regarded as affecting the validity of any trademark or service mark.

Most Alpha books are available at special quantity discounts for bulk purchases for sales promotions, premiums, fund-raising, or educational use. Special books, or book excerpts, can also be created to fit specific needs. For details, write: Special Markets, Alpha Books, 375 Hudson Street, New York, NY 10014.

Publisher: *Mike Sanders*

Executive Managing Editor: *Billy Fields*

Senior Acquisitions Editor: *Brook Farling*

Development Editorial Supervisor: *Christy Wagner*

Senior Production Editor: *Janette Lynn*

Cover/Book Designer: *Rebecca Batchelor*

Indexer: *Tonya Heard*

Layout: *Brian Massey*

Proofreader: *Louise Lund*

Cover Images:
Weather Radio: © Shutterstock/Charlie Hutton
Flashlight: © Masterfile
Water Bottles: © Masterfile
Stormy Field: © SuperStock

This book is dedicated to the men and women who respond to natural and man-made disasters all over the globe, taking time away from their families and putting themselves at great personal risk. —Rod

This book is dedicated to the many thousands of disaster survivors around the world, including the first responders, civilian and military, who heed the call to put themselves in harm's way to rescue others (thank you, BT), and whose memory banks hold too many things that can never be unseen. —Crystal

Contents

Foreword

When I first heard that Rod and Crystal, two emergency preparedness experts, were writing a book about personal preparedness, I was thrilled. I knew their combined 35 years of practical experience would result in a commonsense approach rather than simply theory, which is found in so many preparedness books.

I first learned of Crystal Kline through the City of Tulsa's very innovative and nationally known disaster prevention program, Project Impact. Tulsa was already known for its award-winning benchmark storm water management program. As a Project Impact community, it moved further ahead in its goal to create a disaster-resistant community. In forging creative and innovative public/private partnerships, it built a significant awareness of disaster preparedness among the community.

Tulsa Project Impact inspired true community engagement, and that was the key to its success. The citizens were a vital part of this initiative; without their enthusiasm, input, and hard work, it would have failed. Kline's contribution in building that partnership was significant.

She has worked with organizations in testing their response plans, and she has taken her expertise to Haiti along with my firm, Witt O'Brien's, where as part of the JP/Haiti Relief Organization and the Clinton Global Initiative, she developed curriculum and worked with a team to train residents of Haiti's largest tent city to become their own first responders after a disaster.

Rod Brouhard also is a professional from the trenches. As a paramedic for more than 20 years, he has seen firsthand what happens to individuals who are not in a position to take care of themselves for the first 72 hours after an incident.

During my 8 years at FEMA, we handled 373 major disasters, including the Northridge Earthquake, the bombing of the Murrah Federal Building in Oklahoma City, and the Malibu Wildfires. Since that time, we have built an emergency management company that has helped major organizations and communities with the planning for, response to, and long-term recovery from many of the largest disasters in our nation and around the world.

During that time, I have noticed that in a crisis, people may respond in ways you would not expect. During a disaster, you see the best and the worst in people—most particularly, in the way they respond during the moment of crisis. Some manage better than others, and not necessarily the ones you would expect. The common difference seems to be in how well prepared they are for the unexpected.

A 2009 Citizen Corps National Survey demonstrated that a majority of people rely on emergency responders (fire, police, and rescue) in the first 72 hours of a disaster. However, findings show that in the initial response, those individuals are too involved in actual search and rescue to handle the immediate needs of most of the public. This highlights the need for personal responsibility.

Growing up in rural Arkansas, I used to hear the saying, "If the ox is in the ditch …." The unfinished part of that was "you get in the ditch and get him out." In 1993, the federal standard for managing disasters was to get the ox out of the ditch. But I felt it would be much better and more cost effective to build a fence so the ox wouldn't get in the ditch in the first place.

One of the major ways emergency management has grown is in its success in building fences. Not only have local, state, and federal government learned to build fences, but they have seen the value in teaching their citizens to build fences as well. Today, thousands of training courses are available, as are websites, columns, blogs, books, and videos, all with the mission of making the average business owner, homeowner, school, and family better equipped to meet disasters.

This book is, to some degree, a result of the hard work of many, many people over the past 20 years. It is a book about disasters, about survivors, and about how you can better prepare your family to come through crises. It is an important book in that it highlights the essential role individuals play in their own disaster preparedness.

It is, by its nature, a book about taking responsibility. About being true to yourself and to those for whom you are responsible. I hope that as you read through it, you will be inspired by the real-life stories of people who weathered disasters. Some were more prepared than others, but all survived. They have taken the extraordinarily courageous action of telling their stories; exposing themselves in the hope that their ordeals can be used to help others.

I hope you will honor their courage by reading their stories and then following the commonsense, practical guidance this book offers. Because all the preparedness courses and books in the world won't help if we don't take action, take responsibility, and help ourselves.

Let's get busy and build some fences.

James Lee Witt
Director, Federal Emergency Management Agency (1993–2001)
Executive Chairman of the Board, Witt O'Brien's

Introduction

In 2005, Lesley Smiley, a single woman in her 50s, found herself in a hotel lobby in New Orleans where, for 6 days, she and many others found shelter from Hurricane Katrina. During that time, she and the other hotel guests and staff rationed food and shared living space that had no ventilation and one bathroom that had no running water. Several pet dogs were among the refugees, too.

Jim Lane was a real estate agent in Joplin, Missouri, in 2011. He was eating with friends when the power went out, and the management announced they were under a tornado warning. Jim and the other diners moved to the restaurant's walk-in cooler. When the storm passed, Jim and his friends returned to the dining room, still dark and without power, and finished their meal.

Seven year-old Billy Bass was playing outside his home in Wichita Falls, Texas, in 1964, when the sirens began to sound at nearby Sheppard Air Force Base, where his father worked. A moment later, Billy's mother appeared and announced that they were under a tornado warning and would be taking shelter. But first, they sat on lawn chairs in the front yard with their neighbors, watching the tornado approach across flat terrain that went on for miles. When the mile-wide F-5 tornado came uncomfortably close to Billy's home, he, his mother, and his sisters retreated to a neighbor's storm shelter to ride out the storm.

Debi Gade is a television news producer on a cable network station on Long Island. When Superstorm Sandy approached in 2012, Debi was at the station covering it while her family endured Sandy's direct fury on Long Beach. With no phone lines available, she had no way of knowing how her husband and two children fared. The next morning, Debi frantically drove to the island, only to find the bridges were closed, blocked by National Guardsmen. Debi drove to the next town, parked her car, and walked through the rain to the bridge, only to be told she couldn't pass. Hysterical and determined to find her family, she forced her way past two guardsmen and took off running.

This book is not about surviving the apocalypse. However, in many ways, these and other natural disasters are very similar to what people imagine when they think of the end of the world—the deprivation, horror, and helplessness many experience for days, weeks, or even months. But no bomb, electromagnetic pulse, or other man-made weapon struck New Orleans. It was a hurricane—a hurricane experts had warned could hit the city for years. In fact, city leaders had discussed such a storm in a disaster preparedness exercise called Hurricane Pam practiced just a year before Katrina hit. (Hurricane Pam was eerily prescient of Hurricane Katrina, which makes it even sadder so many in the city were unprepared.)

The twenty-first century has seen a marked increase in both frequency and intensity of natural disasters compared with earlier centuries. In fact, weather-related disasters leading to major losses have quintupled over the past 30 years. Whether or not the human race is responsible for climate change, it can no longer be denied that the oceans are getting warmer and rising or that the polar ice cap and glaciers are melting. These events, in turn, are impacting our weather cycles.

In 2012, global natural disasters combined to cause economic losses of $200 billion—just above the 10-year average of $187 billion. Superstorm Sandy was the single costliest event of 2012. In the months since Sandy ravaged the United States' eastern seaboard, estimated costs have gone from $20 billion to $65 billion to more than Katrina's final cost, projected to be $125 billion. What's more, Superstorm Sandy killed 254 people. Katrina killed 1,836 people. Haiti's 2010 earthquake cost $20 billion and killed 226,431 people. Southeast Asia's 2004 tsunami cost $17 billion and killed 230,000 people.

Natural disasters are becoming more frequent and more intense. They are costing more in terms of lives, property, and overall economic losses to communities and society as a whole. Although natural disasters can't be prevented, you can plan and prepare yourself ahead of time to minimize or even prevent the damage to your home—and your life.

In this book, we highlight common disasters and explain how you can best prepare for them. This is not a handbook for surviving a nuclear attack. We don't include instructions on how to grow your own nonhybrid crops, or how to fend off attacks from neighboring communities who want your food and water. We don't offer suggestions on liquidating your assets and buying gold. We do, however, include sections on what to do about contaminated water resulting from a storm or earthquake. We share tips on putting together a family preparedness kit. And we offer ideas on how you can get involved with your local Community Emergency Response Team in the event that you and your neighbors have to be the first responders on the scene until the official first responders arrive.

We also explore planning for both evacuations and sheltering in place, and how to communicate to the outside world. We look at testing your family preparedness plans with drills and exercises as well as and how to stock up on the supplies you need. We review the various types of assistance offered after a disaster; give advice on staying safe in the first moments and days after a disaster, and explain how unsolicited volunteers and donations can do more harm than good. We address how to cope with stress; go over special needs, medical needs, and sheltering issues, as well as offer pointers on building back stronger and smarter.

Disasters happen. That's just a fact of life. Widespread disasters that impact entire communities can rarely, if ever, be prevented. However, you can lessen the impact they have on you and your family. With the realistic scenarios presented in these pages, along with instructions on how to prepare for those scenarios, you'll be much better equipped to respond to—and recover from— storms, fires, floods, and other horrific events.

It's far too easy to get complacent and believe disasters won't happen to *you* and only happen to other people ... until they happen to you. Only in the first 72 hours after a disaster do you really understand the need to plan and prepare. Once those 72 hours are gone, your life begin to approach something similar to normal and complacency returns.

If you're going to survive more frequent and more intense natural disasters; if you're going to survive the occasional chemical spill or house fire; if you're going to survive this thing called life, you must expect the unexpected, anticipate the unanticipated, and think about the unthinkable.

And *prepare.*

How to Use This Book

We've divided this book into several parts, each of which helps you that much more as you prepare you for disasters or hazards you might face. Sidebars sprinkled throughout the text share more of what we have to teach you and what we feel you need to know.

We've also included numerous checklists, forms, and worksheets throughout the book. Look for them on the last pages of the appropriate chapters to find the information you need. We hope you'll find these pages invaluable as you educate and prepare yourself for surviving the storms of life.

Acknowledgments

My wife, Melanie; my daughter, Marie; and our dogs put up with my absences—both physical and cerebral—for long stretches, and I thank and love them dearly for it. Special thanks to all our real-life subjects for bearing their souls about such vulnerable times of their lives. I'd like to extend a special thank you to my co-author, Crystal. You made this book what it is. —Rod

I would like to express my infinite gratitude to Ann Patton, Roger Jolliff, and Kim Fuller. Thank you for introducing me to the fascinating world of emergency management and for always believing in me. Thanks to Josh and Lindsay Kline for your patience while I was tied to on my laptop. And thank you to disaster survivors Lesley Smiley, Debi Gade, Jim Lane, and Billy Bass for sharing your stories, exposing your pain, and tearing at old wounds in order to help others. —Crystal

1

Before Disaster Strikes

It seems that hardly a day goes by when we don't hear of a disaster—natural or man-made—occurring abroad, a few states away, or even across town. Disasters and hazards are so unpredictable, the value of planning ahead cannot be underestimated. For proof, all you have to do is look at the structural, physical, emotional, and economic tolls communities and families face after failing to prepare for the worst.

By picking up this book, you recognize the need to plan for worst-case scenarios. The very fact that you're thinking about it shows commendable foresight, but simply thinking about it isn't enough.

In Part 1, we talk about planning. We go over the types of information you need for your plan, discuss when to evacuate and when to shelter in place, and also tell you how to prepare your family's preparedness kit. We explore some of the tools and supplies you need, share advice on building a financial preparedness kit, explain how to protect your important documents, and go over some essential information on preparing your house for the approaching hazard.

1

Making a Survival Plan

On August 26, 2005, Lesley Smiley began her drive home from the Orleans Parish Civil District Courthouse, where she worked as a researcher. It was Friday night in New Orleans. Single and in her 50s, Lesley was looking forward to a relaxing weekend with friends after a short Saturday shift at her second job. New Orleans Saints fans were converging on the Superdome with their traditional chants of "Who dat?" and the hot, humid air carried the sounds of live music as street musicians settled into their regular Friday night spots. All across the Big Easy, residents and tourists alike were preparing for a typical weekend night.

Meanwhile, in the Florida Panhandle, people were making preparations of a different sort. For the past week, Hurricane Katrina had been varying in intensity between a tropical storm and a Category 1 hurricane, and it was destined to make landfall in Pensacola.

But that was Florida, which is surrounded by water and often sees a number of such storms. It had been decades since New Orleans had taken a direct hit from a hurricane. Sure, it had suffered damage from hurricanes that made landfall nearby, such as Georges in 1998 and Ivan in 2004. But the last hurricane to wreak devastation on New Orleans had been Hurricane Camille in 1965, and even that wasn't a direct hit.

Camille made landfall as a Category 5 hurricane, but the scope and intensity of her destruction was credited in part to the fact that she arrived with very little warning. The storm was predicted to make landfall in the Florida Panhandle, but it never took its expected eastern turn and, as a result, less than 50 percent of the population west of Pass Christian evacuated. Because she caught so many unprepared, Camille became the third-deadliest hurricane in the twentieth century.

That was in 1969; this was 2005. Meteorology had improved so much over the last several decades. What were the chances that another hurricane would hit New Orleans with so little warning? Meteorologists had been watching Hurricane Katrina throughout the week, and the storm was predicted to hit the Florida Panhandle by late Sunday or early Monday.

But as Lesley drove toward her home in the West Bank, she heard a radio news report that made her stomach sink. Nearby Plaquemines Parish had been placed under a mandatory evacuation order. Hurricane Katrina would barely miss the Florida Panhandle, and the storm was heading straight for New Orleans.

When Disaster Looms

Lesley had lived in New Orleans for 15 years. She had experienced tropical storms and some hurricane activity, but the short notice of this warning stunned her. By 6 P.M., Katrina's sudden shift toward New Orleans with an expected Category 5 strength was all over the news.

Lesley remembers conflicting feelings of denial and an urgency to come up with a survival plan. She called several friends, but no one answered. She began to seriously consider her options, and the outlook wasn't good. "I knew my car wouldn't make it to Baton Rouge because it had a cracked radiator," she remembers. So she went through the Yellow Pages, calling car rental companies to see if any vehicles were available—and pushing back the sense of urgency that was getting a little too close to panic.

PREPARATION SAVES LIVES

We cannot stop natural disasters but we can arm ourselves with knowledge: so many lives wouldn't have to be lost if there was enough disaster preparedness.

—Petra Němcová, Czech model, author, and philanthropist injured in Thailand during a tsunami that killed her fiancé, photographer Simon Atlee, after the 2004 Indian Ocean earthquake

---

A native of Tulsa, Oklahoma, Lesley knew from experience the vital significance of being prepared for disasters. Tulsa has seen everything from tornadoes, to ice storms, to wildfires, to floods. Living in Tornado Alley, Tulsans must be ready at a moment's notice when warned to take shelter from an approaching tornado.

But tornadoes are vastly different from hurricanes. A tornado touches down, does its damage, and is quickly gone. A hurricane lasts hours—sometimes even days. And a hurricane often packs wind speeds just as fast and powerful as any tornado.

The one advantage a hurricane has over a tornado is its advance warning. A tornado might be spotted in time to give as much as 20 minutes' advance warning. (The average lead time is 13 minutes.) According to the National Oceanic and Atmospheric Administration (NOAA), preparedness actions are difficult to take with hurricanes once winds reach tropical storm force. Hurricane warnings are issued 36 hours in advance of those expected tropical storm–force winds. New Orleans did not get 36 hours' advance notice of the tropical storm–force winds that preceded Katrina's landfall.

Lesley's upbringing in Tornado Alley was a huge benefit when Katrina veered toward New Orleans. She knew she needed to have a plan.

AWARENESS ISN'T ENOUGH

Having enough awareness to know you need a plan and actually taking the actions to develop one are two completely different things.

No rental cars were available. It was late, and Lesley had to work the next day. Work had not been called off yet, and Lesley hoped against hope that it wouldn't have to be. She went to bed with no solid plan in mind for how she was going to escape Katrina.

The Importance of Advance Planning

Disasters happen—and they don't wait until you're prepared for them. How well you come through a disaster could depend on how prepared you are when it strikes.

Planning for a disaster is similar to planning for any of life's contingencies. You know there's a possibility you might someday experience health issues, so you purchase health insurance. Or to avoid leaving the cost of your medical bills or funeral to loved ones or bickering about your estate, you purchase life insurance, write a will, and leave instructions on how you want your money and possessions divided.

Planning for a disaster is no different. It's a responsibility you should take as seriously as purchasing insurance—even more so, in fact, because proper planning could save your life. Your plan doesn't have to be detailed and complicated. It can be as simple as "When you hear the sirens, get into the shelter."

Billy Bass was almost 7 years old on April 3, 1964. He remembers the day was warm, and he and his sisters spent much of it playing outside in their Wichita Falls, Texas, yard.

Then his mother, who had heard the sirens from nearby Sheppard Air Force Base, came outside and announced that a tornado was coming. Before seeking shelter, however, Billy, along with his mother and his sisters, joined their neighbors already watching the tornado approach.

"The area was flat and hilly," Billy remembers. "You could see [the storm] coming …. It was a mile wide. Enormous. We watched it for several miles …. When it got to within about a mile of us, … things got dead still. There were no sounds of animals, of birds chirping—it just got dead still … without so much as a breeze blowing. And you could actually feel the pressure, … it was like it was sucking the air out of your mouth. The air became a kind of green, a real eerie color." At that point, Billy's mother ushered the family into the storm shelter.

Billy's house was damaged, but it survived the storm. His neighborhood lost more than 100 homes that day, and throughout Wichita Falls, the tornado left 7 dead and more than 100 injured, destroyed about 225 homes and businesses, and caused approximately $15 million in property damage. Meteorologists rated the tornado an F-5 on the *Fujita scale*.

DEFINITION

The **Fujita scale** (F-scale) is a method of measuring or rating tornado intensity, based on the damage inflicted on buildings and vegetation. It was replaced with the Enhanced Fujita scale (EF-scale) in 2007.

In the 1960s, folks were advised to crack open windows in their homes and cars to alleviate the pressure a tornado caused. That idea has long been debunked—cracking the windows actually generates a *lifting* force, making it *easier* for the storm to rip off the roof of a house or pick up a car. But in 1964, the idea of cracking the windows to normalize the pressure seemed to make sense.

So when the sirens went off, Billy's father, who was at the nearby Air Force base, went out to crack the windows on his car—locking himself outside the building in the process. Unable to get back inside the building, he rode out the tornado in his car.

The base took a direct hit, and the tornado picked up Billy's father's car and turned it nearly 360 degrees without rolling it over. A great deal of dust got sucked into the car, and Billy's father came home covered in mud but otherwise unharmed.

Billy's family had experienced several tornadoes before this one, and their plan was simple: take shelter and ride it out. Had they not been prepared with a plan, the outcome could have been far worse for all of them.

In this chapter, we help you put together your own plan so you're not caught unprepared when warning sirens go off.

Communication Is Key

A family preparedness plan is just that: a *family* preparedness plan. It's vitally important that each member of your family participates in and contributes to your plan and that each member feels a sense of ownership over the planning process. Otherwise, they might not be familiar enough with it to actually use it when the time comes. Or fear might lock them in their tracks. Fear of the unknown is one of the biggest barriers to getting through a disaster smoothly.

Schedule a series of family meetings in which you discuss the hazards your family faces—fires, tornadoes, earthquakes, severe thunderstorms, and other potential hazards that could hit your area—as well as the various components of your plan. Communicate with each other, but also communicate with yourself. It's vitally important to be realistic about the risks you face and about your responsibility to prepare for them.

CHILDREN AND DISASTERS

Children can be sensitive and frightened by the various what-ifs you'll discuss during your planning meetings. Remember, by talking about drills as games, and with the use of play and pretend, this planning time can also give them a feeling of empowerment and control.

Plan for each possible hazard to take place at anytime during the day or night, and take into account that each member of your family might be in different locations such as home, school, work, or a friend's house. Come up with a plan for how and where to meet after a disaster.

It's important that all family members have memorized names, addresses, and phone numbers, so you can get in touch with one another if you're separated. Cell towers may be overwhelmed or completely disabled after a disaster, and making phone calls on your cell phone could be difficult at best. In some situations, cell phones might not be able to send or receive local calls, but can receive them from out of state. So have an out-of-state friend or relative designated for everyone to check in with to ensure everyone is okay.

Even though your ability to make phone calls may be hampered, it may still be possible to text because texting is done on a different frequency. So if your calling capability is cut off, your phone might still be able to send and receive texts.

Assessing Your Risks

One of the first steps to developing your family's disaster plan is identifying your local risks and vulnerabilities. Knowing what disasters you're likely to face means you can successfully plan and prepare for possible outcomes.

For example, do you live in an area at high risk for earthquakes? Do you live in Tornado Alley, or maybe in a coastal area where hurricanes and tropical storms are common? Do you live near a body of water such as a lake or river? Even a small creek nearby could put you at risk of flooding.

Perhaps you live in an area that puts you at risk for man-made disasters—close to oil refineries or chemical plants, for instance. Or do you live or work near a railroad that transports many dangerous chemicals through your community on a frequent basis?

Make a list of your family's potential hazards. And think about what other hazards you might encounter—oil spill? refinery explosion?—and add these to your list, too (see "Worksheet: Your Family Survival Plan" at the end of this chapter).

OVERPLAN RATHER THAN UNDERPLAN

It might seem excessive to plan for each and every hazard or disaster you could encounter. But remember, it's better to overplan for potential disasters than be caught off guard by something you didn't consider and, therefore, plan for.

Thinking about the possibilities and discussing them together as a family helps you take ownership over what happens. It gives you a sense of security, of control in circumstances that are generally beyond your control. No plan will be perfect; there will always be bumps and glitches, unforeseen and unexpected. However, planning, preparing, and discussing these things gives you an advantage and a level of peace and security. The ability to remain calm and in control, and to act quickly and with purpose when necessary, are valuable benefits of taking the time to plan and prepare.

Evacuate or Stay Put?

Saturday, Lesley and the other employees were sent home after only a couple hours. At that point, she felt as though her options were closing in on her. With none of her friends answering their phones, and no rental cars available, Lesley knew she had to evacuate, but to where?

Using the Yellow Pages again as her guide, she began calling every hotel in the area. After several solid hours of calling, she finally found a hotel that had vacancies and reserved a room for two nights.

"That's what people do if there's a hurricane," she says. "They go the route of *vertical evacuation.* They go to a high-rise hotel, taking just enough pieces of clothing and personal items for about two days. Because they figure, okay, it's going to hit, and there's going to be a lot of glass, and it will take the city possibly two, three, or four days to clean it up. But you know that's not what happened."

Lesley moved what furnishings she could to interior rooms, away from the windows. She also removed her curtains so they wouldn't get wet and mold. And then she made her way to her hotel.

DEFINITION

Vertical evacuation means to move to a higher floor or ground, to get as far above sea level as possible. For Lesley, that meant staying in a hotel above the projected water surge. In a tsunami, it means going as far inland and upward as possible, as quickly as possible.

When you have your list of risks—natural and man-made—your next step is to think about each separately and ask yourself, "When this disaster occurs, do I evacuate, or do I shelter in place?" Add the answer to this question to your survival plan (see "Worksheet: Your Family Survival Plan" at the end of this chapter).

The following sections offer an at-a-glance look at where you should weather out a storm or other hazard—at home or inside another structure, or completely away from the danger zone. Chapter 9 offers much more in-depth information and specifics for different kinds of disasters, so be sure to review that chapter, too. And for further guidance on how to prepare for risks, check out the Federal Emergency Management Agency's (FEMA) site, fema.gov; FEMA's ready.gov, and The American Red Cross's readyrating.org.

If you have any doubts on the appropriate plan of action, your local news or emergency management should have instructions. These are often given via television, radio, and warning sirens; NOAA weather radios; and even social media.

If your community emergency management officials or meteorologists tell you to take cover immediately, do exactly as they say. The same is true for instructions to evacuate. These aren't suggestions made casually. Your safety and well-being are too important to disobey.

Earthquakes

When an earthquake hits, how you should respond depends on where you are. If you're indoors, get on the floor, take cover under something sturdy, and stay protected until the earthquake is over. If you're outside, stay outside, and move away from buildings, power lines, and other potential hazards.

NATIONWIDE HAZARD

We tend to think of earthquakes as being a West Coast hazard, but 45 states are at high-to-moderate risk for earthquakes. The New Madrid fault line responsible for the 1811 New Madrid earthquake that shook homes as far away as Washington, D.C., stretches southwest from New Madrid, Missouri, and has the potential to affect Missouri, Arkansas, Illinois, Indiana, Kentucky, Tennessee, and Mississippi.

Extreme Heat

In extreme summer heat, stay inside as much as possible and keep your body cool and damp. Turn on the air conditioner or fans, and take cool baths to keep your temperature from rising with the thermometer outside.

If you must be outside, try to stay in the shade as much as possible. Wear wide-brimmed hats, use sunscreen, and continually drink water.

HEAT WAVE

The heat wave of summer 2012 killed 82 people in the United States and Canada. July 2012 was the hottest month in U.S. history, with average high temperatures soaring above 100°F (38°C).

Fires

If your home is on fire, and you can't quickly put out the fire with a fire extinguisher, get out. To avoid potential smoke inhalation, drop to the ground and crawl your way out if you have to. If your clothes catch on fire, stop, drop, and roll back and forth until the fire is out.

If wildfires are burning in your area, pay attention to local emergency instructions. If you're told to evacuate, do it. If you're not instructed to leave, and you plan on sheltering in place, keep an eye on local reports. Wildfires can change directions quickly. Also check your roof and surrounding yard regularly for sparks or burning embers that could erupt into flame.

Floods

When floodwaters begin to rise, so should you—get to higher ground. Evacuation versus shelter in place depends on where you are.

Generally speaking, most emergency management professionals advise staying indoors. If you're inside a multistory building, go to higher floors using the stairs, not the elevator.

And never, *ever* drive on water-covered roads.

BEWARE WATER-COVERED ROADS

On Memorial Day weekend 1984, Tulsa, Oklahoma, experienced thunderstorms that dumped 12 inches of rain within just a few hours. Most Tulsans were unprepared for the storms because meteorologists had predicted a beautiful and sunny weekend. The flooding caused $180 million in damages and killed 14 people. All 14 were killed while driving on water-covered roadways.

Hurricanes

With hurricanes, the best thing to do is evacuate. If you can't evacuate, shelter in place.

As mentioned earlier, hurricanes differ drastically from tornadoes in the amount of notice given. There's a pretty big difference between 13 minutes and 36 hours before tropical storm–force winds arrive.

Tornadoes

In the case of a tornado, shelter in place—unless you live in a mobile/manufactured home. If you're in a mobile/manufactured home, go to the nearest storm shelter immediately.

MOBILITY = VULNERABILITY

The very thing that makes mobile/manufactured homes mobile—their lightweight structure unattached to a foundation—is what makes them so vulnerable during tornadoes. In the March 12, 2012, tornadoes that struck Kentucky and Indiana, 24 people were killed inside mobile/manufactured homes that were slammed, tossed, flipped, or crumbled. That number represents a full two thirds of the total of 34 people killed. Emergency managers are loathe to encourage people to leave one shelter for another during a tornado warning, but they highly recommend it if you're in a mobile/manufactured home.

Winter Storms

Obviously, stay indoors if you can, and stay as warm and dry as possible by layering on clothes and blankets.

If a winter storm catches you in your car, stay in your car. Turn on your hazard lights, and get out of the way of traffic but somewhere where you can still be seen. Don't get out of your car and walk in a blizzard unless a shelter is within just a few steps.

Man-Made Disasters

When referring to a tornado or other natural disaster, "sheltering in place" means staying inside a safe shelter as opposed to fleeing the area. However, when referring to a man-made disaster, such as a chemical spill, shelter-in-place has a slightly different meaning.

When dealing with a release of chemicals or other hazardous materials, you should move inside a safe structure and close and lock all doors and windows until given the all-clear by emergency personnel. This means you don't leave to pick up your children from school, go home, or do anything else but stay put. (The school will be sheltering in place also, and won't let you in anyway.) Be sure to close all ventilation systems, too. Be alert to emergency personnel going door-to-door giving the all-clear or providing instructions in case the situation changes.

If you believe you have been exposed to a dangerous chemical, call 911 or your local emergency response number, and seek medical help as quickly as possible.

PREPAREDNESS AWAY FROM HOME

It's important for you and your family to be prepared at home, but you don't spend all your time at home. Find out what preparedness plans are in place at your place of work and at your child's school. If none are currently in place, urge your office's facility maintenance department or your child's school to develop such plans. Your insistence could save lives.

Practice Makes Perfect

You can make exercises and drills fun for children by presenting them as play and pretend. By practicing the steps your family will take during specific events, children learn how to respond when the time comes. Be very clear that drills are only play, you're not in danger, and everyone is and will remain safe throughout the process.

Practice evacuations for fires and hurricanes, and practice sheltering in place for earthquakes and tornadoes. Make a game of practicing "stop, drop, and roll" for fires and "drop, cover, and hold on" for earthquakes. Discuss the best place in the home to go to during a tornado warning, and time the children to see who can get there the fastest. Be sure that if your children are ever home alone during a warning, that they know what the signals are for sheltering in place and they know to go to an upper floor for flooding and to a basement, an inner room with no windows or outer walls, or a safe room for tornadoes.

Teach your children how and when to dial 911 (also be sure they know when *not* to dial 911), and help them memorize your names, address, and phone numbers as soon as they're able to learn them. This will help reunite family members in the case of separation during a disaster.

Practice power outages by turning off the lights. Be sure everyone knows where the emergency preparedness kit is and how to use a flashlight.

Be sure everyone knows where the smoke alarms are located and recognize the sound they make. Use the smoke alarms to kick off your fire drills. Be sure each family member knows where the fire extinguishers are kept and how to use them. Practice using the fire extinguishers on imaginary fires. (Don't start a real fire for the purpose of extinguishing it.)

Practicing, playing, and pretending your family is responding to a disaster creates a much better chance each one of you will survive a real-life disaster. Your family plan will consist of more than a list of hazards and a schedule for drills. To be effective, it needs to address how you will communicate with each other; prearranged meeting places; phone numbers of workplaces, schools, and doctors; insurance information; Social Security numbers; and many other important pieces of information that will be extremely valuable in the case of a catastrophe. If certain family members have special needs, address those needs in your plan. If you have pets, include them, too.

Account for everything and everyone. You can never be *too* prepared.

Creating Your Plan

You can create your survival plan in any number of ways, from writing it down and posting it on the refrigerator to holding a family meeting to discuss your options and deciding on a course of action for every potential disaster your family faces.

Keep the information current, updating it once a year when, for example, you change the battery in your smoke detector.

Store your survival plan in a safe place, such as a safe-deposit box in a bank in another town. (Be sure to record the bank contact information and safe-deposit box number as well.) If you have a safe room, store a copy of your plan there, too, inside a fire-proof safe or a metal box.

Each family member should keep a copy of it at his or her place of work and in his or her car, and each child should keep a copy in his or her school backpack. This information also should be stored on each family member's smartphone, laptop, and tablet.

Above all, be sure everyone knows what to do in case of an emergency, whether they're home or out of the house, at work, at school, at a neighbor's, etc.

Worksheet: Your Family Survival Plan

Use this worksheet to map out your family's survival plan.

Plans for Potential Hazards

Thinking about and planning for the natural disasters and hazards you could encounter makes you better prepared for if and when something does happen.

Natural Disaster/Local Hazard	Evacuate or Shelter in Place?

Family Meetings, Drills, and Meeting Places

Schedule your meetings during times when your family is all together—at the dinner table during dessert or an evening snack perhaps. During those meetings, discuss your reconciliation plans—how you will communicate and where you all will meet after a disaster. Likewise, when scheduling and planning drills, each family member needs to participate either in the planning or the play. Their participation during each step of the process ensures that the information thrown at them during the real thing is "old data," which will take less time to process.

Family meetings to discuss the survival plan are scheduled for:

Family disaster drills and exercises are scheduled for:

_____

_____

_____

In case the family is separated during a disaster, our predetermined meeting place is:

_____

_____

_____

Family Contact Information

Include information for each family member here. (Add more as needed for additional family members.) If you live alone, add contact information of close friends as well as family who live elsewhere.

Father's workplace: _____

Address: _____

Phone: _____

Father's cell phone: _____

Father's email: _____

Social media URLs: _____

_____

_____

Mother's workplace: _____

Address: _____

Phone: _____

Mother's cell phone: _____

Mother's email: _____

Social media URLs: _____

_____

_____

Child's school or workplace: _____

Address: _____

Phone: _____

Child's cell phone: _____

Child's email: _____

Social media URLs: _____

_____

School teacher or main contact person: _____

Teacher's email: _____

School website: _____

School social media URL: _____

What's the school's disaster plan?

_____

_____

_____

What are the procedures for parent/child reconciliation?

_____

_____

Is there a shelter on the school campus? Where do teachers and students go to shelter in place? What are the evacuation plans?

_____

_____

_____

Child's school or workplace: _____

Address: _____

Phone: _____

Child's cell phone: _____

Child's email: _____

Social media URLs: _____

_____

School teacher or main contact person: _____

Teacher's email: _____

School website: _____

School social media URL: _____

What's the school's disaster plan?

_____

_____

_____

What are the procedures for parent/child reconciliation?

_____

_____

_____

Is there a shelter on the school campus? Where do teachers and students go to shelter in place? What are the evacuation plans?

_____

_____

_____

Medical and Insurance Information

If you or members of your family are seriously injured or ill and hospitalized as a result of the disaster, having the following information with you can expedite the transfer of medical records to the hospital, resulting in more effective medical care with fewer risks.

Family doctor: _____

Address: _____

Phone: _____

Pediatrician: _____

Address: _____

Phone: _____

Hospital: _____

Address: _____

Phone: _____

Health insurance issuer: _____

Phone: _____

Policy number: _____

Life insurance issuer: _____

Phone: _____

Policy number: _____

Auto insurance issuer: _____

Phone: _____

Policy number: _____

Homeowner's insurance issuer: _____

Phone: _____

Policy number: _____

Property restoration company: _____

Phone: _____

Out-of-State Contacts

List the names of predetermined out-of-state friends or family members to check in with after a disaster.

Name: _____

Phone: _____

Name: _____

Phone: _____

Name: _____

Phone: _____

Name: _____

Phone: _____

Name: _____

Phone: _____

Safe-Deposit Box Information

If you have a safe-deposit box, make a note of the bank in which it's located along with the box number.

Safe-deposit box bank branch: _____

Safe-deposit box number: _____

Emergency Pet Shelter

If you have pets, you need to prepare in advance for their survival during a disaster. If you can keep your pets with you, by all means do so. If you need to provide alternate shelter at a friend's or family member's, record that information. Some hotels accept pets, and these might be alternative options for shelter during a storm.

Friend or family pet-sitter: _____

Phone: _____

Or:

Pet-friendly hotel: _____

Address: _____

Phone: _____

Pet-friendly hotel: _____

Address: _____

Phone: _____

Pet-friendly hotel: _____

Address: _____

Phone: _____

Social Security Numbers

Keep the following confidential information in a safe-deposit box or safe. Do not distribute copies in children's backpacks or at work for risk of identity theft.

Social Security numbers of each family member:

Name: _____

SS#: _____

Name: _____

SS#: _____

Name: _____

SS#: _____

Name: _____

SS#: _____

Name: _____

SS#: _____

2

—— ◦◦◦ ——

Your Family Preparedness Kit

As Lesley prepared her apartment for the approaching storm—moving her furnishings to the back of her apartment, removing the drapes, and taping the windows—she also quickly went through her files and grabbed all her important papers and documents. She put them in a plastic box and placed the box in the trunk of her car before she left for the hotel room she'd booked.

Fortunately, Lesley was able to ride out the storm and immediate aftermath in the hotel. Also lucky for her, her car was protected during the storm in the hotel's interior parking structure, and her papers were still there weeks later when she went back to get her car.

But what if Lesley hadn't been able to book that hotel room? What if she was forced to evacuate elsewhere? And what if she hadn't been able to find that interior spot for her car? What if she had parked outdoors? In all likelihood, she would have lost her car and the documents stored inside.

Lesley needed a plan, and she needed a preparedness kit.

The Importance of a Preparedness Kit

In Chapter 1, you learned how to create your family's survival plan before a disaster strikes. But planning is only a part of your disaster preparedness efforts. You also need to test your family's plan with drills and have a family preparedness kit assembled and at the ready the moment a hazard occurs.

A kit is necessary whether you evacuate or shelter in place. You'll be grateful for it when access to fresh water is cut off and you have plenty in your kit, or when the ground is covered with glass, nails, or other debris, and you can pull on the boots you packed months ago.

In this chapter, we explain how to assemble a preparedness kit with items that will help you and your family get through the first several days after a disaster. (We look at testing your survival plan by running your family through practice drills in Chapter 6.)

Creating Your Kit

Your kit can be very basic and contain just the essentials you think you need, or it can be very comprehensive and include everything we recommend in this chapter. Building a comprehensive kit can be expensive, so it's best to build it a little at a time. By adding one new item each week, you can slowly assemble a comprehensive family preparedness kit that will be a lifesaver in case of emergency.

You can use anything to house your kit, depending on the amount of items you pack and how many people and pets are in your household. Large plastic lidded totes work well. You might need a few of these, depending on your situation and how comprehensive you make your kit.

Now let's take a look at what you should pack in your family preparedness kit.

Water

Water is one of the most important items you should pack in your kit. But how much is enough? The recommended amount of water for drinking and sanitation is at least 1 gallon of water per person per day for 3 days. So for a family of 4, for example, you'd need a minimum of 12 gallons. Children, nursing mothers, and those suffering some kind of physical illness might need extra, and more could be required for medical emergencies, so pack a few additional gallons.

To be sure you have the safest water in your preparedness kit, use commercially bottled water. Keep it in its original container, and don't open it until necessary. Store the water in a cool, dark place (this might be with your kit or separate from it) until 2 weeks before its expiration date and then rotate it out with a fresh supply.

We're not done with your water concerns yet. In addition to packing commercially bottled water, you might also consider including supplies so you can treat your own water later if need be. For example, you might find yourself in a situation where your home's water supply has been contaminated and you've used all your bottled water. In that case, you'll have to treat your own water, which is easy to do, but you need to prepare for it.

In your preparedness kit, include containers in which to treat your water. Two-liter plastic soft drink bottles work well. Don't use any containers that have stored milk or fruit juice, though. The organic sugars in those liquids can grow bacteria very easily and make the containers quite hard to clean. Don't use glass either. Glass containers are cumbersome and can break or chip, especially in a disaster.

MAKE MINE A DIET, PLEASE

Repurposing diet soda bottles is better than using bottles that held regular soda. The sugar from regular soda is harder to clean from the bottles.

Before packing them, clean and sanitize your containers with dish soap and water and rinse off all the soap. Add a solution of 1 teaspoon unscented liquid chlorine bleach to 1 quart water, and swish it around thoroughly so the solution touches every part of the bottle. Pour out the solution, and rinse the bottle with clean water. Treat the original bottle caps with the same solution, top the bottles, and pack them in your kit until you're ready to fill them.

Be sure to pack some unscented chlorine bleach and an eyedropper in your preparedness kit, too. You'll need them to treat the contaminated water.

To treat water from a well, or water that's been contaminated in some way as a result of the natural disaster or hazard, add 2 drops unscented chlorine bleach to a soda bottle of water (or 8 drops per 1 gallon) in a sanitized bottle, and let it stand for 30 minutes before using. You should be able to notice a slight chlorine smell in the water. If not, add another 2 drops of bleach and let it sit for at least 15 more minutes.

If your tap water is commercially treated with chlorine by your utility company, further treatment is unnecessary unless you're told differently, with reports of broken water or sewage lines.

If you don't want to use bleach to treat your water, you can use chlorine tablets or water purification tablets instead. You can find these at most sporting goods stores. Any water that has not been commercially treated should be replaced every 6 months. If your supplies run low, don't ration. Drink what you need now and find more later. You can minimize your need for water by being less active and staying cool.

Food

In addition to water, food is another essential to pack in your preparedness kit.

Power outages may accompany disasters, and they may last for several days. After the 2007 Tulsa ice storm, for example, most of the city was without power for up to 11 days. Your area may also be vulnerable to a power outage as a result of thunder storms, ice storms, or even just a transformer being hit by a car, so stock enough *nonperishable* food in your preparedness kit to feed your family for at least 3 days. Keep the focus on foods that don't require cooking or refrigeration, such as canned foods or mixes—and don't forget the manual can opener.

Pay attention to the expiration dates on the food you squirrel away. Date your supplies with a marker if the expiration date isn't clearly visible. Be sure to rotate your supply every so often (see the following table for the shelf life of several foods and beverages), placing the older items at the top or in the front, and the new items on bottom or in back, and use the food before it goes bad. And remember, you don't have to do put together a comprehensive kit overnight. Pick up an extra item or two every week while grocery shopping to add a little to your kit at a time.

When adding food to your preparedness kit, keep a few points in mind: first, stay away from foods high in salt or sodium because these foods cause thirst, making you drink more water, and bloating. Pack low-sodium foods to avoid consuming your water too quickly. Along the same line, choose foods high in water content, such as canned fruits, vegetables, and noncondensed soups that don't require water to prepare.

Also choose foods your family will actually want to eat. Although it likely won't be possible to prepare a fabulous dinner with all the trimmings, it is possible to pack foods that appeal to your family's tastes—and maybe even a few fun foods or comfort foods. There will be enough stress involved in recovering from a disaster without adding to it with food no one likes. What's more, familiar foods offer comfort and security during a time when everyone will be feeling a bit insecure and in need of comfort. Some comfort foods high in calories can provide energy, but be sure the food isn't heavy enough to cause sluggishness.

If some of your family members aren't allowed to have sugar, have allergies to wheat, or have other special food requirements, make a point of having enough food packed especially for them (and a little extra for other family members who might think it looks pretty good). You don't want them to run out of food early on, especially if their health depends on their dietary needs.

The following table outlines some nonperishable foods you might want to include in your preparedness kit, along with their shelf life, after which you'll need to replace them. Also see the "Worksheet: Preparedness Kit Checklist" at the end of the chapter for more foodstuff suggestions.

Nonperishable Foodstuff and Their Shelf Life

Foodstuff	Shelf Life
Ready-to-eat canned meat	Within 1 year or before the expiration date
Canned fruit, vegetables, and noncondensed soup	Within 1 year or before the expiration date
Protein, fruit, or granola bars	Within 1 year or before the expiration date
Dry cereal	Within 1 year or before the expiration date
Powdered milk, boxed	Within 6 months
Peanut butter	Within 1 year or before the expiration date
Crackers	Within 6 months
Dried fruit	Within 6 months
Nuts	Within 1 year or before the expiration date
Canned juices	Within 1 year or before the expiration date
Fun or comfort food	Depends on the food; for best results, use before the expiration date
Baby food and liquid formula	Within 1 year or before the expiration date
Nonperishable pet food	Within 1 year or before the expiration date

Don't forget to include a manual can opener for canned food, as well as some napkins, plastic utensils, plates, and cups. Pack zipper-lock bags, airtight containers, and screw-top jars in which to keep food such as cookies, cereal, or crackers; dried fruits; and nuts. It's often difficult to reseal the original bags or boxes after they're opened, and you want to protect them from bugs and vermin.

If any cans are dented or swollen, don't use them. And check everything for spoilage before using it.

For more suggested foods and supplies, see the "Worksheet: Preparedness Kit Checklist" at the end of the chapter.

FEEDING BABY

Even if a mother is nursing, she may be unable to nurse after a disaster or hazard and will need an alternate method of feeding. If this could apply to you or your family, consider packing some commercial baby food and/or liquid formula. Be sure to stock a few sterile baby bottles, too.

Special Needs Items

If you wear prescription eyeglasses, you'll want to account for them in your preparedness kit, too. You might not be able to include a duplicate of the pair you currently wear, but you could include the last pair you had before the ones you currently wear. Something will be better than nothing should you lose or damage your glasses during an emergency.

If you wear contacts, pack an extra pair of lenses in your survival kit. Be sure to label which is for your left eye and which is for your right if the two prescriptions are different. Include a bottle of cleaning solution and a lens case as well.

If you wear hearing aids, be sure to tuck extra batteries in your kit. Pack them in something larger, like a sandwich-size zipper-lock plastic bag, so they don't get lost.

Include several days' worth of your prescription medications in your preparedness kit. Note the expiration date of each prescription, and rotate out your supply a few weeks before the expiration date.

The "Worksheet: Preparedness Kit Checklist" at the end of the chapter lists further items you'll want to consider including.

For Children

It's important that children feel a sense of ownership over the planning process. This helps them feel more secure if a disaster does happen. Have your children help pack the kit by making a game of it. Give them each the same list, and have them go on a scavenger hunt throughout the house looking for items to pack in the kit.

In addition to their favorite nonperishable foods and snacks, add some children's books and games. Be sure to include music-playing devices such as MP3 or DVD players, along with extra batteries, and that they have access to their favorite music.

KIDS AND DISASTERS

Sesame Street's website offers an excellent section on preparedness activities for small children. "Let's Get Ready! Planning Together for Emergencies" offers printable downloads, games, and videos on such important activities for small children as memorizing their full name and helping pack the family preparedness kit. Learn more at sesamestreet.org/parents/topicsandactivities/toolkits/ready.

For Pets

Your pets depend on you for their survival—no less so during and after a disaster. So don't forget to include your pets in your planning and preparedness efforts.

If you must evacuate your home, **never leave your pets behind.** Survival on their own may not be possible. Some of the saddest sights to see after a disaster are the images of pets separated from their owners; lost on the streets with no idea how to get back home or survive on their own.

Keep your pets' tags current and attached to their collar. Be sure they include your name, address, and phone number. Keep a current picture of your pet in your preparedness kit for identification purposes.

Some public shelters may not allow pets, so you need to have a shelter plan in place for them. This will take some time to research. It may be necessary to have friends or family on standby to take you and your pets, if there's time. Another alternative is a hotel. Find out in advance which ones in your area accept pets, and include this information in your preparedness kit. (You probably already did this in Chapter 1, but if not, do so now.)

Your local emergency management agency or animal shelter might have some local information that will help you in planning for your pet's shelter needs.

As part of your family preparedness kit, create a sub-kit for your pet(s). This kit should include nonperishable pet food (remember a can opener if the food is canned!), water, dishes, leashes, litter box and litter, and more. See the "Worksheet: Preparedness Kit Checklist" for more pet supplies you'll need to include.

Other Items to Pack

A well-stocked first-aid kit is essential, as are a few common over-the-counter medications such as pain killers, antacids, etc.

A weather radio is helpful to have during and after a storm or other hazard, so include one in your preparedness kit. Look for one with tone alert. You can also include a standard AM/FM radio. Don't forget the batteries for either of these.

NOAA WEATHER RADIO

When shopping for a weather alert radio, we recommend getting one with the Public Alert and/or NOAA Weather Radio (NWR) All Hazards logo. Many types and styles are available, ranging from $20 to $200. A weather alert radio with Specific Alert Message Encoding (S.A.M.E.) technology enables you to program your watches and alerts specific to your area. NOAA Weather Alert radios are by far the fastest for receiving warnings. Weather alert apps and weather warnings on TV and radio are good alternates for when you're not near a weather radio, but when at home, the weather alert radio gives you the fastest weather warnings and watches.

Be sure to pack a flashlight or two in case you lose power. Pack plenty of batteries, too. You could also include matches and a charged fire extinguisher.

Pack a whistle in your kit, too. This is good to have in case you get trapped under debris or in any way need to get the attention of search and rescue crews.

Stock two complete changes of clothing for each person—one for warm weather and one for cold weather. Include heavy shoes or boots, regardless of weather, because you'll probably have to walk through large areas of debris with broken glass, nails, pieces of wood, etc. Include a blanket or sleeping bag for each person as well—possibly several blankets if you live in a cold climate.

Something you might not think about until you need it: a local map. This will come in very handy after those disasters where a community loses street signs and all markers that make an intersection or block familiar.

See the "Worksheet: Preparedness Kit Checklist" for more necessary items to include in your kit.

Storing Your Kit

You want to store your preparedness kit someplace where it's easy to get to, but where it's not in the way of your everyday life. Store it in an inner room or closet where you go to hide from tornadoes, in your storm shelter, or in a safe room. A basement is also a good place. Wherever it is, be sure it's ready to grab and go.

It's also not a bad idea to have additional kits at work and in your vehicle. After all, you don't know where you'll be when a disaster strikes. At work, be prepared to shelter for at least 24 hours. Include in your kit food, water, medicine, and walking shoes in case you need to walk a long distance in an evacuation. Be sure your kit is in something you can grab and carry easily.

In a winter storm, you could become stranded in your car. Have a kit packed with water and food, especially protein. Nuts and protein bars are good. Be sure you have jumper cables, flashlights with batteries, a first-aid kit, an AM/FM radio so you can hear news reports and emergency messages, kitty litter to give your tires traction in the snow or ice, a shovel, ice scraper, blankets, and warm clothes, including heavy boots. Flares or a reflective triangle are a good idea, too. If you don't already, keep a charger in your car to charge your cell phone. And don't forget supplies for pets and babies—pet food, baby formula, diapers, and wipes—if you have them.

It's possible you could be on your own for the first several days after a widespread disaster and responders are spread thin. Your preparedness kit may be your lifeline in terms of keeping you and your family nourished, hydrated, and secure until responders reach you. The time and resources you spend preparing your kit is an investment for which there may never be a return, but for which, in terms of value, there is no price.

Worksheet: Preparedness Kit Checklist

We can't stress enough the importance of a preparedness kit. Some of the items on this list, such as pet supplies or baby supplies, might not apply to your family, so tailor the list to meet your family's needs. And remember, you don't have to put together your kit overnight. Take your time, add a little each week, and before you know it your kit will be fully stocked.

Nonperishable food and beverages:

- ❑ Bottled water (1 gallon per person per day for 3 days)
- ❑ Canned fruit
- ❑ Canned vegetables
- ❑ Canned meat (tuna, salmon, or chicken—but know the latter has a much shorter shelf life)
- ❑ Canned noncondensed soup (no water necessary to prepare)
- ❑ Protein bars
- ❑ Fruit bars
- ❑ Granola bars
- ❑ Dry cereal
- ❑ Peanut butter
- ❑ Crackers
- ❑ Dried fruit
- ❑ Nuts
- ❑ Canned juices
- ❑ Powdered milk, boxed
- ❑ Fun or comfort foods (cookies, candy, chips, whatever those may be)

Special needs items:

- ❑ Prescription eyeglasses
- ❑ Extra contact lenses
- ❑ Contact lens solution

- ❑ Contact lens case
- ❑ Hearing aid batteries
- ❑ Prescription medication—periodically rotate to prevent expiration
- ❑ Commercial baby food and/or liquid formula
- ❑ Sterile baby bottles
- ❑ Diapers
- ❑ Diaper rash ointment
- ❑ Feminine hygiene supplies

For children:

- ❑ Children's books
- ❑ Children's games
- ❑ Children's music
- ❑ Children's DVDs
- ❑ MP3 player
- ❑ Portable DVD player
- ❑ Extra batteries in various sizes

For your pets:

- ❑ Nonperishable pet food
- ❑ Manual can opener (if you didn't already include one with the people food)
- ❑ Bottled water in addition to what you have for you and your family (1 gallon per day for 3 days for large pets)
- ❑ Food and water dishes
- ❑ Leash, harness, or pet carrier
- ❑ Kitty litter and litter box
- ❑ Pet first-aid kit
- ❑ Pet medications
- ❑ Veterinarian records
- ❑ Current picture

Other equipment:

- ❑ Manual can opener
- ❑ Napkins
- ❑ Plastic utensils
- ❑ Paper/plastic plates
- ❑ Plastic cups
- ❑ Zipper-lock bags
- ❑ Airtight containers
- ❑ Screw-top jars
- ❑ NOAA Weather Radio with batteries
- ❑ AM/FM radio with batteries
- ❑ Flashlights with batteries
- ❑ Whistle
- ❑ Matches
- ❑ Fire extinguisher
- ❑ Duct tape
- ❑ Plastic sheeting
- ❑ Dust masks
- ❑ Garbage bags
- ❑ Paper towels
- ❑ Moist wipes
- ❑ Antibacterial hand sanitizer
- ❑ Two complete changes of clothing for each person—one for cold weather and one for warm weather, including undergarments and socks
- ❑ Heavy shoes or boots for each person
- ❑ At least one blanket or sleeping bag for each person; more if you're in a cold climate

- ❑ Over-the-counter medication:
    - ❑ Pain killers such as ibuprofen or acetaminophen
    - ❑ Allergy medicine
    - ❑ Cold medicine
    - ❑ Heartburn medication
- ❑ First-aid kit:
    - ❑ Adhesive bandages
    - ❑ Cloth bandages
    - ❑ Gauze and cotton
    - ❑ Scissors
    - ❑ Tweezers
    - ❑ Thermometer
    - ❑ Latex gloves
    - ❑ Antibiotic ointment or creams
    - ❑ Packets of alcohol wipes for cleaning cuts
    - ❑ Burn ointment
    - ❑ Eye drops
    - ❑ Antacids
    - ❑ Laxatives
    - ❑ Antidiarrheal medication
- ❑ Local map

Other:

- ❑ _____
- ❑ _____
- ❑ _____
- ❑ _____
- ❑ _____

3

Gearing Up

Co-author and paramedic Rod arrived in Mississippi just 5 days after Hurricane Katrina wreaked havoc on the state's southern coastline. His first night responding to 911 calls brought him to an apartment complex far enough inland it was spared from the devastating storm surge. Almost all the residents were still at the complex, but they were without power and water. Most didn't even have fuel to drive anywhere.

The night was hot and humid, and the air was eerily still, considering the maelstrom that had just torn through. All around the apartment buildings, trees and limbs littered the pathways, making it difficult to navigate a gurney. As he walked between the buildings, Rod was fascinated by the innovative uses of household items and the camaraderie of the residents. Dozens of kettle-style barbecues dotted the grounds, used as braziers for large wood fires. They certainly weren't needed for heat, but the light from the fires served as security lights for the residents.

Inside the apartment the emergency staff—Rod, a local ambulance crew, and a local fire crew—responded to a man who had had a seizure. Around him, nearly a dozen people were sorting cans of food and other packaged items. It seemed as if the neighbors were gathering supplies to share among the crowd. The man's seizure had stopped, so the emergency crew lifted him onto the gurney and started making their way back across the complex to the waiting ambulance.

To help the responders find their way, residents rushed ahead of them with camping lanterns. The burning kettles helped as well. As they climbed in the ambulance, Rod wondered how long it would be before these folks got power back and could use their barbecues for hot dogs again.

Stocking Up on Survival Gear

You've created your family survival plan and started a preparedness kit. You bought extra food, water, and other items you might need in the wake of a disaster. That's a good start, but now you need to stock up on some survival gear. Much of what you need for disasters you probably already have in your home. Whatever you don't have, you'll want to buy before you need it.

STOCK UP SOONER THAN LATER

If you're missing something on these pages, chances are other people don't have them in their homes either. Specialty items for disaster preparedness aren't common, everyday items stores that usually stock, so you might not find them at your local discount store. So when everyone is trying to stock up at the same time, supplies run out quickly.

This gear—which makes up your disaster kit—should include tools for cooking, communicating and gathering information, personal care and hygiene, treating injuries, and general *surviving*. Keep everything in your disaster kit as low tech as possible, with some exceptions we explain later in this chapter.

The disaster kit you assemble in this chapter is good for your home or on the go. You don't need separate kits for staying home or evacuating. If you're in an area where evacuation is likely (based on the type of disasters you're likely to face), house your kit in sealable containers such as large lidded plastic totes so you can quickly load them into the car when it's time to go.

Kitchen and Food Prep

Cooking in the wake of a disaster is similar to cooking while camping. Assuming you want to enjoy hot food at least a few times while you're roughing it disaster style, you'll need a stove of some sort. (Obviously, you won't have a microwave, so if you consider opening a frozen dinner and nuking it for 2 minutes as a form of cooking, you might want to be sure all your food is edible right out of the package.)

Several types of disaster stoves are available, and any good camp stove will work, too. If you want to be very self-sufficient and you live in an area where sticks and wood are easy to find, a *rocket stove* or other such *biomass fuel* stove will work great for you. These types of stoves don't need gas or kerosene to burn; you can use sticks or pinecones, or you could even use charcoal.

DEFINITION

A tall, double walled, and very low-tech cooking device, a **rocket stove** gets its name from the way it uses heat to create a draft and push the superheated air toward the food. **Biomass fuel** is whatever organic material you can burn to create heat. Most biomass stoves burn small bits of wood, leaves, pinecones, or other organic matter. Most can also burn wood pellets and charcoal.

You can even use an old-fashioned charcoal barbecue grill during a disaster. Even a kettle-style barbecue is capable of burning wood as well as charcoal.

For your first evacuation stove, try a Hibachi grill. It's small, inexpensive, and easy to find. You can store one in an evacuation kit and break it out in any parking lot when it's time to eat.

If being a wood gatherer or cooking over a smoky fire doesn't appeal to you, a gas stove is fine. Keep enough fuel on hand to get through 3 days if you're using a biomass stove and enough to survive 7 days if you must rely on gas. The only way to know how much fuel is enough for 3 days with a biomass fuel stove is to practice.

When using gas, be sure to stock extra fuel in your kit because stores will run out of propane and other camp stove fuel quickly.

Charcoal or wood pellets are the best option for storing portable biomass fuel.

NEVER BURN INDOORS

Never use a disaster stove or camp stove indoors. You run a serious risk of carbon monoxide poisoning when cooking on biomass or gas stoves without proper ventilation. Only cook outside in open areas with plenty of ventilation. If conditions aren't able to sustain outside cooking, eat food that doesn't require cooking first and save the cooking for more favorable conditions.

In addition to a stove, you'll need other food-prep supplies. Knives, can openers, cutting boards, aluminum foil, plastic wrap, and other tools and equipment will all prove helpful when you're cooking after a disaster. See the "Worksheet: Kitchen and Food Prep Checklist" at the end of this chapter for more kitchen and food preparation supplies you'll want to stock in your disaster kit.

Light and Communication

After food and water, light and information are the two most important commodities in a disaster.

Chances are high the electricity will be out after a disaster, so you'll need flashlights and maybe even lanterns to light your way when it's dark.

If the electricity is out, chances are land-line phone service will be out as well. Wireless, or cellular, service also might be out, but you should still have a mobile phone at the ready because wireless service is often restored faster than land-line phone service.

After hurricane Sandy, some of the hardest-hit areas were still without land-line phones as late as March 2013. Cell providers attached makeshift antennas to anything that could serve as a tower after Hurricane Katrina. Generators were parked at the bases of fast-food signs and tall trees all over Mississippi and connected to microwave dishes above.

If wireless service is on and your phone is email and internet capable, you can use it to check the news, get in touch with friends and relatives, etc. If it isn't, you might want to have your laptop or tablet computer with you, too. It's possible you could find a Wi-Fi spot from where you can get online.

TABLETS VERSUS LAPTOPS

Many people have computers these days, and many are laptops. Either a laptop or a tablet computer works as a portable, battery-powered communication tool, but tablets often come with data plans or the option to get them, whereas laptops do not. A tablet might not be as versatile for a full range of computing, but as a portable device to obtain information wirelessly, you can't beat a tablet.

Low tech is better than high tech in a disaster because less can go wrong with low tech. Radio signals are the most low-tech way to broadcast information, so include a portable AM/FM radio in your disaster kit. Two-way radios will come in handy, as well, even if your mobile phone is working.

Every radio needs a set of extra batteries, and phones and other electronics with chargers need an extra charging cable, so be sure to pack these items, too. If multiple items can use the same charger, you only need to pack one or two in your disaster kit.

Anything that requires electricity will need a way to get it. You might not be able to count on the power company in a disaster, so you'll have to come up with alternatives for plugging in electronics.

Several devices can help you stay powered, the first of which is a *dynamo*-powered device. Dynamo radios are emergency radios intended for disaster use, and many also work as flashlights. They have a crank on the side of the device or some other sort of hand-operated charging method. Usually, cranking the handle for as little as 30 seconds is enough to get up to an hour of listening or flashlight time. Some versions include a USB port for charging mobile phones and other devices. You can find dynamo radios at many department stores.

> **DEFINITION**
>
> A **dynamo** is an electricity generator used to power radios, flashlights, and other small items in emergency situations.

Solar-powered devices are more expensive than dynamos, but they passively collect energy as long as they're in the sunshine. Unlike dynamo devices, which are almost always bundled together as a radio and a flashlight, solar power packs are more likely to be sold as standalone energy sources. Several different types are available, ranging from small units that can fit on your car dashboard to large, folding solar arrays you can mount on tripods. Solar power packs are available online or in large warehouse stores.

Look, for external, rechargeable batteries sold for cell phones and tablet computers. These batteries are often charged with USB cables and then have their own USB ports you can use to charge other devices. You can charge them in the car or using a solar charger. When the sun goes down and the car is off, these provide stored power for your communication needs.

For more, see the "Worksheet: Light and Communication Checklist" at the end of this chapter.

Health and Hygiene

Staying healthy during a disaster is paramount because hospitals are likely to be overwhelmed and understaffed. In the aftermath of Hurricane Katrina, for example, only Biloxi Regional Medical Center remained open for patients of Mississippi's Harrison and Hancock Counties. Patients needing care for serious medical conditions were often transferred hundreds of miles away to other states, creating hardships for the patients and their families left behind. And during Superstorm Sandy, two large New York City hospitals had to be evacuated after their backup generators failed.

Health-care provider networks and resources are often stretched incredibly thin during and after a disaster. If you must seek medical care, by all means do so. But understand that the service won't be the same as what you're used to receiving.

There are two distinct parts to staying healthy: dealing with acute illnesses and injuries and maintaining hygiene. You simply cannot ignore the importance of cleanliness and hygiene during a disaster.

Hygiene is ongoing, but let's start there. You'll need to include the basics in your disaster kit: soap, shampoo, deodorant, toothbrush and toothpaste, toilet tissue, and feminine supplies. Contact lens wearers should pack an extra pair of lenses and solution.

It also helps to include a bottle of liquid detergent, hand sanitizer, spray disinfectant, and bleach.

Pack a few garbage bags and a medium plastic bucket with a lid for general use, too. You can't predict all the uses you might have for a container. In many cases, you'll have an opportunity to carry water or food. Never use a container for food or water after it was used for any sort of waste or garbage.

There's no better way to avoid illness than pay attention to proper hygiene. Brush your teeth twice a day, and bathe at least every other day during a disaster, even if you aren't always as diligent about it regularly.

KEEP IT CLEAN

Always brush your teeth with drinking water. If you use questionable water for bathing—water authorities say it's good for bathing but not drinking—do not get the water in your mouth.

Staying clean requires more than bathing and brushing. It also requires a change of underwear now and then. If you have to take your supplies on the road, your evacuation kit should include clothes and bedding, as mentioned in Chapter 2. Even if you seek out an emergency shelter, you might be required to provide your own bedroll.

The "Worksheet: Health and Hygiene Checklist" at the end of this chapter offers a complete list of what you need to stock in your disaster kit.

Emergency First Aid

With 911 and other emergency serviced overwhelmed after a disaster, you might need to do a little more hands-on treatment of minor injuries and illnesses than you'd normally have to take on. Injuries that would definitely warrant a trip to the emergency room on any given Saturday afternoon might have to be handled on your own, at least for a while.

In Part 4, we give you tips on providing first aid during a disaster. We also highly recommend that part of your advance disaster preparation should be to take a CPR and first-aid class.

What you'd keep in your medicine cabinet for run-of-the-mill scrapes and cuts probably isn't enough for even mild disaster situations, so be sure to stock your disaster kit well. Include pain relievers and fever reducers like Tylenol, Advil, Aleve, and/or aspirin in your disaster kit. More specialized over-the-counter medicines like allergy or antidiarrhea meds are good to include, too.

To treat cuts and scrapes, pack antibiotic ointment and first-aid spray. You'll want to pack alcohol wipes and antiseptic hand cleaner as well. You'll be glad you stocked up on anti-insect spray and insect bite swabs, too.

MEDICATION EXPIRATION DATES

Keep all the medications and topical agents together in one container. On the outside of the container, write the date on which the first product expires. Before that day, replace the expiring drug and any more that will expire soon. Each time you check your medications for expirations, update the date on the container.

Also include several sizes of adhesive bandages, adhesive tape and sterile gauze, Ace bandages, SAM splints, clean towels, and cold packs. You'll have to purchase a SAM splint at a specialty store or online. You can use a cardboard splint instead of an aluminum splint, but it will take up much more room.

A thermometer, tweezers, bandage scissors, and extra latex gloves are helpful to pack as well.

If you opt for a readymade first-aid kit from a pharmacy or department store, augment it with the extra items recommended here if they're not included.

Prescriptions and specialty medical equipment will be part of your disaster supplies, but they probably won't stay in your kit all the time. You'll have to remember to pack whatever you or your family needs. Make a list of all the equipment and prescription medications you'll need to take with you in case of an evacuation, and keep it in your disaster kit. This list could include prescription medications, prescription glasses, specialized medical equipment (oxygen, nebulizer, dialysis, BiPAP/CPAP, etc.), and any other specialized medical supplies (dialysis solution, blood sugar testing supplies, etc.).

Much of the specialty medical equipment used at home needs electricity. Most of these machines have battery backup, but those batteries will need to be replaced or charged. Be sure to consider your medical needs when packing or purchasing electrical power options.

We've included a comprehensive list of essential first-aid items in the "Worksheet: Emergency First-Aid Checklist" at the end of this chapter.

General Purpose Tools and Supplies

The last part of your kit is the general purpose gear and things you don't know you need until it's too late to get them, such as items to help you shelter in place if necessary or make quick repairs.

First, you need a toolkit. This will take care of minor repairs to your home or car. What you keep in there depends on your vehicle or your home, but at the very least, you should include pliers, wrenches, screwdrivers, a utility knife, a pry bar, a hatchet or hacksaw, different types of tapes and adhesives, and plastic sheeting.

The following "Worksheet: General Purpose Tools and Supplies Checklist" offers more suggestions.

This is enough to get you started. As we move through the chapters and start preparing for your specific situation, you'll no doubt come across more items to add to your kit.

Keep this kit off the floor and easily accessible. You might need to grab it and load it in the car quickly. If you have the room, keep it close to your food and water supplies.

Worksheet: Kitchen and Food Prep Checklist

Here's a list of kitchen and food prep items you'll need to have on hand after a disaster.

- ❑ At least 3 gallons of water per person (see Chapter 2)
- ❑ Nonperishable food
- ❑ Plastic utensils, plates, and bowls
- ❑ Manual can opener
- ❑ Knives for preparing food
- ❑ Small cutting board
- ❑ Salt, pepper, sugar, and spices
- ❑ Aluminum foil
- ❑ Plastic wrap
- ❑ Zipper-lock plastic bags of various sizes
- ❑ Mixing bowls
- ❑ Measuring cups and spoons
- ❑ Small Dutch oven
- ❑ Frying pan
- ❑ Disaster stove, camp stove, or grill
- ❑ Charcoal, wood pellets, kerosene, propane, or other fuel for your stove/grill

Worksheet: Light and Communication Checklist

These items will be essential tools for staying lit and informed:

- ❑ Flashlights
- ❑ Lanterns
- ❑ Light sticks
- ❑ Mobile phone
- ❑ Laptop or tablet computer (iPad or similar)
- ❑ Portable radio
- ❑ Handheld, two-way radios
- ❑ Batteries for flashlights, radios, phones, etc.
- ❑ Charging cables for phones, computers, etc.
- ❑ Dynamo radios, flashlights, etc.
- ❑ Solar power packs
- ❑ Whistles for each person

Worksheet: Health and Hygiene Checklist

Your disaster kit should include the following:

- ❑ 1 bar of soap per person
- ❑ 3 ounces shampoo per person
- ❑ Comb and brush
- ❑ 1 deodorant applicator per person
- ❑ 1 toothbrush per person and 1 (or more) tube of toothpaste
- ❑ 1 roll of toilet tissue per person
- ❑ Feminine supplies
- ❑ Contact lenses, enough lens solution for a week, and prescription glasses
- ❑ Lip balm
- ❑ 8 ounces sunscreen per person of the highest SPF you can find
- ❑ Moist towelettes
- ❑ Baby wipes
- ❑ Liquid detergent
- ❑ Hand sanitizer
- ❑ Spray disinfectant with bleach
- ❑ Unscented chlorine bleach (could be used for sanitation or for water treatment)
- ❑ Eye dropper (for use with the bleach)
- ❑ Plastic garbage bags with ties for personal sanitation use
- ❑ Medium plastic bucket with tight-fitting lid

Worksheet: Emergency First-Aid Checklist

A well-stocked emergency first-aid kit can be a lifesaver during a disaster situation:

- ❑ Pain relievers and fever reducers: acetaminophen (Tylenol), ibuprofen (Advil or Motrin), and naproxen (Aleve)
- ❑ Aspirin in the event of chest pain
- ❑ Allergy drugs: diphenhydramine (Benadryl) and loratadine (Claritin)
- ❑ Antidiarrhea medicine such as loperamide HCL (Imodium)
- ❑ Triple-antibiotic ointment (Neosporin) for cuts and scrapes
- ❑ First-aid spray
- ❑ Alcohol wipes for cleaning cuts and scrapes
- ❑ Antiseptic hand cleanser
- ❑ Insect bite swabs
- ❑ Bug spray with DEET
- ❑ Petroleum jelly (Vaseline)
- ❑ Hand lotion or moisturizer
- ❑ Several sizes of adhesive bandages
- ❑ 2 rolls each of 2-inch and 1-inch medical adhesive tape
- ❑ 20 (4×4-inch) sterile gauzes
- ❑ 4 elastic Ace bandages for wrapping sprains and swelling
- ❑ 2 triangular bandages for splinting
- ❑ Aluminum SAM splint
- ❑ Bandage scissors
- ❑ Fever thermometer
- ❑ Tweezers
- ❑ Several clean towels
- ❑ 5 instant cold packs
- ❑ Latex gloves

❑ List of prescriptions and specialty medical equipment that won't live in your disaster kit:

  ❑ Prescription medication

  ❑ Prescription glasses

  ❑ Specialized medical equipment (oxygen, nebulizer, dialysis, BiPAP/CPAP, etc.)

  ❑ Specialized medical supplies (dialysis solution, blood sugar testing supplies, etc.)

Worksheet: General Purpose Tools and Supplies Checklist

These items might not seem immediately necessary, but you'll be glad you thought to pack them when the need arises after a disaster:

❑ Toolkit

❑ Pliers

❑ Wire cutters

❑ Set of wrenches, including an adjustable wrench

❑ Phillips and flat-head screwdrivers

❑ Utility knife

❑ Pry bar

❑ Hatchet

❑ Hacksaw

❑ Duct tape

❑ Electrical tape

❑ Industrial glue

❑ Pipe sealer

❑ Plastic sheeting (enough to line an entire room)

4

Financial Preparedness

When we left her in Chapter 2, Lesley had reserved a room, quickly storm-proofed her apartment, and was headed toward her hotel as Hurricane Katrina approached New Orleans. After 6 days at the hotel, and after much uncertainty and frightening situations, Lesley eventually made her way to the Louis Armstrong New Orleans International Airport, where she was stuck for close to 20 hours before getting a flight out to the Lackland Air Force Base in San Antonio, Texas, and from there, a flight to Dallas. Friends then took her to Oklahoma City, Oklahoma.

Each step in Lesley's story of her survival of and recovery from Katrina was excruciating in its uncertainty, not to mention the oppressive heat, the filth and squalor surrounding her, and the fear she felt. Lesley's strength was spent; she was dehydrated and bruised all over; her blood pressure was spiking; and she was suffering from post-traumatic stress disorder that took her some time to recognize.

Like many other Katrina survivors, Lesley, who was in her mid-50s, was not a wealthy woman. In fact, she worked two extra jobs in addition to her position at the courthouse, and even then she still lived paycheck to paycheck.

Now with no job, no home, and no money, Lesley had no idea what she was going to do, where she was going to go, or how she was going to pay for anything.

The Importance of Advance Financial Planning

Although they're essential, having a survival plan and well-stocked prepared-ness and disaster kits alone isn't enough. You must also be *financially* prepared to deal with the aftermath of a disaster. A financial plan to pay your bills and access all your family's financial accounts and records is a vital component to the disaster recovery process and, therefore, needs to be part of your prepared-ness planning.

Rebuilding after destruction costs a great deal—even relatively minor dam-ages to a home can be expensive—and insurance policies may take longer to pay out and then be less than you expect. In worst-case scenarios, you could find yourself in a situation like Lesley's—suddenly relocated to a new city with no home, no money, and no job.

INDIVIDUAL ASSISTANCE

If the president declares your community a disaster area, federal disaster assistance programs may apply. However, most individual assistance is given out as low-interest loans from the Small Business Administration—which must be repaid. If the president has not issued a federal disaster for your area, you won't qualify for assistance.

In this chapter, we discuss how to successfully prepare your family to with-stand the impact a disaster may have on your financial health. We explain how to protect your family financially with the appropriate insurance and offer advice on keeping your financial and legal documents safe. Finally, we highlight the importance of keeping a stash of cash—not credit—safe for a rainy day.

Insured Is Prepared

Your home is your shelter, your safe haven. It's probably your greatest invest-ment, too. Part of protecting your family is protecting that investment.

You can do this in advance of disasters in several ways, including having the appropriate insurance and employing other mitigation practices to help strengthen the actual structure of your home. We look at the physical preparedness you can take to help your home weather the storm later in Chapter 6, but for now, let's talk insurance.

What Insurance Do You Need?

Several types of insurance can help protect your home from natural disasters. But what kind of insurance you need depends on what kind of home you have. (Your insurance agent can help you decide which policy is right for you.)

If you own a home, two types of policy forms are available to you: homeowners and dwelling. Homeowners insurance combines property and liability insurance. Liability insurance could come in handy in case someone is injured on your property. Dwelling insurance covers only the cost to repair and replace the structure.

If you own a mobile/manufactured home, homeowners insurance designed specifically for this type of home covers both the structure and the contents.

Condominium insurance covers your contents and any part of the condo deemed your responsibility as the owner in the condominium rules.

A primary home on a farm or ranch may not qualify for standard home-owner's insurance. A farm owner policy is probably going to be the best way to insure your home.

If you're a renter, renter's insurance covers your possessions. Your landlord should have his or her own coverage on the building you live in.

Important exceptions to most all types of typical insurance policies are flood and earthquake insurance. If you want coverage of either on your home, you need to purchase the policy separately.

Flood Insurance

Flood insurance usually isn't covered in standard homeowners policies. However, if you live in a flood zone, it's a good idea to purchase flood insurance. And if you have a federally backed mortgage, you're *required* to purchase flood insurance from the National Flood Insurance Program (NFIP).

Even if you don't live in a floodplain, still consider flood insurance. In fact, 25 percent of all claims turned in to the NFIP are for homes *not* in a designated floodplain. Floodplains change based on topography and development, so although your home might not be in a floodplain now, it could be next year. The flood zone map might change, and you could suddenly discover that your home is now listed in the floodplain.

When FEMA changes a community's floodplain map, it usually comes as a shock to people who have never considered themselves in the floodplain. NFIP regulations require the publication of public notices each time FEMA proposes new or modified flood hazard information, including Special Flood Hazard Area boundaries and zone designations. These changes can be appealed. The notices are published to begin the required appeal periods for the communities impacted by the changes. Each community does things a little differently, but don't expect your insurance company to stay on top of it.

You can purchase NFIP insurance through your homeowners insurance agent. Remember that although your homeowners insurance might cover damage from wind-driven water, it won't cover damage from rising water. You don't want to take the risk of going without flood insurance and then after a disaster, have to depend on the government for help that you may have to repay later.

CRS COMMUNITIES

If you live in a community that participates in the Community Rating System (CRS), you may enjoy discounts of up to 45 percent off your rates, depending on how your community ranks in its efforts to go above and beyond what's required to protect from storm water damage. To see if you live in a CRS community, and look up rankings in the Flood Insurance Agent's Manual, visit fema.gov.

Be sure you're covered, whether the water is wind-driven or results from rising water from nearby creeks, rivers, ponds, lakes, or the sea.

And don't wait until severe storm season or until a tropical storm starts to form and head your way to purchase flood insurance. Most policies have a 30-day waiting period built in before your policy goes into effect, so make purchasing flood insurance part of your financial preparedness plan—well before a storm or other hazard looms.

Also have a restoration company chosen and programmed into your phone. After a flood, or any large disaster, restoration companies are booked quickly, so having a relationship with one in advance helps ensure you get service quickly and avoid developing mold.

Earthquake Insurance

In the same way damage from floods isn't covered by your homeowners insurance, damage from earthquakes isn't a part of your policy, either. To protect your home and its contents from earthquake damage, you need to add an endorsement to your homeowners policy and pay an extra premium.

Just as flood insurance rates depend on many variables, earthquake insurance rates depend on how close you live to known fault lines. If you live in certain areas of California, for example, your rates will probably be higher than those for homeowners in Oklahoma (which has more seismic movement than most people realize, but it's all small stuff—lots of little tremors as opposed to strongly felt quakes). Other factors influencing your rates include the stability of the soil and what kind of home you own.

Deductibles range from 2 to 20 percent of the replacement value of your home, which can be very high.

Should you purchase earthquake insurance? Your agent can help you decide, but it also might be a good idea to talk to people who have had to make that decision and ask why they decided to purchase or not to purchase.

Cash on Hand

It's always a good idea to save money "for a rainy day" ... or for a flood, a tornado, or a hurricane. Putting a little money aside each month to save toward a disaster can only help. And as Katrina demonstrated, ATMs may not always work in the wake of a storm.

Keep a stash of cash and traveler's checks in a safe but easily accessible place in your home. If you have a safe or a safe room, store it there, with your preparedness and disaster kits. To be extra safe, you could have some additional funds set aside in a safe-deposit box, preferably at a bank in a different city.

How much to have set aside is a personal decision, but small bills are best.

What About Plastic?

As convenient as credit and debit cards are during normal, everyday life, they shouldn't be your sole source of income and purchasing power after a hazard. Credit and debit cards rely on phone lines and wireless internet access for processing, and those systems might not be accessible immediately after a disaster.

Along with the cash you've squirreled away in your preparedness kit, consider also stocking a spare credit card with a low or no balance in your kit or somewhere safe for use later, when phone lines and other structures and systems are restored and your cash has run out.

But in the immediate aftermath of a hazard, if you need to purchase food or supplies, cash is your best friend.

FINANCIAL PREPAREDNESS HELP

Free federal assistance is available to people who wish to financially prepare for disasters. The University of Minnesota Extension offers *Recovery After Disaster: The Family Financial Toolkit* at extension.umn.edu/family/tough-times/ disaster-recovery/family-financial-toolkit. The Financial Literacy and Education Commission also offers resources to help you strengthen your ability to be financially prepared. Learn more at treasury.gov/resource-center/financial-education/Pages/commission-index.aspx.

Being financially secure is a goal every family should strive for. Being prepared for the unexpected should be a very real part of that goal.

Worksheet: Financial Preparedness Checklist

This checklist helps you develop the financial planning part of your preparedness plan. Keep this information with the rest of the plan in the various places you'll need access it: at home, at work, in your car, and even in a safe-deposit box.

- ❑ Update your homeowner's insurance to cover your hazards. Be sure it combines property damage and liability.

- ❑ If you own a mobile/manufactured home, purchase homeowner's insurance that covers both the structure and your contents.

- ❑ If you own a condominium, purchase insurance for your contents, and find out if you're required to insure anything else according to your condominium rules.

- ❑ If you live on a farm or in a ranch house, find out what kind of insurance is available to you, and work with your insurance agent to decide the best policy for you.

- ❑ Purchase renter's insurance, if you rent your home.

- ❑ Purchase flood insurance through the National Flood Insurance Program. (See your homeowners insurance agent.)

- ❑ Make contact with a restoration company and program its number into your phone.

- ❑ If you live in an area at risk for earthquakes, purchase earthquake insurance.

- ❑ Cold, hard cash, in small denominations.

- ❑ Traveler's checks.

- ❑ Spare credit or debit card.

5

Essential Documents

As much as disaster supplies and gear are important for your survival after a hazard (as you read in Chapters 2 and 3), insurance is vital for financial security (as you saw in Chapter 4), and other documentation is essential to keep track of during and after a disaster, too.

But when you leave your home in the midst of a disaster, paperwork is probably the last thing on your mind. Many disaster survivors say that safety for themselves and their families came first, followed by disaster supplies, and then pictures and mementos. Paperwork doesn't even make it into the conversation.

But it should.

Disaster aid can be summed up in roughly two categories: emergency response and long-term recovery. Emergency response doesn't require identification or proof of residency. No one from the rescue helicopter is going to ask to see your ID before they haul you up off the roof of your car in rising floodwaters.

Long-term recovery is different, however. Disaster housing, grants, loans, and a host of other services offered to disaster survivors require applications and approval. You'll need important documentation for these applications: your Social Security number, photo identification, proof of income, and proof of homeowners or renters insurance.

In the event of an evacuation, you might not get a chance to go back to your home after you've left. As you move through the various aid programs, filling out applications and arranging for items and services you need, you'll have to prove certain things. It's possible to complete all the necessary paperwork without documentation, but having all that information on hand will significantly expedite the process.

Gathering Important Documents

During a disaster, paperwork is, understandably, not the first thing you'll grab to take with you. So you have to pack your important papers long before disaster strikes and keep copies in your evacuation kit with all your other supplies.

Perhaps most important, pack a copy of your driver's license. In most states, you're not allowed to drive if you don't have a license with you. A photocopy isn't the same as the physical license, but something is better than nothing. Plus, having a photocopy will make it easier to obtain a replacement license later.

You should also have copies of your passport, birth or marriage certificates, wills, car titles and registrations, important real estate paperwork, and other legal documents.

Make copies of all your important licenses and certifications, too. In Rod's day job, for example, he has to maintain nine different certifications and licenses. If he can't prove any one of those, he can't work.

Use the "Worksheet: Essential Paperwork Checklist" at the end of this chapter to be sure you have everything you need.

You might be thinking all this personal information in one place is an easy target for identity thieves. And you're right. It's important to keep paperwork as secure as possible. Most of it will fit in a portable fire safe with a locking lid. They're heavy, but that keeps the thieves from easily poaching them out of your car or from a shelter.

SAFE-DEPOSIT BOX

Putting the originals or copies of all your documents in a safe-deposit box ensures you'll have what you need in case you get stranded out of your home. Put your safe-deposit key on your car key ring so if you're not home when disaster strikes, you'll still be able to get what you need from the bank. Keep a copy of your safe-deposit key with your disaster kit, too. It's also a good idea to use a bank across town or even in another town. You don't want a neighborhood disaster to keep you from accessing your house and your bank at the same time.

Medical History and Information

If you take prescription medications, chances are you don't remember the dosages—and maybe not even the names—without looking at the bottles. You might be trying to think of them right now as you're reading this. Imagine trying to remember your medications in the middle of a disaster when so many other things are going wrong around you.

Your medications are just part of your medical history. Whatever conditions you might have—what you take the medications for—and any allergies you may have to food or drugs are also important to note.

DRUG VERSUS MEDICATION

Throughout this chapter and the rest of the book, we use the terms *drug* and *medication* interchangeably.

Health-care providers would prefer to know your medical history as they're assessing you, whether that's an everyday checkup at your primary care physician's office or an EMT exam after a tornado hit your house. Knowing this information helps caregivers make decisions about your treatment and diagnoses. They can treat you in an emergency without knowing your medical history, but you'll receive much more focused care the more they know about you.

Your medical history is too important to try to remember during the midst of a medical emergency, let alone during a disaster.

Take Responsibility for Your History

No one will be able to provide your medical history but you, so it's vital you make this important record and have it accessible when you need it. After all, after a disaster, health-care providers might not have the ability to search through electronic health records or contact your doctor as they could any other time. Chances are, if a disaster strikes your hometown, your doctor is taking care of herself and her family, just like you're taking care of yours.

Keep a copy of your medical history, and a history for each person in your family, in your documents kit or safe along with all your other important information as well as a second copy for each person to carry with them.

Like your identification and bank history, this medical history contains information you don't want just anyone to have access to, so store it in a safe place.

Making a Medical History

Really, all you need to make a usable medical history is a piece of paper and a pencil. We've included a "Worksheet: Your Medical History" at the end of this chapter that you can use to create your medical history. Or if you're computer savvy, you could create your medical history in a spreadsheet. That way, you can change it easily as your medical conditions or prescriptions evolve. Every time you update your medical history spreadsheet, print a fresh copy and destroy the older version. Whatever you use to create your history, do it in a format that makes sense to you.

Start with your full name, gender, and date of birth. You don't need to put your Social Security number on your medical history—and we don't recommend you do. In fact, despite a tradition of using Social Security numbers for identification purposes, hospitals and other health-care providers are moving away from the practice. What's more, it's currently illegal for someone to force you to provide your Social Security number.

List all the medications you take on a daily basis. Include prescription and nonprescription drugs, as well as any vitamins or supplements you take.

List all the prescriptions you take on an as-needed basis as well. Health-care providers assume you take over-the-counter pain relievers, allergy medicines, or drugs to relieve other minor ailments. However, prescriptions intended to be taken on an as-needed basis are typically much stronger and more likely to interact with other medications they might give you.

WHAT MEDICINES ARE YOU TAKING?

The combination of erectile dysfunction (ED) drugs like Viagra with nitrates like nitroglycerin can cause a deadly loss of blood pressure. When a health-care provider asks you what medications you've taken in the last 24 hours, *be honest*— especially if you're asked about ED drugs. It might save your life.

Besides the name of the drugs, also include how much medication you take each time (the dose) and how often you take it. For example, you might take 20 milligrams of lisinopril for blood pressure once a day. Write down this information for each drug, vitamin, or supplement you include on your history. If you take it as needed, write that down, too.

As important as your medications are, you also need to include any allergies you might have. Pollen allergies or hay fever aren't that important, but you can include them if you'd like. What health-care providers really need to know is what foods and drugs cause you to have allergic reactions.

Even if you've never had a life-threatening reaction to something, if it makes you itchy or swollen, it counts. Any peanut, egg, latex, or penicillin that's caused you to break out could eventually cause a serious allergic reaction called *anaphylaxis*.

DEFINITION

Anaphylaxis is a potentially life-threatening allergic reaction that includes more than one body system. Usually, anaphylaxis causes reactions in the integumentary system (itchy, swollen skin), the respiratory system (wheezing in the lungs), and the cardiovascular system (dangerous drop in blood pressure).

Some drugs are directly related to food allergies, so it's important to list both food and drugs. For example, if you're allergic to eggs and you receive certain vaccinations, you could have a reaction.

The last thing you want to put on your medical history form is a list of all your medical conditions. People often have a tendency to ignore things that don't bother them anymore. As a paramedic, Rod regularly asks patients if they have any medical problems, and they respond "No." However, on their medical history, they include a list of medications they take on a daily basis. When questioned, they'll say something like, "I don't have high blood pressure as long as I take my medication."

A medical condition that's under control with the help of medication is still a medical condition. It's important to list everything. Put as much detail as you can about your medical conditions. If you have heart trouble, explain that. Did you have a heart attack? Did you have bypass surgery?

For all your conditions, also put the date you were diagnosed—as near as you can remember. Several years of high blood pressure can take a serious toll on the kidneys. A recent stroke is more dangerous than one that happened 10 years ago.

Digital Backups and Documentation

When a storm approaches and you have to evacuate your home, it's natural to want to grab some mementos to take with you, but remember, safety first. You don't want to put yourself or your family in danger simply to retrieve a photograph or trinket.

It helps to have some things packed ahead of time so they're quick and easy to grab as you're evacuating, or stored elsewhere so you know they're safe and sound and you can think about other, more important things.

Well ahead of any disaster or hazard, make copies of all your family photos. If you don't have a scanner at home, most drug store photo departments have self-service scanners. Some camera shops will scan your photos for you, too. You can also create backups of your priceless and irreplaceable videos and rest assured you'll still have those backups should something happen to the originals.

Along with your family photos and wedding videos, use your camera to get an inventory of your possessions. After all, it's a good idea to know what you have—especially your valuables—before something catastrophic happens like a disaster or a fire.

Take pictures of all your jewelry boxes with every earring, diamond, and necklace in its correct place. Then take a picture of each individual piece that's particularly expensive. If you have an appraisal for a valuable or a piece of jewelry, include the appraisal paperwork in the picture, and pack the appraisal with all your documents.

Also walk around your home inside and outside with a video camera, and narrate the video with information on how your home is laid out, any improvements or upgrades you've made, etc. Save the video with your other important information. If you ever have to make a claim for replacements, this will help you prove your losses, and your insurance company will deeply appreciate a comprehensive photo inventory of your valuables. See the "Worksheet: Digital Documentation Checklist" at the end of this chapter for more ideas on what to photograph.

TAKING INVENTORY

Inventory booklets can help you prepare your inventory. One, the "Household and Personal Property Inventory Book," published by the College of Agricultural, Consumer and Environmental Sciences, University of Illinois at Urbana-Champaign, is downloadable from aces.uiuc.edu/vista/pdf_pubs/houseinv.pdf. "Recovery After the Disaster: The Family Financial Toolkit" provides recovery strategies and resources for homeowners and renters alike. Find it at www1.extension. umn.edu/family/tough-times/disaster-recovery/family-financial-toolkit/docs/nss/ financial-toolkit-nss.pdf.

Keep CDs, a portable hard drive, or another memory device with all your digital photos and videos packed in your evacuation kit or in your documents safe. You can also upload your photos and videos to online storage servers such as Google Drive or Dropbox.

No Job Is Finished Until the Paperwork Is Done

When and if the time comes to evacuate your home, take your document kit with you. This will become your lifeline to get help and rebuild. Keep it safe, and don't advertise that you have all this information on you.

Be sure to keep the documents in your kit up to date, too. Make it a habit to check these documents whenever you update the rest of your disaster supplies. You may never understand how important this paperwork is until you need it.

Worksheet: Your Medical History

Complete a medical history for every member of the household. Make two copies; keep one copy safe with the rest of your important paperwork, and give the other to each person to carry.

Name: _____

Date of birth: _____

Gender: _____

Daily medications:

Name	Dose	Frequency

As-needed medications:

Name	Dose	Frequency

Allergies—food and drug:

_____

_____

_____

Medical conditions, with date diagnosed:

_____

_____

_____

_____

Worksheet: Essential Paperwork Checklist

Use this worksheet to be sure you have all necessary documents. Check off anything that pertains to your family and be sure you can account for it. (Feel free to cross out anything on the list that doesn't apply to you. Not everyone has adoption papers, for example.)

- ❑ Driver's license
- ❑ Passport
- ❑ Other identification documents
- ❑ Birth certificate
- ❑ Marriage license
- ❑ Divorce papers
- ❑ Adoption papers
- ❑ Child custody agreements
- ❑ Death certificates
- ❑ Wills and living wills or advanced directives, and powers of attorney
- ❑ Social Security cards
- ❑ Property records—leases, deeds, mortgages
- ❑ Automobile titles and registrations
- ❑ Insurance policies—home, car, life
- ❑ Loan documents
- ❑ Bank account information
- ❑ Recent paystubs and bank statements
- ❑ Most recent tax returns
- ❑ Debit and credit card numbers and statements
- ❑ Login, password information, and personal identification numbers for all financial accounts
- ❑ Spare keys to home, car(s), and safe-deposit boxes
- ❑ Important certifications and licenses
- ❑ Medical history

Worksheet: Digital Documentation Checklist

Some documents don't have to be in hard copy. Photos and large inventories can be transported much more easily in digital form. Use this worksheet to help you organize your digital information.

- ❑ Copies of important family photos on CDs, on flash drives, or online
- ❑ Photographs of all contents of home:
    - ❑ Jewelry—expensive and otherwise, with appraisals
    - ❑ Every room in your home
    - ❑ Extra buildings
    - ❑ Landscaping
    - ❑ Automobiles
    - ❑ Recreational vehicles such as boats, personal watercraft vehicles, three and four wheelers, bicycles, and motorcycles
    - ❑ Outdoor recreational activity equipment such as swing sets, play houses, and trampolines
    - ❑ Furniture
    - ❑ Closets full of clothing
    - ❑ Fur coats, leather coats, etc.
    - ❑ Kitchen appliances
    - ❑ China, cookware, silverware
    - ❑ Washer and dryer, water heater, and other appliances
    - ❑ Cell phones
    - ❑ MP3 players
    - ❑ Computers, tablets, electronic reading devices
    - ❑ Stereo equipment
    - ❑ Televisions, movie-playing devices, and movie collections
    - ❑ Electronic video game consoles
    - ❑ Children's toys and games

❑ Musical instruments, sound equipment, book collections, or any other kind of valuable collections such as coins, stamps, baseball cards, or other memorabilia

Other:

❑ _____

❑ _____

❑ _____

❑ _____

❑ _____

❑ _____

❑ _____

❑ _____

❑ _____

❑ _____

❑ _____

❑ _____

❑ _____

❑ _____

❑ _____

❑ _____

❑ _____

❑ _____

❑ _____

❑ _____

❑ _____

❑ _____

❑ _____

❑ _____

- ❑ _____
- ❑ _____
- ❑ _____
- ❑ _____
- ❑ _____
- ❑ _____
- ❑ _____
- ❑ _____
- ❑ _____
- ❑ _____
- ❑ _____
- ❑ _____
- ❑ _____
- ❑ _____
- ❑ _____
- ❑ _____
- ❑ _____
- ❑ _____
- ❑ _____
- ❑ _____
- ❑ _____
- ❑ _____
- ❑ _____
- ❑ _____
- ❑ _____
- ❑ _____
- ❑ _____
- ❑ _____

6

Securing Your Home

In an earlier chapter, we discussed properly insuring your home as part of protecting your finances. The appropriate insurance is one very important element of protecting your home, and by extension, your financial health, but you can do some additional things to cover yourself.

In this chapter, we discuss protecting your home by strengthening the structure through a variety of mitigation techniques that enable it to better weather natural disasters, lessening the impacts in a way that can save lives and reduce property losses.

All these mitigation methods require a financial investment—some small and some significant. However, it's important to note that according to a 2005 study by the National Institute of Building Sciences, for every $1 spent on mitigation, $4 is saved in recovery costs. So for the purpose of financial preparedness, structural mitigation measures are quite worthwhile and should be part of your disaster preparedness plan as a homeowner.

If you're a renter, this is a conversation worth having with your landlord. The types of structural strengthening discussed in this chapter will not only help you, the renter, in terms of the safety of your family and your contents, but also help the homeowner in terms of the potential amount of money he could lose or save in future disaster losses, depending on actions he takes now.

Earthquakes

Earthquakes are the result of the constant movement of the earth's crust. Older, conventionally built homes may suffer significant damage from the shaking earthquakes cause; modern technology has provided the capability to build structures that move with the earth.

Just as a willow tree is likelier to survive strong winds because it is more flexible than other trees, bending with the wind instead of breaking, the same principle has been implemented when building structures in areas known for their high earthquake risk. However, not all structures are designed with earthquakes in mind, and even those built to be more quake-resistant can still suffer a great deal of damage when a quake occurs. In addition to the structural damage to the foundation, the frame, etc., there's the added risk of fire or water damage due to broken gas lines and burst water pipes.

To reduce damages from earthquakes, you want to try to keep your home from shifting with ground movement. Keep it as stable as possible, focusing on the foundation and walls.

Securely bolt the sill plate to the foundation of the house, and secure the walls with hold-downs. How you do this depends on the type of structure you have. Contact a contractor or your local building department for recommendations.

Unbraced cripple walls can move during a quake, damaging the home and possibly causing injury. Cripple walls are located between the first floor of a building and its foundation. Adding horizontal supports between the vertical studs at the top and bottom of these walls braces the walls and reduces the risk of damage. Add nails to ensure the supports are securely attached.

HIRE IT OUT

If you're not qualified or equipped to manage the kind of structural amendments noted in this chapter, call a qualified contractor for these projects.

Inside, try to prevent heavy items such as furniture from falling over and injuring someone. Be sure the heaviest books and objects are on the lower shelves, while the lightest items are on upper shelves. Store breakables such as china, glasses, and bottled items like wine and olive oil in closed cabinets— no glass doors, please—with latches.

Fasten shelves sturdily to walls, and fasten your pictures and mirrors securely, too. Place the heavier ones away from areas where they could fall on people, such as over sofas and chairs or beds. Brace your overhead light fixtures, too.

Water heaters commonly topple over during earthquakes and can cause injury. To prevent this, strap the water heater to wall studs to secure it, and bolt it to the floor. Do the same for refrigerators, furnaces, and gas appliances.

Floods

Water damage in the home can be extremely expensive. Even just an inch or two can cause tens of thousands of dollars in damage. And the longer you wait to fix it, the worse and more expensive the problem becomes. After 72 hours, you not only have a water damage problem, you also have a mold problem. The longer you wait to fix a mold problem, the worse and more expensive it gets. See a pattern here? According to the National Flood Insurance Program, between 2007 and 2011, the average residential flood claim was almost $30,000.

The best way to prevent loss from flood is not to build in a known flood zone. But as mentioned earlier, floodplains change based on topography and development. Just because your area has never flooded before doesn't mean it won't in the future. If it rains where you live, it can flood. However, if you do live in a known flood zone, you can lower your risk.

When it comes to flood-proofing, elevation is key. Elevate your electrical switches, sockets, wiring, and circuit breakers at least 12 inches above your home's projected flood elevation. Also elevate your furnace, water heater, washer, and dryer on cement blocks at least 12 inches above your home's projected flood elevation. Don't know your home's projected flood elevation? Call your community's floodplain manager for that information as well as what zone you fall into on the floodplain map.

Confirm that your sump pump is in working order. In case of a power failure, install a battery-powered backup. If you have fuel tanks, anchor them. Also clear debris from your gutters and downspouts.

One of the most effective ways of protecting your home from floodwaters, however, is by elevating the entire structure. If your home is in a designated Special Flood Hazard Area, or has been severely damaged after a flood, you may be required to elevate it to comply with local floodplain management ordinances or to be or remain eligible for flood insurance under the NFIP. (The NFIP defines an elevated home as one that has no basement and has its lowest elevated floor raised above the ground by foundation walls, shear walls, posts, piers, pilings, or columns.)

ABOVE THE FLOOD

"Above the Flood: Elevating Your Floodprone House" is a FEMA publication that illustrates how homes were elevated in southern Florida after Hurricane Andrew. The publication includes a number of different elevation techniques. Find it at fema.gov/media-library/assets/documents/725?id=1424.

Hailstorms

Hail is associated with tornadoes and severe thunderstorms. Hailstones can be as small as tiny pebbles and cause little to no damage or as large as soccer balls and cause unthinkable damage. Hail damage causes nearly $2 billion in damages each year in the United States.

Your home's roof takes the brunt of the damage hail causes, but you can mitigate against potential hail damage by making your roof stronger. Impact-resistant shingles, class 4 shingles, and roof decking are designed to withstand the impact of hail during storms. Many insurance companies offer discounts to homeowners who use impact-resistant roofing materials. You can probably find these shingles at most home improvement stores.

For a list of impact-resistant shingles and roofing products approved by Underwriters Laboratories, visit amfam.com/pdf/insurance/roof.pdf.

HAIL!

Hailstones 7 inches wide and 18.75 inches around fell in Nebraska on June 22, 2003. On July 23, 2010, hail was found in South Dakota measuring 8 inches wide and 18.625 inches around.

Hurricanes

In a hurricane, the wind is the greatest threat to your home. By beefing up your roof, garage door, doors, and windows, you can make your house more impervious to hurricane-force winds.

Impact-resistant shingles and roof decking can protect your room from the wind and flying debris. Using tie-downs, wind clips, or hurricane straps can secure your roof and make it more resistant to being lifted from your house.

Your garage door is your biggest entryway, and if it isn't secure, it can be breached—in which case the rest of your home suddenly becomes much more vulnerable. And if your garage door goes, your roof could be next. You can retrofit your current garage door, or you can upgrade it with a wind-resistant garage door. Most retrofits are budget-friendly. You can hire out the work or do it yourself if you feel comfortable.

Braces are one retrofit you can make to your garage door. Add braces to meet wind-load standards in your area, attaching them to brackets in the door frame. These braces aren't permanent; they're only attached when anticipating a storm. They take about 5 minutes each to install and are easily removed. This is probably the cheapest way to strengthen your garage door.

Hurricane panels are another option. These metal or aluminum panels attach to the outside of the garage door. These are the same panels many homeowners use to protect windows and entry doors. The panels are more expensive than bracing, and local building codes may require special permits before you can install them because they're permanent fixtures.

You also could replace your current garage door with an impact-resistant door. This, obviously, is a more expensive method. You might get a better deal by shopping around during the hurricane off-season. Some impact-resistant doors are tested to withstand 150-mile-per-hour winds and airborne 2x4 studs traveling at 34 miles per hour. Check your community's building codes to be sure your door is in compliance.

Storm shutters or impact-resistant windows and doors protect your home from debris. Like strengthened garage doors, they prevent the roof from being lifted and help you avoid greater destruction when it comes to your home.

PROACTIVE MEASURES

It's important to note that although some winds might be too strong for many buildings to resist, taking these proactive measures provides significant protection in most high-wind events. For example, a roof without ties may be lost in even some weaker tornadoes such as an EF-1 or EF-2. However, with ties or hurricane clips, your roof will be much more likely to stay secure during these events. And that means the rest of your structure—as well as the lives of the people within—is more likely to remain secure.

Lightning

Each year, thousands of lightning strikes occur in each state, often causing fire and electrical damage, endangering both people and property. Lightning is a hazard every homeowner faces, regardless of region.

Lightning can damage a home's electrical wiring, telephones, computers, and more. In a worst-case scenario, a home may catch fire as a result of a lightning strike. And according to the National Weather Service, deaths from lightning in the United States average 62 per year, with 300 injuries.

Surge protectors are affordable and easy to use, and they're an effective way to protect your electronic appliances from most electrical surges.

Lightning rods and other lightning protection systems provide a direct path to ground the lightning, avoiding the house itself. If you're interested in one of these systems, contact a qualified contractor to install. And be sure to check your local building codes and ordinances for requirements regarding exterior lightning mitigation devices.

Whole-house surge protection systems are installed on your home's electric meter to protect your electronics and appliances. Contact your local power company to install, or hire a qualified electrician.

Power Outages

Power outages are common during and after severe weather. Depending on the time of the year, they may result in anything from loss of food to heat exhaustion, from freezing to loss of life.

In some cases, you *will* lose power due to storms or bad weather. An alternate source of power comes in handy in times like this. Gas-powered generators and batteries can provide electricity when the power's out.

GENERATOR SAFETY

If you opt for a generator, take the time—in advance—to learn how to use it safely. Do not bring it inside; keep it outside to avoid poisonous gas fumes. Also check it several times a year to be sure it's running correctly. There's nothing like finding out your generator isn't working—during a power outage.

It's smart to have a licensed electrician regularly check your home for short circuits, old wiring, and overgrown trees that may interfere with power lines. Taking small steps like this now may save big problems later.

Tornadoes

Tornado Alley runs from Texas to Minnesota and experiences the greatest intensity of tornadoes. However, tornadoes can happen anywhere. More than 1,000 are reported each year, causing death, injury, and destruction.

The same mitigation measures apply for tornadoes as for hurricanes. The goal is to make your home strong enough to withstand high winds and debris. Strengthening your windows, doors, garage door, and roof goes a long way toward protecting your home.

Although an expensive option, you could invest in a safe room or storm shelter to further protect your family and some of your important documents and items. One option is to retrofit a room or shelter on your current home, building into the structure. Alternatively, you could purchase a modular unit to be anchored to the foundation. Above-ground and below-ground shelters are available. The most appropriate shelter for your family may depend on your region, the soil density, water tables, and other factors.

Whatever shelter you decide on, it's important to be sure it's certified by the National Storm Shelter Association (NSSA). NSSA certification standards have been made code in many states. NSSA-certified shelters are tested by shooting a 2×4 piece of wood from a cannon at 100 miles per hour—the speed that best simulates the same debris being blown in 250-mile-per-hour winds.

Wildfires

In an average year, 140,000 wildfires burn 14.5 million acres in nearly every state in the United States. To mitigate against potential damages to your home by wildfires, pay special attention to your roof and landscaping.

Some roof coverings are more susceptible to fire than others. Wood shingles should be avoided as they pose the greatest fire hazard. Some areas have outlawed them, and in places where they are allowed, many insurance companies charge higher premiums for the risk. Be aware that some fire-resistant roofs are more vulnerable to hail damage, so the roof you choose depends on which hazards you are most likely to face.

Certain landscaping can cause fire to spread toward your home more quickly or protect your home from fire. Keep your yard free of dead brush and shrubs, and develop an area around your home with only the most fire-proof vegetation. That will depend greatly on your region's climate.

To find out what plants are more fire-proof, ask at local nurseries or greenhouses. Online research might be of use, too.

Winter Freezes

Winter storms may cause flooding, storm surges, and downed power lines, as well as destruction of thousands of trees in the affected areas. And they can cause significant damage to your home by causing water pipes to freeze and burst.

To prevent initial problems from becoming worse, it's important to catch any problems in the beginning—better yet, catch them before they start. This means regular maintenance of your home.

Drain outside faucets of all water when temperatures start to drop toward freezing, and shut off the water supply to the home at the inside valve. Keep your indoor faucets slightly open during hard freezes, too. This prevents your pipes from freezing and bursting—a disaster many homeowners face during the winter. Once water floods the inside of the home, what began as a minor disaster has just become exponentially worse.

Also, be sure to keep gutters clean and clear of brush and other debris to prevent iced dams from forming in the gutter and on the roof.

Inside, keep your house warm, even if nobody's home. This helps prevent water pipes from freezing and bursting.

If your power goes out, you can use a gas-powered generator for heat and to keep your pipes from freezing. Just remember to keep the generator outside so you're not filling your house with fumes.

INSULATED CONCRETE FORM

Building a new home? To save money on heating and air conditioning and create a stronger, safer house, Insulated Concrete Form (ICF) structures are a great alternative to the standard wood frame. ICF construction can add 3 to 5 percent to your construction cost (above grade) but allow for up to 60 percent smaller heating and cooling equipment to heat or cool the same square footage, cutting the cost of the final house by an estimated 75¢ per square foot. ICF homes can qualify for green tax incentives; require less energy to heat and cool; and are less vulnerable to earthquakes, floods, tornadoes, and other natural disasters—and that means lower insurance rates.

Many labor under the idea that disasters can't be prevented. Along the same lines is the often-lamented, "If it's my time, it's my time, and there's nothing I can do about it." But with proper planning and the wise use of technology, you actually can do a great deal about it.

We know floods occur partially as a result of development, and when we don't develop in the floodplain, we don't increase our risk of flooding. We know if we obey our local fire ban, we're less likely to start a wildfire. We know if we build our homes stronger, we're less prone to loss during wind events. And we know if we practice for disasters, we're more likely to respond quickly and efficiently.

Disasters do happen, and most of the time, we can't prevent them. But the good news—actually, the really great news—is we can control the severity of the damage we suffer and the extent of our losses by thinking, planning, and acting in advance.

By implementing some of the mitigation practices highlighted in this chapter, you increase your odds of surviving physically and financially.

Worksheet: Mitigation Checklist

Enacting structural mitigation measures in your home can reduce the impact a disaster might have on your finances by decreasing your potential losses. The following checklist provides some actions you can take to make your home more structurally able to withstand a disaster.

- ❑ Bolt down or otherwise secure heavy items like large furniture, paintings, appliances, and the water heater to prevent them falling.

- ❑ Elevate air conditioners, furnaces, and water heaters to at least 12 inches above the projected flood level.

- ❑ Anchor your home's foundation.

- ❑ Brace cripple walls.

- ❑ If you're at risk for hail, replace your roof with impact-resistant or class 4 shingles.

- ❑ Tie down your roof with hurricane ties, straps, or wind clips.

- ❑ Replace your garage door with a wind-resistant garage door, or retrofit it with braces or hurricane panels.

- ❑ Protect your windows with impact-resistant glass or storm shutters.

- ❑ Use surge protectors throughout your home.

- ❑ Have a qualified, licensed electrician install a lightning protection system.

- ❑ Install whole-house surge protectors.

- ❑ Purchase and practice using a gas-powered generator and batteries to use as alternate power sources.

- ❑ Have your home's electrical system inspected.

- ❑ Add a safe room or storm shelter to your home—retrofit, build into a new structure, or add a modular unit.

- ❑ If you're at risk for wildfires, replace your roof with fire-resistant shingles.

- ❑ Protect your home from wildfires by fire-proofing your landscaping.

- ❑ In preparation for a freeze, drain faucets of water, shut off outside water valves from inside the house, and keep pipes warm to avoid them freezing and bursting.

- ❑ Keep gutters cleaned and cleared of brush to avoid water/ice collection.

2

A Storm Is Brewing

Are there dark clouds on the horizon? Is a hurricane forming off the coast? Maybe the banks of your local river are reaching maximum capacity.

Whatever the hazard, hopefully by this point, you've sat down with your family and begun to discuss your options in various disaster scenarios. Maybe you've developed your family plan, and perhaps you've started to build your family preparedness kit. Do you think you're ready for a disaster? None of us are ever truly *ready,* but you can be *readier.*

In Part 2, we discuss the importance of knowing what to expect in various disaster situations. The best way to do that is by having family drills and exercises to test your emergency plan.

We also talk a bit about how your brain takes in data, and why you respond the way you do when something unexpected occurs. We look at last-minute preparations you can take, as well as evacuation and sheltering in place procedures. We also address what to do when faced with specific disasters, such as tornado, wildfires, and power outages among others, to help you get *readier.*

7

Are You Ready?

Debi Gade was a television producer for a news station on Long Island, where she had worked for 17 years. It was late October 2012, and Debi was the producer in charge of covering the upcoming presidential election. On October 22, Tropical Storm Sandy developed in the western Caribbean Sea. Within days, meteorologists were predicting the highly unusual spectacle of a fusion between then Hurricane Sandy and a cold front, earning the predicted amalgamation the nickname "Frankenstorm," due in part to its proximity to Halloween. This wasn't the first time New York had been under a dire hurricane warning.

"They predicted it to be bad," Debi said. "But I've lived here for 30 years, and they've predicted other storms to be bad that never turned out to be as bad as they said."

Debi's family took the routine precautions at their home on Long Beach, in sight of the bay from one vantage point and sand dunes from another. They brought their outdoor furnishings inside and moved items from the first floor to upper stories. They sandbagged their basement, boarded up their windows, and moved their cars to higher ground. Neighbors were evacuating.

The news waits for no man, however, and both in spite of and because of the imminent "Frankenstorm," Debi found herself at work on October 29. After all, this storm was breaking news. The station put up the news crew in a hotel, which eventually lost power; guests had no light and no heat. But Debi had access to a radio and was able to keep in touch with her family by phone for at least part of the night while the radio news continued to emphasize the beating Long Beach would receive.

Debi's daughter told her later how the bay came up like a tsunami. It rose and fell, filling Debi's home in less than 15 minutes. It engulfed the basement and then flowed into their first floor living area—through the basement, through the ground, through the front door. Water was coming in everywhere, filling their home.

Debi's husband and their 17-year-old son were at home, helpless, with no way to prevent the rapid rush of water. Across the street, Debi's neighbor lived in a home that had been rebuilt and elevated after Hurricane Irene. Debi's 10-year-old daughter and several other neighbors waited out the storm there. That home survived Sandy with minimal damage.

By the next morning, Debi found herself without phone access and cut off from her family. With no way of knowing if they were safe, Debi frantically attempted to drive to Long Beach. The city was cut off, with the National Guard, state police, and local police blocking all entrances. Debi parked in the next town and walked through pouring rain to the bridge, where she was told she could not enter.

Desperate, Debi took off running on the bridge, and others followed. "It was like an angry mob," she said. "I busted through two police lines to get into the city because I had to find my family and see my house."

For the first several days, Debi's family stayed on the second floor of their home, in shock. They had no power, no heat, and no lights. They tried to clean and clear things out of the house during the day, but at night, with no power, it was pitch black.

"There was no food. No running water. We would go to the basement with pails, fill them with water, and then pour the water into the toilets so we could flush them."

As the tide receded, so did the water, but that brought a new element to the disaster. The sewer systems in Long Beach overflowed, raw sewage mixed with the sea water, and as the water receded, it left a layer of brown sludge on everything it touched—both inside and out.

Debi is a very organized person. As a successful news producer, her life is neat and tidy. A multitasker, problem-solver, and ardent yoga enthusiast, Debi found her inner resources failing her amid all she was going through.

"People were walking around like zombies," Debi said. "I couldn't function. You just can't believe that this is your life. It was like an out-of-body experience. It was sheer destruction everywhere you looked. All the schools, businesses, and buildings were gone. Cars and boats were strewn everywhere. It was overwhelming."

Cool Heads Prevail

Responding quickly to a disaster with calm presence of mind is essential. But this calm presence of mind isn't something that just happens. It's the result of training.

According to research in disaster behavior, humans respond appropriately to disasters when they know what to expect. It has everything to do with the speed with which we process data. If it's information we've previously processed, either by practicing and planning for disasters or by actually experiencing them, we can operate on autopilot. If it's new data, it will slow us down, causing what Debi called the "zombie" experience.

In spite of days of dire warnings from meteorologists, Debi was not the only one who was unprepared for what met her when she crossed the bridge into Long Beach, and for the long recovery period ahead.

Regardless of how we've trained our brains to process information during a disaster, one thing that decades of research has shown is that panic is rare. Although it's the one thing authorities most fear from the public, the truth is that during disasters, most people respond calmly, even altruistically, helping strangers and reassuring one another. Panic is not the enemy. Lack of data and lack of experience, the unknown, causes the brain to process slowly and react slowly. The unknown is the enemy.

KNOWLEDGE

Knowledge is going to make you stronger. Knowledge is going to let you control your life. Knowledge is going to give you the wisdom to teach your children. Knowledge is the thing that makes you smile in the face of disaster.

—Avery Brooks, actor

The brain can be trained to successfully handle disasters by practicing with drills and exercises, or even by simply imagining how you'd respond in a particular scenario.

How often do you go into a movie theater and immediately note the exits? How well do you listen to the flight attendant who goes through the safety procedures? Instead, do you plug in your iPod, close your eyes, and tune her out?

By taking a little extra time and interest in finding the exits inside a large building and imagining yourself going through the motions of a calm evacuation, you not only better enable yourself to think and act quickly when necessary, but you also give yourself a certain piece of mind.

Although it seems counterintuitive, spending some time thinking about the worst-case scenarios and imagining how you'd handle them can actually help ease your mind and give you a sense of security should something actually happen.

At home and with your family, talk about the potential hazards you face. Run through drills to strengthen your ability to think quickly on your feet while staying calm. Your disaster preparedness plan will cover how to respond to each of your family's hazards. In addition to training your brain to respond properly to each hazard, drills also test your plan for any flaws, which you'll want to correct as soon as you can.

In the following sections, we run through a few drills for the most common disasters you and your family might face—earthquakes, fires, and tornadoes. But take time to review the list of potential hazards you made in Chapter 1 and come up with your own drills specific to the disasters on your list.

After each drill, make note of any issues that cause concern, such as doors that may not open easily or hallways that may be blocked with clutter.

For these and other potential hazards, it's also productive to discuss the scenarios—what you would do and how you'd communicate if you get separated and cell phone service is interrupted. What if a tornado, or earthquake, or fire occurs when children are home alone? Be sure you have a plan for every possible circumstance.

Make your family preparedness an integral part of your family traditions. Knowing that you and your family take the time to address the possibilities and you know what to do during an emergency will add to your family's sense of safety and security.

Earthquake Drills

If you have small children, you can make an earthquake drill fun. Explain before the drill that an earthquake may start with a low rumbling noise. Then, count down from 10 to 1, begin to make a humming noise, and have the rest of the family join in, getting louder and louder as you go. When you're ready, yell "Earthquake!" At that point, everyone should act as though the ground is moving and the house is shaking—gyrating, shuddering, pretending like they're losing their balance.

Very loudly yell, "Duck!" and have everyone duck to the ground. Explain to your kids that if they drop to the ground, they lessen the chances of getting knocked off balance and falling.

Next, yell "Cover!" Everyone should find his or her cover under something like a sturdy table.

"Hold on!" Now everyone holds on to their cover.

During each step, continue the shaking and gyrating. After a full minute of holding on, calmly say, "It's over. All clear."

When the all-clear is given, have the family members survey the room, pretending there's debris strewn about, and find the safest way out of the building.

Be sure that during the drill, everyone stays away from windows, tall pieces of furniture, and anything heavy hanging on the walls like large mirrors, paintings, or flat-screen TVs. Remind your children that during a real earthquake, these will be potential hazards.

Fire Drills

In your preparedness plan (from Chapter 1), think about how you'll escape from each room in case of a fire, and plan two exit routes from each room if possible.

Give each person an assignment so everyone has a role. Put someone in charge of getting the small children out safely. Put someone in charge of helping anyone with special needs or elderly family members. Put someone in charge of any overnight guests staying with you.

Plan on where everyone will meet outside. Make it a centrally located spot a short distance away from the house so you're all out of harm's way.

Begin the exercise by setting off the smoke alarm. You can do this by pressing the test button.

Evacuate as quickly as possible. Practice evacuating from your bedrooms as if it were the middle of the night, and practice evacuating from a fire that starts in the kitchen or the living room. Practice being able to open all doors and windows as escape routes, and note any difficulties.

FIRE EXTINGUISHER SAFETY

For a small fire, be sure all family members know where the fire extinguisher is located and how to use it.

Go to your meeting place, and be sure everyone is safe and accounted for. In a real fire, a parent would make the 911 call, but if the parents are still inside, the children should be instructed not to go back inside to find them, but instead call 911.

Practice "stop, drop, and roll." Have everyone pretend his or her clothes are on fire, stop where they are, drop to the ground, and roll back and forth until you tell them the fire is out.

Tornado Drills

When notified of a tornado warning via the television, radio, NOAA weather radio, or through a smartphone app, take shelter immediately.

Before running your drill, be sure all family members know where in your home is the safe place to go. If you don't have a basement or safe room, take shelter in an interior room with no windows. If you have time, cover everyone with pillows, blankets, or even a mattress if possible. The point is to protect yourself and your family from flying debris, which causes most injuries and fatalities during a tornado.

Don't open windows to "alleviate pressure." This is an old myth that actually puts people at greater risk because allowing the wind in can create a lift that has the potential to rip off the roof. (In a very strong tornado, such as an EF-4 or EF-5, that may be a moot point because the tornado will do whatever damage it can whether the windows are open or not. But for weaker tornadoes, the closed windows could make a difference.) However, you might not have time to pay attention to whether the windows are open or closed, and that's okay. When the warning comes, get far away from the windows and take shelter immediately.

Begin the tornado drill by making siren sounds. To make it more fun for children, time everyone to see who gets into the shelter or the safe room the fastest, and offer a small prize to the child who arrives and covers him- or herself with blankets and pillows first.

Safety First; Possessions Later

People who have researched disaster behavior note a tendency to do what's called "gathering." Once people are on notice that they must evacuate, it usually takes a number of confirmations before people believe it—and even then, they often don't leave without gathering their belongings first.

Whether the belongings are necessary and whether they're practical, it doesn't matter. It appears to be an instinct, which if there was time, might be a good survival instinct. However, when your building is on fire, or your house is on fire, or a tornado is headed your way, you don't have time to grab your luggage, your family photos, or your important papers.

Tell your children and other family members the importance of ensuring their own safety first and worrying about "stuff" later. With drills and exercises, you can overcome this gathering tendency.

Remember, things can always be replaced. You and your family members can't be replaced. When it's time to get out, get out. Don't gather. Don't delay. It's not worth your life.

Worksheet: Exercise and Drill Checklist

After you've developed plans for different types of disasters, practice following them. This worksheet helps you keep track of the drills you run with your family. Try to run through your emergency plan at least once a year.

Earthquake drill   Date: _____

Fire drill   Date: _____

Tornado drill   Date: _____

Other:

_____   Date: _____

_____   Date: _____

_____   Date: _____

_____   Date: _____

_____   Date: _____

8

---•◦•---

Should You Stay
or Go?

The waters of California's Merced River had been rising steadily for days. A few more inches higher, and the river would breach its levees. Local volunteer firefighters tried to keep residents up to date on how close the water was getting, but residents near the levees were constantly reporting new leaks as fountains of muddy water bubbled out and flooded pastures or farms.

Many of the dairy and hog farms near the river were flooded long before the water got to critical levels. Farmers tried relocating their livestock, but the sheer number of animals who needed to be protected was overwhelming and growing rapidly. In desperation, farmers simply opened the gates and let the animals find their own way to higher ground.

Melanie Martinez moved to the rural area of Mountain View, California, less than a year before. Such flooding was rare, she was assured. Locals said this was called a "hundred-year flood" because the water only got this high once a century.

Melanie and her then-fiancé, co-author Rod, were preparing to evacuate. They had protected the lowest areas of their home with sandbags, and all their valuables were either packed in the truck or placed on high shelves. Rod was a paramedic and a captain at the volunteer fire department. He was dealing with flooding in other parts of the county while trying to help Melanie pack. As the water peaked at its highest point only inches from the tops of the levees, Melanie and Rod waited for the official order to evacuate.

Melanie was in the garage, picking up the last few items and moving them to higher areas. When she finished, she opened the door from the garage to the backyard, screamed, and slammed the door closed.

Concerned, Rod came running out to the garage. Frightened, Melanie told him she saw a "giant dog" or something in the backyard and it was growling. Rod grabbed a baseball bat and went to the door, planning on scaring away the animal.

He opened the door, paused, and began to laugh hysterically. Outside stood a 350-pound sow. The pig looked at Rod, snorted, and continued to root around, looking for something to eat. Once Rod was able to stop laughing enough to explain what Melanie had seen, she sheepishly came to the door to marvel at the beast. Melanie fed the sow, and it waited out the rest of the flood danger in their backyard. No order to evacuate ever came.

Evacuation Decisions

Whether you evacuate or stay put during a disaster or other hazard depends on a lot of variables, including the type of disaster, the amount of advance warning you receive, the threat level to your home, what options you have for evacuation, and more. If you live in the city and don't have access to your own vehicle, for example, your options are limited by public transportation services. Or if you live in a rural community, there might not be enough population to support setting up a shelter in your area.

Many of these issues should be addressed by the preparedness plan you created in Chapter 1. You should already have planned for the types of disasters you face and know what you'll do—leave or stay put—for each type of disaster you could face.

Disasters that come with warnings—most floods, hurricanes, and severe storms, to name a few—are the easiest to determine whether you'll stay or go. You probably decided that back in Chapter 1. You've probably already packed a kit in case you need to leave, and you have enough supplies to stick it out for at least 3 days and preferably a week.

You can't decide ahead of time exactly what you'll do when the time comes. You can't know for sure that you'll be able to stay or that you'll definitely evacuate. You have to make those decisions in the moment based on your current circumstances. And depending on the situation, the decisions might be made for you.

Mandatory Evacuation

If an official knocks on your door and tells you to leave or the phone rings and you hear a recording from officials telling you it's time to evacuate, you're probably facing mandatory evacuation. Officials will indicate whether the evacuation is a suggestion or an order.

WHEN YOU'RE ORDERED TO EVACUATE

With mandatory evacuations, authorities usually identify the best routes to use to get out of the danger zone. You'll see folks directing traffic to help you get out of the area as safely and efficiently as possible. Listen to the evacuation order, and take notes on the instructions. If officials come to your door, ask for any handouts they might have with directions. Also write down any radio frequencies or phone numbers where you can get more information if necessary.

Mandatory evacuation doesn't mean someone is going to force you to leave your home at gunpoint. It means emergency services are heading for safer ground, and they won't be around to help you if you stay. Depending on who's telling you to leave—local, state, or federal governments—and on the laws of your area, defying a mandatory evacuation order could be a violation of the law. You probably won't be arrested—emergency services likely don't have the resources to arrest everyone who doesn't leave—but you might be cited and fined later.

Losing emergency services is a big deal, however. If the situation is so dangerous that the folks with specialized training and equipment are heading out, you should leave, too. The chances you'll require their services if you stay are pretty high.

Voluntary Evacuation

In many ways, mandatory evacuation orders are easier than voluntary evacuations. When officials *suggest* you evacuate rather than *order* it, you're left to make decisions about your own fate, often without all the facts.

When deciding whether to stay or go during voluntary evacuation orders, take into account several things:

How close is the disaster? If you don't have enough time to get away, it's better to shelter in place. You don't want to be stranded on the road when the disaster hits.

How safe is your home? If you live on the highest point of the neighborhood, your home is probably safe from a flood. If you have the only safe room in town, your home might very well be the best place to stay during a tornado. On the other hand, if you live in a mobile home or on the thirtieth floor, staying during a hurricane or tornado is out of the question.

Will emergency services be available? If emergency services are evacuating, no one will be left to help you in case of a problem. You should leave.

Are you ready? If you've planned and prepared to shelter in place and have received no mandatory evacuation orders, you'd be better off staying.

Do you have pets? Later in this chapter we discuss pets and livestock in detail, but for now the question is whether to evacuate or shelter in place. Your pets are a part of that decision, and you'll have to find a shelter or hotel that accepts animals. If you're ready to shelter in place and have heard no order for mandatory evacuation, your pets will have a better chance with you at home.

Make your decision to stay or go quickly but not out of fear. You've planned for this, remember? If you're staying, it's time to batten down the hatches and get ready to ride out the storm. Whether you're staying or not, it's time to pack up the car, just in case. There's no time to mull it over. If you're going to go, you need to get on the road. Now.

Packing Up

What Melanie and Rod were doing is typical of disasters. Despite all the planning and preparation, we can't live our lives all packed up and ready to evacuate at a moment's notice. There will always be photo albums in the bookshelf and important papers in the desk accessible for everyday use. During the last few hours or minutes before a disaster strikes, you should get things together to be mobile if you have to.

THE OPTION OF MOBILITY

Even if you plan to shelter in place, the option of mobility is important. It would be horrible if you made the decision to stick it out and weren't prepared to leave when circumstances changed and forced to go.

Move all your evacuation supplies into your car, and fill up your gas tank if it's not full. Pay attention to local news so you get the word quickly if an evacuation order is given. If you have time, charge all your portable electronics—phones, radios, laptops, tablets, etc.

If there's time, you also could grab a few photographs or mementos. But keep it light, and *do not do this* if it's time to go. If at any time during this process you get the word that it's time to evacuate or circumstances change and you have to leave, drop what you're doing and hit the road.

See the "Worksheet: Emergency Mobility Checklist" at the end of the chapter for more things to do to be sure you're equipped to evacuate at a moment's notice.

Last-Minute Preparations

You've decided (or been ordered) to leave. The car is packed. The gas tank is full. Now for the last-minute details before you go. These things—closing and locking all the doors and windows, loading the car with your evacuation supplies, notifying your out-of-town contacts, etc.—should take you less than 5 minutes to complete. Don't panic. Move quickly but methodically.

Work together. Everyone in the family can have a job, even the kids. Their responsibility might be to climb in the car and buckle up on their own, but every bit of autonomy helps get you on the road faster.

See the "Worksheet: Last-Minute Checklist" for more.

Pets and Livestock

This disaster is affecting your pet as much as it's affecting you. Animals don't always understand what's happening, but they're hardwired for self-preservation. That means an animal left outside might try to go find someplace safer. Unfortunately, in many cases, there's nowhere safer a pet can get to on foot. It's your responsibility as a pet owner to be sure your pet is safe.

Never leave a pet behind. Always take your animals with you if you evacuate.

If you shelter in place, keep your animals inside with you. Dangerous predators, like snakes, can be pushed out of their usual habitats by some disasters. Leaving pets outside may put them at risk.

Also, be sure you have enough emergency supplies for your animals as well as yourself. Remember: each dog and cat counts as a person when calculating your water supplies.

Keep a copy of veterinary records for all your pets, too. If you need to shelter your dogs and cats, you may need to provide copies to the shelter.

EVACUATING WITH BIRDS

If you're forced to evacuate and travel with birds, be sure the cage has a thin cover to restrict the bird's vision but still allow light into the cage.

All pets should have proper identification. It's best for dogs and cats to have microchips and for their information to be on file with animal control and their veterinarian. You should still have the animal's medical records, however, because local animal control centers and veterinary offices could become damaged or destroyed in the disaster.

Even though you should **never leave an animal behind,** circumstances sometimes force you to do the unthinkable. Understand that if you do leave a pet behind when you evacuate, there's a very good chance your pet will die. If you do take this risk, never chain your pet outside during a disaster. Lock them in the house, free to roam from room to room. Leave them plenty of food and water, too. For additional water, prop up or remove toilet seats and remove toilet tank lids. Don't forget to prop open bathroom doors so the animal can get to the toilets. Also put a notice on a window indicating the number and types of animals in the house—tape it on the inside facing out so it doesn't blow away. Include your phone number on the notice. And if you haven't already, take a picture of your pet to identify it if it runs away or gets hurt.

Pets are part of the family, but whether we like it or not, they're second-class citizens when it comes to disasters. Most public shelters don't accept pets, so if you have your pet with you on the road, you might have to find alternatives to a public shelter.

Not all disaster shelters turn away animals. In some areas, authorities have found that evacuees are more likely to use shelters if their pets are allowed, too. The only way to know is to ask. If you can, call the shelter to see if it allows pets. Even if the shelter doesn't allow animals, someone there might be able to direct you to a shelter that does. If there aren't shelter options, attempt to find somewhere to take your pets before choosing to leave them at home.

Check with local hotels (preferably before the disaster) to identify which ones accept pets. Or try to find kennels and pet boarding either locally or outside the disaster area. If all else fails, check with local animal shelters to see if any of them provide emergency boarding for pets. Obviously, space will be limited even if you can find a shelter that provides emergency relief.

Large animals such as cows, pigs, and horses provide a much more complicated challenge. Long before a disaster strikes, call your local animal control office to ask about regional disaster plans with regard to livestock.

Be sure your animals are identified as yours with proper documentation. Arrange to have enough trailers, vehicles, and qualified drivers to move your animals if needed, and identify where you'll take your animals if you need to evacuate them. Map out at least two routes to get the animals to their destination.

Know that if you haven't created a specific plan for your large animals, there's very little you can do on short notice. If you don't have the time to evacuate your animals before evacuating your family, either turn the animals out (like the pig Melanie discovered) or be sure the animals have adequate shelter, food, and water.

Worksheet: Emergency Mobility Checklist

Regardless whether you plan to leave or stick around during a disaster, you'll need to be prepared to hit the road if things start to turn bad. Here are some last-minute things you need to do before the stuff hits the fan:

❑ Move all your evacuation supplies into your vehicle.

❑ If you don't have a full tank of fuel, go get gas.

❑ Park your vehicle outside next to the building—close enough to get some shelter from the building if you decide to stay, but far enough away that it won't be damaged or trapped in the garage.

❑ Tune the TV or the radio to a channel that keeps you updated on local information. Situations can change quickly, and you want to hear what's happening as soon as the information becomes available.

❑ Dress in long pants and sturdy shoes with a long sleeve shirt—and stay dressed that way until the disaster is over.

❑ Put a bag or container next to the door you can add last-minute items to. Put the car keys in that container so you can't accidentally leave without it.

❑ Put all your prescription medicines in the container next to the door.

❑ Put your wallets, passports, and cash in the container.

❑ Be sure your communication plan is established, and make contact with your out-of-town person. Explain your plans, and give a timeline for your next contact.

❑ If you have enough time, charge everything: phones, radios, computers, tablets, etc. Everything with a rechargeable battery should be at 100 percent or as close as you can get it.

❑ Be sure all your charging equipment is next to or in the container by the door. Don't forget to take the chargers.

❑ If you have time, take a look at your evacuation supplies. Are they all there? Do you have supplies for the kids and pets?

Worksheet: Last-Minute Checklist

These last-minute items can be done by more than one person so you get it done quickly. For instance, someone in the car can be getting maps ready while someone else is calling the out-of-town contact and a third person is locking up the house.

❑ Close and lock all doors and windows. Never leave a window or door open, especially during tornadoes or hurricanes.

❑ Load the last-minute evacuation supplies container into the car.

❑ Be sure you have your phones and radios.

❑ Unplug all appliances.

❑ Know where you're going. Pick a shelter or a rendezvous point to drive to, and find it on your GPS and on a paper map.

❑ Call your out-of-town contact to let him or her know you're leaving.

❑ Follow any instructions given by authorities on the radio.

9

Disaster Strikes

You've made your plan, and you've put together your preparedness kit. The event you've prepared for has happened. What do you do?

The most important thing to do is to work your plan. But remember that the plan is not meant to be a strict set of instructions you have to stick to no matter what. It's a work in progress. With each drill or real-life event, you learn new things, and as a result, you can add to or change some things about your plan that don't quite work.

In this chapter, we take a look at some disaster scenarios—natural as well as man-made—and offer some additional action plans you can include with your own family plan.

Earthquakes

It's impossible to predict when and where an earthquake will occur. When an earthquake hits, how you respond depends on where you are.

If you're indoors, duck, cover, and hold on. Drop to the floor, take cover under something sturdy, and hold on until the shaking stops. Stay away from windows, outer walls, and anything that could fall—think tall bookcases, china cabinets, big-screen TVs, large paintings and framed photographs, and chandeliers and other light fixtures. Stay away from other heavy items like water heaters, furnaces, gas appliances, and refrigerators. (Although you already secured these to the walls and bolted them to the floor after reading Chapter 6, right?)

If the earthquake happens while you're in bed, stay in bed and protect yourself with your pillows, holding your arms protectively over your head.

Do not use elevators.

If you're outdoors, don't go indoors. Stay outside, and move away from any buildings and power lines. Just as most tornado deaths and injuries don't come from a person being thrown by the twister, but instead from flying debris, so it is with earthquakes. Most deaths and injuries come from falling debris and shattered glass as nearby buildings collapse.

Extreme Heat

Extreme heat is dangerous. The summer heat wave of 2012 killed 82 people in the United States and Canada. July 2012 was the hottest month in U.S. history, with average high temperatures over 100°F (38°C).

During extreme heat, it's all too easy for people to suffer from hyperthermia—very high body temperature. During times of extreme heat, you must keep your body cool and damp. Remain indoors as much as possible, and use air-conditioning, fans, and cool baths to keep your body temperature down. If air-conditioning isn't available, remember that heat rises, so remain on lower, shaded floors as much as possible. Keep the blinds closed and the drapes drawn to keep your surroundings cooler.

If you must be outside, try to stay in the shade as much as possible. Wear wide-brimmed hats, use sunscreen, continually drink water, and avoid overexerting yourself.

Find places to go that are air-conditioned such as malls, libraries, or churches. See if your community offers shelters for people to escape to during oppressive heat.

It's extremely important to remain hydrated during heat waves. Drink water continually, all through the day. And instead of eating three heavy meals a day, eat four or five light meals. The heavier the meal, the more energy your body needs to digest it, increasing your body's heat.

Be sure your pets are protected from the heat, too. Constantly check that they have plenty of water and someplace cool to be.

THE DANGER OF HOT CARS

Never leave children or pets in hot cars, even just for a minute. Since 1998, 560 children have died of heatstroke when left in cars; the number of pets is probably higher. The heat wasn't preventable; the deaths were.

Check on any elderly or frail neighbors. Older people are often on a restricted budget and don't feel they can afford to use their air-conditioning. Some can be stubborn on this to the point of danger. If necessary, invite them to your home for some iced tea and to soak up some air-conditioning. In addition to ensuring they stay cool, you're also doing your part to create neighborhood bonds, and possibly giving some much-needed attention to a lonely neighbor.

TREASURES OF THE HEART

There are no greater treasures than the highest human qualities such as compassion, courage, and hope. Not even tragic accident or disaster can destroy such treasures of the heart.

—Daisaku Ikeda, Buddhist philosopher

Fires, House

House fires cause damage to the tune of $7.3 billion—and kill more than 2,000 people—each year across the United States. Home fires are a different from most disasters, in terms of preventability. Most aren't started by natural causes such as lightening or wildfires but instead by carelessness in the kitchen, electrical problems, cigarettes, outdoor grilling, space heaters, fireplaces, irons and other heat-producing appliances, and children playing with matches. And most people who die in home fires die of smoke inhalation, or inhalation of poisonous gases, rather than open flames.

It doesn't take long for a fire to get out of control. In fact, you might not know a fire is burning somewhere in the house until the smoke alarm goes off. If the fire quickly passes the point it can be put out with a fire extinguisher, you must evacuate—*quickly*. You won't have any time to gather items. You may have only seconds to get out.

If your clothes catch fire, remember "stop, drop, and roll"—stop where you are, drop to the ground, and roll back and forth until the fire is out. Flames can also be smothered with a blanket.

As smoke gets thick, you may need to crawl along the floor. Smoke rises, and the air is more breathable near the floor.

If you have to open a door, first touch the knob to see how hot it is. Also feel the door itself. If either is hot, try to find another way out because there could be fire on the other side of the door.

If someone in your home is blocked from escaping, don't risk your own life to help. It might sound selfish, but you need to get out as quickly as possible and immediately call 911 for help. You can't help anyone if you are passed out from smoke inhalation.

Fires, Wild

As more and more people settle in areas known for hot, dry summers, drought and wildfires become realistic hazards. Some wildfires begin with something as simple as a dropped match or cigarette, while others are caused by lightning. The problem can be worse in an area where highly flammable brush hasn't burned in many years and builds up an incendiary stockpile. Regardless of how they begin, wildfires spread quickly, consuming everything in their paths—brush, trees, and unfortunately, homes.

If wildfires are burning in your area, stay calm, pay attention to air-quality forecasts, and carefully listen for instructions.

If you're told to evacuate, or if you feel you should evacuate, go to a hotel, the home of a friend out of the danger area, or to a public shelter. If you see damaged or fallen power lines and poles as you go, avoid them.

Don't re-enter your house until authorities tell you it's safe to do so. If you become aware of heat or smoke when entering a damaged building, evacuate immediately. And if you return home and find a color-coded sign on your home, don't go inside. The sign was placed there by a building inspector, so you need to find out what it means and whether it's safe to enter. Be sure you or a neighbor or some other trusted person keeps an eye on your home until you're able to re-enter.

If you remained in your home, check your roof and attic for sparks or embers after the danger has passed. Put out any sparks or embers you find, and keep rechecking for smoke, sparks, or other signs of fire on your roof, your property, and throughout your home for several hours. Watch out for hot spots in burned areas, too. They can suddenly flare up. Look for ash pits and mark them. Tell your family and neighbors to avoid them. Wet down debris to help alleviate the dust in the air.

Always protect your hands and feet when working outside in burned areas. Leather gloves and hard-toed, heavy-soled shoes are required.

BEWARE OF BURNS

If you or a family member suffers burns, cool and cover the burns to reduce the chance of infection, and call 911 or seek other immediate help. Turn to Part 4 for further instructions on treating burns and other first aid.

Inside, dispose of any food that has been exposed to the heat or smoke. Also dispose of all household chemicals such as cleaning products, paint, and fuel containers. And don't use water that may be contaminated for anything.

Floods

Realize that if it rains, it can flood. Just because an area's history hasn't designated it as a floodplain doesn't mean it isn't one—or won't become one.

Floodplains are created as a result of changing weather, topography, and development. The more an area is developed, with open spaces covered with concrete and buildings, the less area remains for water to drain so it accumulates. A developing community may see flooding begin to get worse, more frequent, and more intense.

To protect your home, be sure your furnace, air conditioner, and water heater as well as any electrical panels are up off the ground. If possible, sandbag entrances to prevent water from entering. If you're inside a multistory building, go to higher floors using the stairs, not the elevator.

If you take nothing else away from this section, remember this: *the number-one most dangerous thing you can do during a flood or flash flood is drive on water-covered roadways.* No matter how well you know the route, if you can't see the road beneath the water, there's no way you can know for sure the road is still there. It may be washed away or collapsed. It takes only 6 inches of water to cause a car to stall, 12 inches to cause it to float, and 2 feet of water to move it—even larger trucks and SUVs. Before long, the driver is caught in rushing waters, with no control, and water pressure sealing the doors shut. This is an extremely dangerous position to be in.

As inconvenient as it might seem to come to a spot of road that's flooded and turn around to find another route, do it anyway. And if signs or barricades are blocking water-covered roads, do not drive around the barricades to take the road.

If you do, and you're lucky enough not to drown, the likelihood is that you'll get stuck and have to call 911. Emergency personnel will have to come rescue you, possibly even requiring a helicopter rescue. Whatever the method, it will be expensive, and it will endanger the lives of the fire, police, or medical personnel who come help you.

STUPID MOTORIST LAW

Water rescues had become a problem for Arizona, where heavy rains often cause dangerous flooding. So in 1995, Arizona enacted the "Stupid Motorist Law." This law states that people who drive into areas where roads are covered by water, or where they're warned of dangers of rushing waters, will be responsible for the expenses of being rescued by emergency personnel. Drivers may also be fined for reckless driving, charged for a criminal offense, and in all likelihood have to deal with the resulting auto insurance fallout (a company may raise premiums or drop the policy altogether).

Driving into flooded areas is a dangerous and expensive mistake—a risk not worth taking.

Hurricanes

The options for hurricanes are pretty simple: evacuate; if you can't evacuate, shelter in place.

Plan ahead of time for evacuation. Know what evacuation route you'll use, and whether *contraflow* is used on interstates. In the case of Hurricane Katrina, the eastbound lanes of Interstate 10 were closed coming into New Orleans, but the westbound lanes were open to Baton Rouge.

DEFINITION

Contraflow is alteration of the normal flow of traffic. In emergency evacuations, contraflow doubles the number of lanes available for outbound traffic by reversing the flow of lanes heading into town so all the lanes—both inbound and outbound—are now outbound lanes. All incoming traffic is blocked until the evacuation is complete.

You should have your supplies already organized in an emergency preparedness kit, as you learned in Chapter 2. Preparing your kit well in advance ensures you have everything you need and prevents you from overlooking something important or having to make a run to the store … along with everyone else in town. In New Orleans, the first three items stores ran out of were bottled water, Vienna Sausages, and bread. Remember, you should have enough nonperishable food and bottled water to last 3 days, with 1 gallon per person per day.

An ax is an important tool to have in your preparedness kit if you live where hurricanes are common. It'll come in handy if water surge forces you onto your roof. One elderly couple who survived Katrina used an ax to break through their attic roof. The wife had one leg in and one leg out, while the husband held on to his wife's leg. They held onto the roof and each other that way all through the night until a rescue boat arrived to take them to safety.

Be sure your car is running well and that your gas tank is full—preferably before the long lines begin to form at the gas stations. There's nothing like waiting in line for 45 minutes to get to the pump only to find that the person in front of you got the last of the gas.

Cover your home's windows, too. Storm shutters, the best option for window protection, are a common sight on the Gulf Coast. A good alternative is boarding your windows. Move things to interior rooms, away from windows if possible, and remove your curtains, too, so they don't get wet.

Wind clips, mentioned in Chapter 6, are a good option to install on your roof—long before a storm looms. Tying down your roof makes it more secure and less likely to be blown away. Beefing up your garage doors, also discussed in Chapter 6, is another way to fortify your home. Both of these actions can also be used to prepare for tornadoes. Of course, not much can withstand direct hits from Category-5 hurricanes or EF-5 tornadoes, but these actions can help protect against weaker-category winds.

Bring anything inside that isn't tied down, such as patio furniture, trash bins, toys, bikes, etc. If you have a boat, plan ahead for temporary storage. By the time the hurricane hits, your boat should already be in storage. After Hurricane Katrina, many boat owners found their boats in nearby neighborhoods, parking lots, and neighbor's yards; some never found their boat after the storm.

Power Failures

In August 2003, the largest electrical blackout in U.S. history occurred, the result of a software bug in the alarm system at First Energy Corporation in Ohio. The blackout affected 10 million people in Ontario, Canada, and 45 million people in 8 American states. The blackout lasted from between 7 hours to 2 days, with some areas being restored sooner than others.

If you're struck with a power outage, keep your refrigerator and freezer doors closed. This helps keep your food as cold as possible. Before eating any food that was frozen or chilled, check it carefully for signs of spoilage.

Turn off or disconnect appliances or electronics that were on or in use the time the power went off. When the electricity comes back on, it may come in a surge that can damage some items such as air conditioners, computers, furnaces, or refrigerators. Leave on one light, however, so you'll know when the power has returned.

If you have a generator, only operate it outside in a well-ventilated, dry area far away from air intakes. Never operate it indoors, even in your basement or garage. Generators are powered by engines that emit carbon monoxide—an odorless and colorless gas that poisons without its victims ever knowing what's happening. Misuse of generators killed five people after Hurricane Katrina and sickened many more. These were easily preventable deaths. Be sure to read the instruction manual that came with your generator carefully.

Generators work with electrical power, which if not connected and grounded properly, can shock or kill you. Check your generator's instruction manual for correct grounding information, and be sure your generator is properly grounded.

Don't plug a portable generator into an electrical outlet in your home or garage. It can backfeed power into the utility company lines, placing utility workers in danger while they're working on downed power lines. Instead, use a heavy-duty, outdoor-rated power cord to connect to the generator. Then connect appliances to the power cord.

Also don't overload your generator. Use it only when necessary and only to power a limited number of appliances. Don't try to power your entire house at one time on a single generator. You could damage your appliances and maybe even cause a fire in your power cord.

HARD-WIRED GENERATORS

If you want to hard-wire a generator to your home so you have emergency power at a moment's notice, first check with your local utility company. Then hire a licensed electrician to install it with an approved cut-off switch that will automatically disconnect your home from the power grid while the generator is in use.

Keep a traditional landline phone—not a cordless phone—so you still have phone access during a power outage. Your cell phone will require charging at some point, and battery power may run out before power returns.

Remember that in widespread power outage, ATMs, elevators, and gas pumps may not work. As part of your preparedness, be sure your car's gas tank is at least half full at all times. Traffic signals might not be working either, creating traffic slowdowns. Don't travel by car if it isn't necessary.

If it's hot outside during a power outage—go to a "cooling station," if your community has those. Or go to a mall, library, or movie theater. If you have small children, your community may have parks with splash pads, which are cool, fun, and free. Remember to wear lightweight, lightly colored clothes, and drink plenty of water, even if you're not thirsty. Wear a wide-brimmed hat outdoors to protect your face and head.

Put up temporary reflectors in your windows, like cardboard covered with aluminum foil. Hang shades, curtains, or even sheets in your windows that get direct sun in the morning or afternoon to keep that heat and light outside and your home cooler.

Eat small meals, and eat more often. Eating heavily causes your body to burn more energy to digest food, creating heat.

Heat exhaustion, marked by dizziness and nausea, can sneak up on you before you're aware of it. See Chapter 19 on heat and cold exposure for more information on recognizing and treating heat exhaustion.

If it's cold outside during a power outage, put on extra layers of warm clothing. Don't use your gas oven as a source of heat, and never burn charcoal indoors. If the power is going to be out for a long time, go to a friend's or relative's home or to a hotel to keep warm.

Tornadoes

Shelter in place is the best plan with tornadoes, unless you live in a mobile/manufactured home, in which case you should evacuate. Know where the nearest storm shelter is located and how quickly you can get to it. If you don't live in a mobile/manufactured home, shelter in place, and stay inside your house away from windows. Go to a storm cellar, safe room, or basement. If nothing else, go to an interior room, closet, or bathroom on the lower level.

STAY INSIDE

Do not go outside to see the tornado approach. As fascinating as tornadoes are to watch, and as many hits as you might get when you post the video online, it's not worth the risk.

Protect yourself from flying debris by covering yourself with blankets, cushions, or a mattress. Mobile/manufactured home residents aside, most deaths and injuries during tornadoes result from flying debris. A bicycle helmet offers excellent head protection.

If driving, or if you're outside away from a sturdy building, pull your car off the side of the road, taking care not to block the road. Leave your car, and flatten yourself in a ditch or a low spot, keeping flooding in mind. Do not try to outrun the tornado. And contrary to popular thought, do not try to ride out a tornado under a highway overpass. An overpass essentially becomes a wind tunnel during a tornado. Winds are actually sucked through it, taking with them anything or anyone not tied down.

Tsunamis

Tsunamis are giant waves produced by earthquake movement along the ocean floor. They can move 100 miles per hour and hit land with waves as high as 100 feet tall. The most destructive tsunamis have struck along the coastlines of California, Oregon, Washington, Alaska, and Hawaii, although the Gulf Coast, U.S. Virgin Islands, and Puerto Rico also have been hit. Tsunamis are fairly rare on the U.S. east coast.

If an earthquake occurs and you're in a tsunami-risk area, listen to the radio for tsunami warnings. If you're on a beach and you suddenly see the waters recede, consider that a warning. What goes out must come back, and the water will come back with a vengeance. Take heed and get out immediately.

If evacuation orders are issued, evacuate immediately, taking your animals with you. Don't stop to gather any of your possessions. There isn't time.

As in all floods, go to higher ground. Move inland and farther up to higher ground as quickly as possible. Try to get to an area higher than 100 feet above sea level and as far as 2 miles inland, away from the coast line. Go as high and as far as you can.

Don't stay to see the tsunami. Get out, and get up as quickly as you can. If you can see the wave, it could be too late to reach safety.

Winter Storms

Sheltering indoors, staying dry, and keeping yourself warm is a no-brainer when it comes to winter storms. The greatest danger posed by winter storms is loss of heat, which can be caused by power loss due to ice-covered power lines or by loss of natural gas. Most people who die in winter storms are killed driving on ice-covered roads or from hypothermia.

If you lose power or heat, stay inside until after the blizzard or ice storm has passed and streets are treated or plowed. Then seek shelter at a local desig-nated public shelter or with a friend or relative. Wherever you are, stay dry and warm as possible by bundling up with clothes and blankets and sharing body heat. If you use kerosene oil for light, be sure your home is properly ventilated. Avoid candles if possible, due to the fire risk.

When walking or driving on snow or ice, be very careful because *black ice* can be particularly deceptive.

DEFINITION

Black ice refers to ice so thin it's completely transparent, allowing the black asphalt underneath to be completely visible through it. Because the ice is so thin, it's difficult to realize that a parking lot, street, or sidewalk is covered in it, hence the threat.

If you must be outside to shovel snow, care for animals, or do other such tasks, change into dry clothes as frequently as necessary. Dry clothing insulates the body, whereas wet clothing promotes rapid loss of body heat.

Watch for signs of frostbite such as numbness and general loss of feeling in your toes, fingers, nose, and earlobes, as well as pale skin in these areas. If you detect signs of frostbite, seek medical help immediately.

Hypothermia is a common danger in cold weather. You've probably seen a character on TV or in the movies who, when stranded in extreme cold, begins to talk about being very sleepy and just wants to lie down in the snow and go to sleep. That's hypothermia. Other symptoms can include extreme shivering, an inability to think clearly, disorientation, and slurred speech. If you or someone you're with starts to exhibit symptoms of hypothermia, change out of your wet clothes and get warm as quickly as possible from the inside out. Blankets, dry clothes, and warm drinks are a good start. Get medical help immediately.

A great way to keep your body warm in cold weather is by movement. Running in place or doing jumping jacks when inside can help warm the body. If outside, shoveling snow can warm you up. But be careful to avoid overexertion.

If you have to travel during winter storms, carry sand and a shovel in your car in case you get stuck in snow or ice. Also pack boots, blankets, snacks, and a flashlight.

If you do get stuck in your car, turn on your emergency lights and if possible, park out of the way of traffic but where your car can be seen. Don't get out of your car and walk in a blizzard unless you can see there's a shelter from your car within just a few steps. If you have to stay put, turn on your engine and heater for only 10 to 15 minutes each hour, but be sure to crack a window to avoid carbon monoxide poisoning.

Man-Made Hazards

Man-made hazards such as accidental chemical spills; domestic terrorism like the 1995 bombing of the Murrah Federal Building in Oklahoma City, Oklahoma; and international terrorism such as the September 11, 2011, attacks on New York's World Trade Center and the Pentagon in Washington, D.C., show us that attacks and other non-natural disasters fall somewhere on the risk spectrum between "likely" and "possible." Not as likely as a tornado in Oklahoma, perhaps, but a more likely than an electromagnetic pulse wiping out civilization as we know it.

Therefore, it's prudent to address such hazards in this chapter so you know what to do should something like this occur.

Biological Agents

A biological attack is the release of biological agents that can kill or make you sick. Think anthrax, smallpox, plague, or ricin. The most likely group to be used as weapons would be bacteria, viruses, and toxins. Symptoms of exposure may be the first evidence of an attack. Even for minor symptoms like sore throats and mild fevers or headaches, call 911 if they strike multiple people at the same time. Authorities might be able to track multiple 911 calls to identify an attack in progress.

If you see or become aware of a suspicious substance—white powder in an envelope, for example—get away from the substance. Cover your mouth and nose with several layers of fabric, such as heavy cotton, that can act as a filter. Several layers of paper towels may also help, or use a face mask if you have one available.

If you've been exposed, call 911 and seek medical assistance. Remove and bag your clothes. Follow the instructions of doctors and other public health officials for disposal of any contaminated clothing or personal items. Wash yourself thoroughly with soap and hot water, and put on clean clothes. You may need to be to quarantined or put in isolation from others.

Watch your family members for symptoms, too. Remember that symptoms of biological attacks may overlap with symptoms of other illnesses and may not be related to biological attacks.

If a biological emergency has been declared, stay away from crowds where others may be infected. Monitor the news via radio, TV, or the internet. It may take time for authorities to know what the illness is, the agent involved, who is in danger, and what you should do. As information is made available, the media will tell the public what signs and symptoms they should look for, who is in danger, and what vaccines or treatments are available.

Bombs

As we've unfortunately seen, terrorist attacks do happen. Bombs are planted. Buildings are blown up. People are killed.

If you find yourself in a place that has just suffered an explosion, you can take action that may save your life. If things are falling around you, duck and cover under a desk, table, or other sturdy, protective place until the debris has stopped falling. When it's clear, leave immediately. Watch out for unstable floors or stairs, don't use elevators, be aware of falling rubble, and be careful around glass doors and windows. If you see or smell smoke, get down on the floor and crawl out of the building.

People in situations like this have a tendency to gather together and to make phone calls. Do not gather. Do not make phone calls. Do not hold meetings to debate whether to stay or go. Go. Get out. Don't use your cell phone for calls or texts, as the frequencies may set off secondary devices. Turn your phone off to avoid incoming calls or texts.

Once outside, move away from sidewalks or streets to make room for responders and for others still evacuating.

If you're trapped in debris, cover your nose or mouth with anything you have. If you're wearing a cotton shirt, that could work to filter out the dust. Don't shout unless you just have to. Shouting uses air that may be in short supply. It also causes you to breathe in dust. Instead, signal your location by using a flashlight if possible or tap on something like a pipe or a wall to let rescuers know you are there. If you have a whistle on you, use it.

Chemical Threats

Whether they're the result of terrorist action or simply an accident, chemical threats are dangerous. Chemical agents come in various forms, including poisonous vapors, liquids, aerosols, and solids. Many toxic chemicals react at different speeds and in different ways. Some symptoms to look for include difficulty breathing; eye irritation; nausea; burning in the throat, nose, and lungs; or loss of coordination.

Remember the miner's canary: toxic gases in a mine would kill the bird before affecting the miners and, thus, the canary's death served as a warning for the miners. In much the same way, the presence of many dead birds or even insects might warn of a chemical agent release.

If you suspect a chemical threat, try to figure out where it's coming from, if possible, and the extent of the impacted area.

If the contamination is in a building, leave immediately, being careful to avoid the contaminated area. If it isn't possible to evacuate, move as far away as possible from the contaminated area and shelter in place. Close doors and windows, shut off the air-conditioning, and close all ventilation systems. Take your disaster kit and go to an internal room to put as many walls between you and the outside as possible. Seal the room with duct tape and plastic sheeting, and stay put. Listen to the radio for further instructions, and don't come out until you're given the all-clear.

If you're outside in or near a contaminated area, move upwind of the source. Find shelter immediately and shelter in place, or move away from the area toward cleaner air, whichever is faster.

If you believe you've been exposed to something dangerous, call 911.

911

Reserve calls to 911 for life-threatening emergencies only. Calling 911 for more information or for reassurance prevents emergency calls from getting through and places others in greater danger. Listen to radios or television—powered by batteries or generator—to stay updated.

Epidemics

An epidemic is an outbreak of a flu or virus that spreads rapidly. (A *pandemic* is a much wider spread of an epidemic that may sweep a region, or even move from country to country.)

One way to try to avoid catching what's going around is to wash your hands with soap and warm water often and thoroughly—long enough to sing "Happy Birthday" to yourself twice, or about 20 seconds.

Use hand sanitizers, and keep surfaces clean. If you're around people with flu, wear a mask, and keep plenty of tissues and trash receptacles around.

If you're sick, stay home. Cover your cough to protect those around you. Be sure to wash your hands after coughing, sneezing, or blowing your nose. If you need it, acetaminophen and ibuprofen can help bring down a fever and reduce aches and pains.

It's a scary world out there. The man-made hazards sometimes can be more frightening than the impersonal and much more likely natural hazards. But whether we're discussing hurricanes, power outages, an accidental chemical release, or bioterrorism, the same principal holds true: knowledge is power, and power is control. Loss of power doesn't have to mean loss of power.

Thinking ahead, developing a family preparedness kit, and implementing a family preparedness plan strengthened with family drills and exercises provides your family a greater level of protection. Plus, you get an increased sense of security knowing you have more control than you previously thought in a situation often thought out of your control.

3

The First Seven Days

Part 3 builds on what you've learned so far and looks at your first steps after a disaster has struck. We review your first steps to take that first hour postdisaster, putting into action the plan you've worked so hard to build. We address the possibility of your plan failing and offer advice on how to adapt to the things you didn't plan for.

We address your food and water situation, tell you how to safely cook food without your usual equipment and resources, and teach you how to ration and purify your water. We also explain how to assess your home's structural integrity so you can make an informed decision on the safety of staying or the wisdom of leaving. And we go over the safe use of fire, share tips on remaining secure and free from harm socially unstable situations, offer advice on how to deal with rumors, and review what to expect of officials.

What if your family winds up in a shelter? We talk about how to locate shelters, what to expect of them, and how to contribute toward making your shelter a pleasant and safe environment in spite of the stress everyone is under.

Part 3 ends on a discussion of the challenges facing urban dwellers and those who live in the country during a disaster. You'll see that the "country mouse" and the "city mouse" have some challenges in common, while other challenges are specific to each area.

10

The First Hour

On Sunday, May 22, 2011, Jim Lane, a longtime Joplin, Missouri, real estate agent, was in his office chatting with co-worker Donald Lansaw. Don, a former football player, was a young go-getter. Even if a bit inexperienced, he had a good instinct for networking and great people skills. As they talked, the phone rang.

"It was a friend of mine wanting me to go to lunch with her," Jim remembers. Jim left Don at the office and went to meet his friend Heather at a local restaurant. During their meal, the power suddenly went out, and the management ushered all the customers into the restaurant's walk-in cooler. "Then they said, 'hey, it's over,' so we just went back into the dining room and finished [eating] in the dark."

As Jim and Heather drove back to his house, they got lost because Jim no longer recognized his neighborhood. It was in total destruction. Jim stopped the car, and Heather, a registered nurse, immediately jumped out and ran across debris to see if anyone needed help.

Together, they helped people down from second-story floors and loaded the injured onto pickup trucks for transport to the hospital, using doors for gurneys. No one knew yet that the hospital, St. John's Regional Medical Center, had been hit especially hard by the EF-5 tornado that ripped through the area. The roof had blown off; the backup generator failed; and of the 161 people they would learn died that night, 6 were patients in the hospital.

And Jim did not yet know Don was one of those casualties.

In a heartbreaking story recaptured in the *Kansas City Star,* after leaving the office, Don had gone to meet his wife, Bethany, for frozen yoghurt. They had just returned home when the storm approached, the sirens sounded, and they saw the storm moving in. With no basement, Don's wife climbed into the tub, where Don covered her with blankets and pillows and then climbed on top of her, his body a final layer of protection.

When the storm was over and Bethany climbed out of the tub, she saw that Don had been pierced in the abdomen with flying debris. She ran to get help, but Don died before she returned.

Jim's home was gone—the roof had been ripped away, and from there, the destruction had commenced. Insurance eventually would assist him in replacing his home.

A New Reality

The first minutes, even the first hour after a disaster can expose you to the world, to a new reality, in a way few other things can. What you do in that time is a strong indicator of how well prepared you are.

Research indicates that people suddenly faced with a disaster fall into three categories: 10 to 15 percent stay calm. They show great presence of mind, acting quickly, decisively, and efficiently. Another 15 percent panic and completely lose control. Not only are they unlikely to save themselves, but they get in the way of evacuation attempts and endanger others as well as themselves. The rest don't do much. Their brains operate in slow motion, like a computer that's struggling to process too much data at once.

The difference between those who think quickly and calmly on their feet after a disaster and those who disintegrate into hysterics or suddenly can't think or function at all is preparedness.

Studies show it takes the brain roughly 8 to 10 seconds to process new data. When bombarded with too many pieces of new data at once, your brain experiences a crash—a slow-down of your ability to think and move.

When you imagine how you'd react in certain scenarios, and practice your responses through drills and exercises, you're turning new data into old data, so when the real thing comes along, you don't experience that slow-down but are able to operate calmly, with presence of mind and a built-in knowledge of how to respond.

When Jim and Heather drove into Jim's neighborhood, it was her training as a nurse that moved her to jump out of the car and begin acting. Jim followed suit, and soon the two of them were engaging in search-and-rescue actions—almost without consciously thinking about it. This shows how vitally important preparedness is. When you think and prepare for these events ahead of time, you train your brain to respond later, when reality hits.

The First Hour

Let's take a look at your possible responses during that first hour after a disaster for several types of hazards, as you put to work the plan you've been building.

NAVIGATION PLAN

Problems show up like the rocks in a bay when the tide is out. You can develop a navigation plan. When the water is up, you don't know where the rocks are. Use downturns to find areas that need to be improved.

—James Morgan, CEO, Applied Materials

No matter what kind of disaster causes the damage, at some point you should call your insurance company and the property-restoration company you identified earlier as part of your preparedness planning. Do this sooner rather than later because rapid response is key in preventing more, worse problems down the road. Understandably, depending on what else is happening that first hour, it might not be your first priority, but do get to it as soon as you can.

Earthquakes

If after an earthquake, you're trapped in a closed-off area, use a flashlight. Be careful not to use matches or lighters in case gas fumes are present.

Be careful to avoid breathing in dust. Cover your mouth with a piece of cloth to filter any dust. Avoid movement that will stir up dust, and don't shout if you don't have to. Instead, get rescuers' attention by knocking on a pipe or some other hard surface. If you have a whistle, use it.

Be sure everyone around you is well, if you can. Check yourself and others for injuries. Don't move seriously injured people, unless it's to avoid further injury. Call for help immediately.

Check your building for structural damage. If it doesn't look like it's going to hold, get out as quickly as possible. You should expect aftershocks, and be careful of further structural damage.

Clean up any flammable liquids, if possible, and check your utilities for damage. If you hear a hissing sound or smell gas, open a window and evacuate. Shut off the main gas valve outside. Turn off the electricity at the fuse box or circuit breaker, and shut off water supply at the main valve.

If family members are separated at various locations, follow your plan for meeting or communicating. Remember that phone lines may be jammed, so try texting. Texting is carried through a separate frequency.

Stay away from damaged areas to free up emergency crews to do their work. If your home was fortunate enough to avoid damage, do not go to damaged areas to gawk. Traffic from curious observers may prevent responders from being able to get through.

LOOKY-LOOS

On May 30, 2013, an EF-2 tornado touched down in Broken Arrow, Oklahoma. Within minutes, Highway 51 was clogged with what meteorologists called "looky-loos" going to check out the damage. Fire, police, and emergency medical crews had to drive off the highway to get around all the traffic—most of which had no business being there. This kind of obstruction can prevent emergency crews from rescuing people and treating the wounded quickly enough.

If it isn't necessary for you to travel during this time, stay off the roads. If you do need to drive somewhere, be very careful and watch for fallen trees, downed power lines, and damaged roads or bridges.

Fires

After a home fire, do not reenter your home if it's been damaged by fire until you're given the all-clear by your local authorities. Watch for smoke or heat that may indicate the fire isn't out yet as well as for structural damage.

Do not try to reconnect your utilities yourself. Hire a licensed electrician to inspect the electrical wiring before turning the power back on. The same with your other utilities.

If you need a place to stay until your home is cleaned and repaired, the Red Cross may be able to help provide lodging as well as food and some personal items.

During a wildfire, your first order of business is to find shelter, whether you feel your home isn't a safe place to be or you've been told to evacuate.

FINDING SHELTER

If you have no safe place to go during a wildfire, or any disaster, you can text SHELTER and your zip code to 43362 (4FEMA) to find the nearest shelter in your area.

Don't re-enter your home until given the all-clear by fire officials or building inspectors. It is possible that when you return you will find a color-coded sign on your home, placed there by a building inspector. Don't go inside until you get more information and instructions about what exactly that sign means and whether it is safe to go inside. If you smell smoke or sense heat when going inside your house or any building, get out immediately.

If you didn't evacuate, check your roof as soon as the fire danger is over, putting out any roof fires, sparks, and embers you may find. Remain vigilant for several hours, continuing to check and recheck for smoke, sparks, and embers on and around your house.

If you or any of your family have suffered burns, seek immediate help. Call 911, and cool and cover the burns until help arrives.

And as always, be careful around any damaged or fallen power lines, poles, and wires.

Floods

If you're in an area that's flooding due to heavy rains or storm surge, get to higher ground.

Turn off your home's utilities at all the main switches and/or valves. Don't touch electrical equipment if you're wet. As you travel, avoid downed power lines.

Don't walk or drive through moving water. If roads are blocked with barriers or signs, *do not go around them.* Turn around, and find an alternate route. If a road is covered with water but isn't blocked with signs or barricades, don't assume it's still there. It might have washed out with the floodwater. Don't take the risk. Turn around; don't drown.

Avoid drinking the water and using the toilet until you know there are no problems with sewer lines or contamination. When cleaning up, use household bleach to disinfect flooded areas.

Beware of snakes and other animals looking to escape the high waters. They'll want to seek higher ground, too—and that could be inside your house!

FOR RENTERS

If you're a renter and have damage from a disaster, call your landlord. Much of, if not all, the responsibility for repairs and preventing further damage falls to the owner.

Hailstorms

After a hailstorm, but before climbing up on your roof, check your trees and shrubs for damage. These can be easy indicators of roof damage. Your gutters may be another indicator of roof damage. If your trees, shrubs, and gutters show signs of damage, your roof is likely damaged, too.

Stop any leaks you find. Place tarps on your roof to cover any holes, and board up broken windows. Know that some roof damage isn't readily apparent and may not even show up in the form of leaks for several months, so if you suspect damage, have a professional come check your roof.

Check your car for damage, too. It may be best to wait until the sun is shining again because some small hail dents can only be seen in the light.

Hurricanes

After a hurricane, stay where you are. If you evacuated, don't return home until local officials give the all-clear.

If you're not someplace safe, move to where you are out of danger. Avoid flood waters, moving water, flooded areas, and downed power lines. Watch for broken glass, nails, and other debris. Wear gloves and hard-toed boots, and cover your legs while moving through damaged areas.

Don't drink tap water or use the toilets until you know there are no problems with the sewer lines or water contamination. Use household bleach in cleaning and disinfecting flooded areas.

As with floods, watch out for wildlife that might think your home is a safe place to escape high waters.

If you think your home might have mold, call an independent hygienist to inspect your home. If he or she finds mold, call the restoration company you sought out earlier in your preparedness planning to treat it. Getting rid of water damage within the first 72 hours is the best way to prevent mold, but if that's not possible, address the problem sooner rather than later. The longer you wait, the worse and more expensive your mold problems will be.

RED VERSUS GREEN

After many disasters, volunteers or emergency workers go door-to-door to check on residents. You can let them know if you need help or that everyone inside is okay by putting up a sign on the front of your house or in a front window. A red sign or large red X indicates you need help. A green sign or large green X means everyone is okay and no assistance is needed. If no signs are present, emergency response crews will stop and check.

Tornadoes

Check yourself and your family members for injuries. Apply direct pressure to any bleeding wounds. Do not try to move injured people, however unless they're in danger and must be moved. Call for help immediately. In the meantime, you might have to treat injuries until help can arrive (see Part 4).

Many people are injured after rather than during the tornado as they attempt to make their way through their damaged home or place of work, through outdoor debris, during rescue attempts, or during cleanup. Be extra careful when walking through broken glass, bricks, and pieces of wood with nails sticking out. Wear hard-toed boots and gloves, and cover your legs as you move through damaged areas. If you see downed power lines, stay away from them, and call the police and utility company to report them.

Be aware of possible damage to your home in the form of structural damage, electrical wiring, or gas leaks. When inspecting your home in the dark, use a flashlight instead of a lighter or candle.

If you suspect structural damage, get out until a structural engineer or building inspector gives you the all-clear to enter. If you smell burning odors or see sparks, shut off electricity at the main circuit breaker and call the electric company. If you smell gas, turn off the main gas valve. Open all the windows and immediately get out of the house. Call the gas company or the fire department. Don't turn on the lights, use matches, smoke a cigarette, or do anything that could set off a fire or explosion. Don't go back inside until you've been told it is safe to do so.

Continue to monitor the radio or TV (powered by batteries or a generator) for further information and instructions, and follow any instructions you're given.

POSTDISASTER PROCESSING

After a disaster, people often need to emotionally process what's happened. Shock, fear, mood swings, anxiety, nightmares—all these and more are common after a disaster. It might take time to adjust; give yourself or your loved ones that time. Telling your story is often a cathartic step; even writing down your experiences can help. Exercise can help, too. Routine is important for children, but even adults can benefit, especially after something as life-shaking as a disaster. Regular meal times, regular family time, and regular bed time can help restore a sense of normalcy and security. Mental-health professionals can be of assistance, too. Don't be afraid to ask for help if you need it.

Follow Your Plan

You know the critical importance of having a disaster preparedness plan, and you've begun to work with your family to develop your own plan that addresses your responses to the most likely hazards your family faces.

It's equally important to actually *follow* your plan after a disaster occurs. So if you're in your home facing a tornado, and your plan says you shelter in place, don't jump in your car and try to outrun the tornado.

But what if, like Jim, you're not home when the disaster occurs? How do you follow your plan when your plan is at home?

Naturally, some parts of your plan will stick in your memory and you'll just know what to do, no matter where you are, because you've planned, prepared, and practiced ahead of time. You're not likely to have memorized every part of your plan, though. That's why it's a good idea to have more than one copy and to keep those copies in the places you're likely to be when a disaster hits:

- Keep a copy in your home in a safe place.
- Keep a copy in a safe-deposit box.
- Keep a copy in your office.
- Keep a copy in your car's storage console.

Your plan will not only contain information on how to respond, but also have the important information about your family members' medical conditions, your family doctors, your school's parent/child reconciliation plans, family reconnection and communication plans, and all the important contact information you'll need.

It's important that you follow your plan as closely as you can. You have invested a great deal of time and effort into putting your plan together. It can only work if every family member has access to it and follows it.

Avoiding Plan Failure

Failure of your plan at some point is not only possible, but likely. The purpose of practicing your plan with drills and other exercises is to find out, in advance, where the weak spots are and take corrective action to adapt and strengthen the plan, well before something happens. The last thing you want is to discover your plan's shortcomings during a real disaster.

If you've developed a plan but haven't taken the time to practice it to weed out any potential failures, you're courting failure. When faced with a real disaster, you and your family members could forget what to do, which could then result in catastrophic consequences.

Regularly practicing your plan with drills and exercises significantly decreases the likelihood of your plan failing.

Adapting to the Unforeseen

Hurricane Katrina made landfall as a Category 3 hurricane. The storm was supposed to strike the Florida panhandle, but it unexpectedly turned toward New Orleans, giving the city much less than the advance notice it normally would have received to implement disaster plans and evacuate. The short notice was one reason so many people were still in the city when the hurricane hit.

Another unanticipated factor of Katrina—and the deadliest—was the levee breaches. The levee failures are considered the worst civil engineering disaster in U.S. history. Even before levee breakdowns, Mayor Ray Nagin called Katrina "a storm that most of us have long feared" as he issued the city's first-ever mandatory evacuation orders on August 28, 2005, the day before Katrina hit New Orleans. At that time, he had no idea the levees would fail in 53 different places, causing a submersion of 80 percent of the city. Many people remaining in the city had to quickly adapt their plans to the rising surge of sea water that invaded the city in addition to the powerful hurricane.

You can prepare, practice, and plan down to the smallest detail. But nature doesn't follow your plan. Chances are, you'll be hit with complications you hadn't anticipated.

Adaptation to the unforeseen is an important part of resilience, the ultimate goal of preparedness planning. Resilience is the ability to anticipate, sustain, and recover from different kinds of shocks. Adaptability is the ability to learn, to build on knowledge and experience, to make decisions while recognizing the need to remain flexible.

BEND WITH THE WIND

The seemingly wispy and weak willow tree is actually the heartier tree because of its ability to bend with the wind without breaking, unlike other trees. For this reason, the willow tree has long been a symbol of an adaptive spirit, the person with the ability to adapt to life rather than fight against it.

There's no end to the list of possible complications for which you don't—and can't—plan, but let's take a look at a few of the more likely potential complications to disasters that require you to adapt, to bend with the wind.

Evacuation Traffic Jams

Often, mandatory evacuation orders result in traffic jams on most major routes out of the city.

To prepare in advance for this, know your community's evacuation routes (if they have them; not all cities do). Carry maps in your car, in addition to your GPS system. Figure out in advance an alternate route, perhaps using rural roads. Take the time to go out and drive some of these routes, figuring out any quirks and possible problems ahead of time.

Unexpected Flooding

If you're caught in a tornado's path while driving, storm water ditches are one safe place you can find shelter. But if it's raining, the ditches can fill with water, presenting you with a second danger, drowning.

If you find yourself in this position, don't seek shelter in a ditch. Instead, lie flat on the ground, face down, away from any areas filling with water.

Problems with Meeting Place

Part of your plan assigns a safe place for your family members to meet during or after a disaster. However, several potential factors out of your control could cause this part of your plan to go awry.

Streets could be closed off or blocked, or buildings could be locked. And if the phone service has been cut off, it may be impossible to communicate a change of meeting place, or the information that one of your group is unable to get there.

Designate a secondary meeting place everyone knows to go to should your first place be unavailable or unreachable. And test your phones for the ability to text, even if they can't make or receive calls. Also test their ability to call out of state.

Backup Power Failure

After a disaster, oftentimes the power is out. And even if you have a generator, it might not work when you need it. As you wait for the power to be restored, you'll have to pull out the dynamo devices or flashlights and batteries, the nonperishable food, and the books and games for the kids.

Lack of Mail Service

After some disasters, mail service could be interrupted for extended periods of time. If possible, find the nearest post office that's up and running and rent a post office box there. Then have all your mail diverted to that post office (PO) box until your local branch is open again.

No Banks, No ATMs, No Money

If your bank and its ATMs are damaged during a storm or other hazard, you might be unable to access your money. After Katrina, for example, many banks and ATMs were underwater for weeks, unavailable to their customers.

If you've used your cash reserves and cannot access your bank account in any way due to the incapacitation of your bank, you might have to rely on friends or family for help in terms of lodging, food, and transportation until you're able to get payouts from your insurance company or federal individual assistance.

NEW BEGINNINGS

A crisis isn't usually the end. More often than not, it's the beginning.

—James Lee Witt

Disasters are never smooth-flowing events. Myriad opportunities exist for things to go wrong, adding layers of complications to the best-laid plans. The key is to plan ahead as much as possible, practice your plan, and be prepared to be flexible and resourceful when unanticipated factors block your path.

11

Managing Food and Water

As soon as the disaster calms down and you're certain everyone is safe, it's time to assess what food and water supplies you have on hand. In these first few days, you must carefully maintain your food and water supplies to ensure they stay clean, sanitary, and safe for your family to consume.

In this chapter, we help you take stock of and manage your food and water stores so you have plenty to sustain your family for as long as you need.

First Things First

If you're safe in your home after a disaster, you may be counting yourself lucky, and rightly so, even if you're without power. But don't celebrate just yet.

One of the first things to remember, especially if you're without power, is to keep your freezer and refrigerator doors closed. Do not open them to casually check what's inside like you might be guilty of doing when the power is on.

Why? Because generally speaking, food stays frozen in a full freezer for about 48 hours—so be sure you stock your freezer well before a disaster! In a half-full freezer, food stays frozen for about 24 hours. You have about 4 hours of cold in a refrigerator after the power goes out.

Each time you open the door, however, the temperature inside goes up, as does the temperature of the food housed therein.

Perishable food must be kept below 40ºF (4.5ºC) at all times. If the power is off for more than 4 hours, you'll have to transfer all meat, dairy, eggs, and fish to a cooler and pack it with ice to keep it cold. (More on this in the next section.) You also need to frequently check all your food with a digital thermometer and discard anything warmer than 40ºF (4.5ºC) to reduce the risk of food-borne illnesses.

Food-borne illnesses can come from several organisms. Typically, those organisms produce toxins that can cause gastroenteritis, an inflammation of the gastric system that often results in nausea, vomiting, and diarrhea; severe cases can even lead to dehydration. After a disaster, you and your family have enough to deal with without adding food-borne illness to the list.

Taking Stock

At the risk of repeating ourselves: do not open the freezer door if your power is out, especially on the first day after the disaster. If the power comes back on tomorrow, you'll be able to use the freezer and consume the food within as if nothing had happened. If the power doesn't come back on tomorrow, that's another story. Don't open the refrigerator door either, for now anyway.

Although you might not know exactly what's in your refrigerator and freezer, that's okay right now. You can still assess what other food and water you have available.

Check your cabinets first. Go through each one by one, and take an inventory of the foods you find inside. If you have an inventory for your emergency food supplies, start with that. Or use the "Worksheet: Food and Water Inventory" at the end of the chapter.

Put perishables—bread, fruit, vegetables, etc.—in one category. Group all canned products in another category, including jars. Lastly, group all boxed products together.

Take stock of all your water supplies, and determine how many gallons you have total. Also count your water storage containers. How many do you have clean and ready to store water? How much can each container hold?

Now for your refrigerator. Before you get started, get a cooler and some ice. For a typical 48-quart cooler, you need about 15 to 20 pounds of ice.

WORK QUICKLY

If the only ice is in your freezer and you're certain the power will be out for longer than 4 hours, this is the *only* time you should open your freezer. Working quickly, open the door just long enough to get the ice and shut it again immediately.

Get someone to help you with this. One of you transfers items from the refrigerator to the cooler while the other keeps a running inventory of what goes in the cooler.

Transfer all meat, dairy, eggs, and fish to the cooler first, and pack them in ice. Next, transfer all fruits and vegetables from the refrigerator into a resealable container or bag, and place in the cooler. Finally, transfer leftovers in sealed containers. Discard leftovers not in sealed containers, such as those in take-out boxes from restaurants.

Anything shelf stable you like to keep in the refrigerator so it stays chilled, such as ketchup, pickles, mustard, etc., can stay in the refrigerator for now. If the jar has been opened, move mayonnaise into the cooler.

Now that you have a running inventory of food supplies, make a plan for how you'll use your food. Start with the perishables, especially those requiring ice to stay fresh, followed by more shelf-stable foodstuffs.

Cooking Safety

Keeping food chilled to below 40°F (4.5°C) prohibits bacteria from producing toxins. It doesn't kill them, however. That's where cooking comes in.

Cooking food to a temperature higher than 140°F (60°C) kills most bacteria and helps you avoid food poisoning. These are the important two numbers to remember for food safety.

In a disaster situation, the safest food to eat is the kind you don't have to cook. However, to use perishables first, you might want to cook any meat you have in the first day or so. (We tell you how to cook using fire in Chapter 13.)

Even if you like your steak rare, in a disaster situation, your food needs to be well done. Now is not the time to go gourmet. Use an instant-read thermometer when you cook meat, and be sure you get it hot enough:

- Cook ground beef, lamb, pork, and veal to an internal temperature of 160°F (71°C).

- Cook red meat (beef, veal, and lamb) cuts to at least 145°F (63°C).

- Cook poultry to 165°F (74°C).

- Cook raw pork and ham to at least 145°F (63°C).

- Reheat precooked ham to at least 140°F (60°C).

- Heat leftovers and casseroles to 165°F (74°C).

When prepping your food, never cut meat on the same cutting board you use later for vegetables, fruits, and other food. It's not safe to do at any time, for fear of contamination, but in a disaster, cleaning your work surfaces is harder than usual.

SKIP THE SEAFOOD

When medical resources are scarce, stay away from seafood, especially shellfish. If you must, you can cook fin fish until the meat is white and flaky.

What About Water?

The most important thing you need after a disaster is water. You can go a long time without food, but your body needs water nearly every day.

You have to be adequately hydrated to control your body temperature and maintain your strength. Dehydration can lead to fatigue and confusion, which in turn could cause you to make poor decisions or get hurt.

How Much Is Enough?

How much water each person needs each day is very personal. The amount has been studied for years and probably is still the most misunderstood of all human needs.

Myths about water abound, including the one that says you need to drink 8 cups of water per day. There is no universal amount of water each and every person must consume, and in fact, drinking too much water can be as dangerous as not getting enough. Drinking too little water can lead to dehydration, a potentially life-threatening condition. However, drinking too much water can lead to hyponatremia, or water toxicity. To make matters worse, the symptoms of dehydration and water toxicity are similar.

No scientific basis exists for drinking a set amount of water every day. If anything, the total intake of fluids for the average adult is about half a gallon. That includes water, milk, soup, juice, coffee, tea, soda, and any other food or beverage containing water. Water is the basis for all *potable* liquids, so drinking soft drinks, milk, juice, and sports drinks count toward your water intake and help keep you hydrated. What's more, caffeine isn't as strong of a diuretic for people who consume it daily, so coffee, tea, and soft drinks can count toward your total fluid intake. (If you don't regularly consume caffeine, however, it *can* act as a diuretic.)

DEFINITION

Potable fluids are safe to consume. Potable water and other fluids will keep you hydrated.

Thirst is a pretty good indicator of when you should drink, so when you're thirsty, drink. Your body should tell you when you need hydration, and chances are you won't drink more than you need.

Never ration your water. Authorities focus on distributing drinking water very quickly after a disaster—it's their first priority. So drink what you need today, and find more tomorrow.

In your preparedness kit, you packed at least 1 gallon of water per person per day for 3 days. For groups of several people, that amount is fine. However, for individuals, the per-person amount is more. In other words, if you are alone, you'll need more than 1 gallon a day for yourself.

This might seem backward, but it's true, in part because a portion of your water supply goes toward washing utensils, dishes, and cookware. You can get away with disposables for some of those things, but you'll have to wash things eventually. You'll stretch your water resources further when washing lots of dishes and utensils at once rather than washing one set at a time.

Remember to count your pets as people for the purpose of storing water. A large dog can drink as much as a human; a cat or small dog, on the other hand, needs less.

Storing Water

In Chapter 2, we discussed stocking water with your other family preparedness supplies. Now that the disaster has happened, you'll have opportunities to get additional water from authorities. The best way to store water is to buy it prepackaged in sealed containers. Keep it in a cool, dark place, and use it before the expiration date. (Light, especially sunlight, and heat encourage bacteria growth.)

If you run out of containers for storing water, you can repurpose containers, but you must be very careful to get—and keep—the containers clean. If you need it, turn back to Chapter 2 for a refresher on how to clean, sanitize, treat, and store water in plastic soda or water bottles.

Alternate Water Sources

If it comes to it, water is available in your water heater tank as well as in your house's pipes.

To remove water from the water heater, first turn off the water supply going into the water heater. Open the highest hot water faucet in the house, such as one on the second floor if you have a second story. Then, open the drain valve on your water heater, and drain the water from the tank into a container.

Treat the tank water the same way you treat tap water. If authorities are telling you to boil tap water, you should boil whatever comes out of your water heater, too. There's a good chance contaminated municipal water could have gotten into your house's pipes before you became aware of the contamination.

If you hear of any sewage leaks or flooding—or if authorities tell you about possible contamination—turn off the incoming water supply to your home. Go to your house's main water supply and turn the valve to the *off* or *closed* position. It's important to locate this valve before you need it, so you can turn off the water in a hurry if necessary.

Purifying Water

We explained how to purify water with unscented liquid chlorine bleach, chlorine tablets, or water purification tablets in Chapter 2. If you don't have any of these items on hand, you can purify your water after a disaster by simply boiling it.

A tea kettle works best for most jobs. Fill the kettle, and heat the water over a flame until the kettle whistles. Remove the whistle from the spout, and continue boiling for 1 more minute. In larger pots, bring water to a rolling boil for 1 minute.

To improve the taste of boiled water, you can aerate it by pouring it back and forth between two clean containers. Two or three pours should do the trick.

Worksheet: Food and Water Inventory

Make a list of all the food in your home. Start with perishable foods and then add shelf-stable goods. Cook and eat the perishable foods before the shelf-stable items. Make note of how much water you have as well as how many extra storage containers you have on hand, too.

Perishables:

- ❑ _____
- ❑ _____
- ❑ _____
- ❑ _____
- ❑ _____
- ❑ _____
- ❑ _____
- ❑ _____
- ❑ _____
- ❑ _____
- ❑ _____

Canned and jarred goods:

- ❑ _____
- ❑ _____
- ❑ _____
- ❑ _____
- ❑ _____
- ❑ _____
- ❑ _____
- ❑ _____
- ❑ _____
- ❑ _____
- ❑ _____

Boxed foods:

- ☐ _____
- ☐ _____
- ☐ _____
- ☐ _____
- ☐ _____
- ☐ _____
- ☐ _____
- ☐ _____
- ☐ _____
- ☐ _____
- ☐ _____

Water:

Gallons total: _____

Number of storage containers: _____

Volume of storage containers: _____

12

Assessing Damage to Your Home

The ambulance pulled up to the driveway to find a sign made of red spray paint on an old door. It read, "Welcome to Jim & Lydia's 'Open House.'" All four relief paramedics and EMTs inside the ambulance shared a chuckle at the sight. Surrounded by debris and uprooted trees stood the shell of a multistory house; they couldn't ignore a good sense of humor amid all that.

The house was devastated. Half of it was just gone, leaving a skeleton of thick wooden beams and steel girders, although the roof was still in surprisingly good shape.

Jim and Lydia from Diamondhead, Mississippi, thought their home of sturdy beams and steel girders would stand up to Hurricane Katrina.
(Photo by Rod Brouhard)

Jim and Lydia came out to meet the ambulance and accepted bottled water and food but turned down medical care. As they visited, the couple told the ambulance crew their story.

The house was built to withstand a hurricane like Camille, a Category-5 storm that made landfall on the Mississippi coast on August 17, 1969. Jim and Lydia were pretty sure their house could handle the lesser Category-3 Katrina, so they packed emergency supplies and rode out the storm in their house.

The storm winds were ferocious, but the house stood its ground. It was the flooding that caught them off guard, as the waters rose higher than they had anticipated. Boats from the nearby marina floated inland on the storm surge and smashed into homes and outbuildings. Several of the homes in their community, Diamondhead, were completely washed away, especially those closer to the water's edge.

Jim and Lydia weren't sure how high the water would get. They watched as it flooded their above-ground basement (a feature common in homes this close to the ocean) and continued to rise until it ripped the walls off the main floor. The couple climbed higher and rode out the rest of the storm in the third floor attic space, where they were still living, 6 days after the storm.

Evaluating Your Home's Structural Integrity

When disaster struck, you were either in your home, sheltered in place to ride it out, or you had evacuated to safer shelter elsewhere. Either way, after the disaster you have to make a decision: is your home safe enough to stay in, or return to?

Eventually, authorities or an insurance company representative will make a formal inspection of your home to determine if it's safe to occupy. However, in the first days after a disaster, authorities are likely overwhelmed with more pressing issues of life safety. So for now, the decision whether to stay in your home or find other shelter is entirely yours.

It's a pretty good bet that your home has been compromised to some degree. Floods, earthquakes, hurricanes, wind storms, tornadoes, and even severe ice storms have been known to bring down buildings. Just because your house is standing after a disaster, there's no guarantee it will stay that way.

You must decide based on your own inspection and situation if you should stay or not. There's no shame in leaving after the storm surge subsides or the winds die down. What was once a sturdy home could now be a house of cards, ready to fall at the first aftershock or high wind.

Before you decide to go, or if you are returning and must decide whether or not to stay, first do an inspection. You're probably not a structural engineer, so your inspection likely will be very rudimentary and might miss things.

First things first: pay attention to any warnings or caution tape already left at your home by authorities. *Do not enter your house if it's blocked by caution tape or if it's surrounded by floodwater.*

Pay attention to warnings or signs left by authorities. Do not enter your home until you find out what the signs mean. Signs could include, among other things, the date the house was checked, the organization that checked it, and notes on the soundness of the structure or contents within.
(Photo by Rod Brouhard)

Don long pants, long sleeves, gloves, and sturdy shoes—preferably boots—before you check out your house. There will likely be plenty of sharp edges and hidden dangers you won't immediately see.

Don't do your damage assessment in the dark. Wait until the sun is shining before you attempt an inspection. When you go into dark areas, use a flashlight. Never try to do an inspection in a house with candles, lanterns, or flame of any kind. There could be gas leaks or other potentially flammable situations.

As you go through your home inspection, take pictures of everything you find.

TAKE LOTS OF PHOTOS

After a disaster, a camera—even your cell phone camera if that's all you have—is your friend. Any photos you take will be a big help with your insurance company later when you're submitting claims and need photographic proof of damage. This is especially true if you plan to live in your home in the coming days. You'll undoubtedly clean up some things before the insurance adjuster gets a chance to come to look over everything, and you need to be able to show how it looked right after the disaster.

How's the Exterior?

Take your time and read through the following sections and then start with a visual inspection of your home's exterior. Use the "Worksheet: Evaluating Your Home" at the end of the chapter as you go. Note this information applies for homeowners as well as renters.

Is it leaning? First and foremost, is your house standing straight? If the house is damaged enough to be leaning, it isn't safe to be inside.

Downed power lines? Do you see any loose or broken power lines running to your home? If the power is on—or when it returns—power lines touching the wrong spot can electrify areas of your home and put you in danger. Don't enter your home if you see downed power lines touching it.

Broken pipes? If any of the pipes leading into the home are broken, it could mean there's a water or gas leak. If the pipe is a water pipe, check to see if the water main is turned off. (Look for a large valve, probably on the street side of your home.) If the pipe leads to a gas meter, leave immediately, even if you don't smell anything.

Do you smell gas? If you do smell gas, don't enter the house, even if you don't see broken pipes. If either the smell of gas, hissing sounds, or the sight of broken pipes suggests the possibility of a gas leak, retreat several hundred yards from the house and call the fire department.

How's the propane? If you use a propane system (if you do, you probably have a big white tank somewhere on your property), turn it off and call your propane supplier. After your system is inspected, you might be able to use it again.

See any cracks? New cracks in the foundation of your home could mean the house isn't safe. If you see any large foundation cracks, stay out of the house. Small cracks in stucco or drywall aren't as dangerous, but they could still indicate significant damage. Take note of any cracks, even if you decide it looks safe enough to go inside.

What shape is the roof in? Is it intact? You can repair some holes in the roof temporarily to get you through the next few days. However, if the roof is askew, it could mean the house isn't structurally sound. Don't go inside if the roof is not at the correct angles.

How's the Interior?

Now that you've walked around the house to inspect it on the outside, it's time to take a look inside. Be very careful when entering your home. Even if the structure looks straight, the right angles might not be perfect.

You are in more danger inside than outside. Only one or two people should go inside at a time, and they should go in single file. Move slowly, and only proceed when you're sure the spot you're in is safe.

Carefully try a door. If it doesn't open, don't force it; it might be providing support for part of the structure. On the other hand, it might just be swollen or have something pressing on it from inside. Try another door, and we'll come back to this one.

TRESPASSING ANIMALS

Beware, too, of any animals who might have decided it's much better to be in your house than outside, especially if the disaster tore some holes in the walls. Make noise and tap on things to let the potential rodents and snakes know you're back home again.

Notice anything sagging? Slowly work your way into the house, taking careful steps. If any areas of the floor sag under your weight, don't walk there; the integrity of the floor in that spot has been compromised. To make the area safe to walk on, nail down subfloor plywood at least ¾ inch thick and 8 to 10 inches wider than the sagging area of the floor. You can also build a bridge over the sagging area by nailing down 2×6 boards at least 8 inches longer than the sagging area.

Look up, too. If the ceiling is sagging, it's probably waterlogged and, therefore, dangerous to be under. Never turn on ceiling fans or lights when the ceiling is wet or sagging.

You can drain the water to make it safe, but you'll need to wear eye protection and be ready to deal with the water mess you'll create. To drain the water, you'll need something long and tough enough to poke holes in the drywall on the ceiling. Depending on how high your ceiling is, you might be able to use a fireplace poker or a shovel.

Using the small, handle end of the shovel rather than the blade, poke holes in the sagging ceiling around the outside of the sagging portion. Don't poke the center of the sagging mass first, because the whole thing could rip away and come tumbling down. Usually, when the drywall is no longer soaked, the ceiling will go back to being relatively flat. It still will be damaged and will need replacing, but it'll be safe to walk under.

Do you have power? The safest and easiest way to check for power is to simply turn on a light switch. If the lights don't come on, check the circuit panel. If the main breaker is tripped (switched off with the on/off switch only moved partway), do *not* turn it back on. Call the power company and explain the situation. You might need to have an electrician look at your home's wiring. If the main circuit is on and only a few of the other breakers are tripped, don't try to use those circuits. Call the power company.

Never mix electricity and water. Stay away from any standing water or soaked carpets and drywall, especially when you're working with outlets or the circuit panel box.

Check for leaks. Look for water damage in walls and cabinets. If you see anything that looks like a leak—water stains along pipes or isolated areas of soaking in an otherwise dry area, for example—shut off the main water supply. Have a plumber come to inspect and repair the pipes before turning the main supply back on.

Check your phone. Regular, hardwired (not cordless) phones might work even if the power is out. Electric, cordless, and internet-based phones (VOIP phones, or the kind bundled with television service through a cable or internet company) might work without power if they have a battery backup. Be sure every phone in the house is hung up for at least 60 seconds and then check to see if you have a dial tone.

Now that you've made it inside and had a look around, let's go back to that door that was stuck and reexamine it.

Is it blocked? Look to see if something is blocking the door, causing it to stick closed.

Is it square? The concern here is that the wall might no longer be straight and the door is actually providing support. Look at the jamb, or frame, around the door. Is it square, or are there bigger gaps between the door and the jamb in some places and other spots where they're touching? If the door's not square, do not try to open it.

Is it swollen? Wooden doors are prone to swelling, especially if they've gotten really wet. Does the door have cracks indicating it got wet and has swollen? Depending on how bad the swelling is, you might not be able to open the door normally. It's best to leave it closed until you can have it fixed professionally.

You're standing in your own home amidst the debris, with lots of emotions and memories probably clouding the moment. You have to decide if you want to seek shelter elsewhere or stay put for the long haul. Your decision hinges on how prepared and resourceful you are.

Unfortunately, there's another potential threat that might help make your decision for you.

Dealing with Contamination

Contamination due to bacteria, chemicals, or radiation can happen in all sorts of disasters. Flooding is the most common because floodwaters are notoriously dirty. However, homes can become contaminated in other ways, too.

Floodwater Contamination

In disasters that include flooding—or if structural damage to your house leads to sewage or drain flooding—anything the floodwater touches is considered contaminated. Floodwater mingles sewage, waste, oil, gas, and other chemicals together in one big, nasty soup. It often takes professional help to adequately clean and restore a home after a flood.

Limit your contact with areas that are soaked with floodwater, and avoid standing water. Contact can lead to infections, especially of the gastrointestinal system. Residents and responders to flooding disasters regularly report cases of severe diarrhea, nausea, and vomiting.

TAP WATER SAFETY

Water supplies can become contaminated all too easily after a disaster. In some cases, municipal supplies can become tainted by floodwater or cracks in the cisterns or pipes that carry water to customers. Authorities will tell you if tap water is safe and give you one of three options: the water is safe to consume right out of the tap, it must be purified before drinking, or it's not safe for any use. It's much harder to know if well water is safe. Do not drink the tap water until you can have it tested.

If you have a septic tank or leach line, check to see that it's intact. Any damage to your septic system may contribute to contamination and must be high on your priority list to fix.

Floodwater could even be electrically charged by power lines under the surface that you can't see.

Something you might not immediately think of being compromised due to the floodwater is the food in your refrigerator and freezer. Check the food in both places, and discard anything touched by the water.

Other Types of Contamination

Chemical contamination can occur when some sort of chemical has been spilled nearby or chemicals in your home have spilled, mixed, or been exposed to air. It's imperative that you follow the orders authorities issue when it comes to chemical contamination. If you're ordered to leave, evacuate immediately, even if you rode out the storm at home.

If authorities tell you to evacuate because of radiation, you don't have a choice. You must leave the area.

Choosing to Stay or Go

After you've assessed the damage to your home, you'll have to decide if it's safe enough to stay or if you'd be safer residing elsewhere.

If you have kids with you, if you don't have adequate shelter from the elements (intact walls and a roof), or if there's no infrastructure in the area (emergency services or support organizations such as churches, neighbors, etc.), you'll need to find shelter elsewhere. If flooding has created large areas of your home that you can't get to, even after a day or two, then your home isn't safe. You should evacuate and find another place to stay. Large areas of flooding from outside floodwater or from drainage or sewage inside your home are just too dangerous to stay, even while attempting to clean it up.

Assuming your home is habitable enough for you to stay, or you have shelter nearby and you'd like to work on the house to make it livable, you'll need to clean it.

First remove any standing water. Mop up shallow puddles, and pump out any water more than an inch deep.

Anything exposed to water must be dried. Separate everything to allow it to dry. Spread furniture and appliances outside, weather permitting, and allow everything to air-dry. Don't do this if there's any chance of precipitation in the next few days. Remember, it will take some time to move everything back inside if the weather takes a turn.

Separate any furniture that has multiple parts or pieces to allow faster drying. Open or remove drawers. Pull apart tables with removable leaves. Let as much air circulate between and among the pieces as you can.

Open windows and get air moving throughout the house to help things dry, too.

Launder everything you can—rugs, cushions, doilies, curtains, tablecloths, etc. Anything contaminated with floodwater that can't be laundered should be discarded; there's just no way to adequately disinfect those items. This includes carpeting and other floor coverings floodwater has soaked through. A good restoration company can help you determine what's salvageable and what's not.

Thoroughly disinfect all surfaces with a solution of 1 part bleach to 10 parts water. Empty out all drawers, and completely wash and disinfect all utensils with the bleach solution before use.

BLEACH AND AMMONIA

Household bleach is very useful during disasters. You can use it to purify water and clean anything from basic dirt to serious mold. One thing you must *never* do is mix it with ammonia. When bleach and ammonia mix, a gas results that can render you unconscious in a matter of seconds and kill you with prolonged exposure. Don't mix bleach with any other household cleaners, either, because they might contain ammonia. The only household cleaner you can safely mix with bleach is basic dish detergent.

As you work, identify any other sagging areas in the floor you might have missed during your first walk-through, and reinforce them with subfloor plywood as explained earlier. Patch up holes in the walls and broken windows with plywood. Be sure to leave some windows and doors accessible.

Dealing with Mold

Moisture equals mold. You have 24 to 48 hours to get your home and possessions dry before you run the risk of mold. The molds that grow after flooding are nasty. Besides being a health hazard if you breathe the allergens created by the spores, it can also eat through wood and cause structural damage.

If you're going to tackle mold on your own, first dry everything thoroughly. Don't even start trying to clean mold until the areas where it's growing are totally dry.

Wear the appropriate protective clothing: long rubber gloves, goggles, and a respirator mask. The Centers for Disease Control and Prevention recommend an N95 mask, which you can get at hardware stores. Never try to clean mold without the proper protection. Breathing or touching mold spores can make you extremely sick.

Porous surfaces like ceiling tiles or carpet trap mold and make it nearly impossible to completely eradicate it. Throw out any moldy porous items.

Scrub mold off hard surfaces such as wood with bleach solution. Don't scrub the mold while it's dry, or you risk filling the air with spores. Spray the mold with the bleach solution and then scrub it off. Remember, use 1 part bleach with 10 parts water. If the bleach solution isn't strong enough, or you see a lot of discoloration from the fungus, try 1 part household detergent and 20 parts water to 10 parts bleach.

Leave large areas of mold—anything larger than 3 feet square—to a professional. This is even more important if the mold was triggered by wastewater or outside flooding.

No one can decide for you whether you should stay home or evacuate after disaster strikes. The advice in this chapter is to be used as a guide, but only you know how much damage you can tolerate. Jim and Lydia never lost their collective senses of humor or of adventure. That's the lesson they taught: survival is mostly about attitude.

Worksheet: Evaluating Your Home

When inspecting your home to determine whether you can stay or need to find shelter elsewhere, be sure you can check off each of these items before entering the house:

- ❑ All walls are straight with no leaning
- ❑ No standing water is touching the house
- ❑ No power lines are touching the house
- ❑ No obvious broken pipes
- ❑ No smell of gas or propane
- ❑ No large cracks in the foundation
- ❑ No sagging or missing roof

Take notes about your home's condition. Take pictures, and video if possible, for insurance claims later.

Doors—able to open/close, location, and condition:

_____

_____

_____

Holes in walls or sagging floors:

_____

_____

_____

Power—which circuits work and which don't:

_____

_____

_____

Obvious leaks in walls or cabinets:

_____

_____

_____

Stay or go? Use this list to help you decide whether to stay or go. If you can check off everything on this list, you can probably stay, at least temporarily:

- ❑ There is an area within the house that's habitable and not contaminated
- ❑ You have a way to get in and out without becoming contaminated
- ❑ The roof is adequate to keep you dry
- ❑ Emergency services are available
- ❑ You have enough water and food supplies to last at least 72 hours—or you have a process to get water and food

If you cannot check all five boxes, consider seeking shelter elsewhere

13

Playing with Fire

We take fire for granted these days. We contain it and control it, and thanks to modern technology, we're even able to replicate the heat and the light of fire without the danger of an open flame.

Disasters can change all that. When we lose the capability to control heat and light, we may be left with the need to make use of that open flame.

Caution with Candles

In everyday life, candles are fine. They're pretty, and they smell good. After a disaster, however, they're not the best idea. In an emergency, it's always better to use a flashlight or a battery-powered lantern than a candle with an open flame.

But just because they're not the *best* choice doesn't mean you can't or won't use candles. Plenty of folks keep candles around as a backup to other, more high-tech options. They're effective, low tech, and reliable.

Anytime you use an open flame, though, you run the risk of causing a fire. After a disaster, the fire department's resources might be needed elsewhere, and they might not be able to fight a house fire as they normally would. Using a candle in that sort of situation could lead to a second disaster potentially more devastating than the first.

In a disaster situation, candles are not for decoration or ceremony; they're tools for survival. If you choose or are forced to use them, it's vitally important to treat candles as dangerous but necessary tools. Burn them only while you're awake, never leave them unattended, and extinguish them before leaving or going to sleep.

CANDLE FIRES

According to the U.S. Fire Administration (USFA), 20 percent of all candle fires are caused by candles left burning unattended. Even worse, candles start more fires when they're used for light. More than a third of all candle fires start in the bedroom, and half of all deaths related to candle fires happen between midnight and 6 A.M.

Use sturdy candle holders—preferably of metal or glass—that won't tip or burn and are large enough to collect any hot wax that drips down.

Keep candles away from clothing, books, magazines, curtains, and other flammable materials. Keep all open flames away from flammable liquids, too.

Trim all candle wicks to ¼ inch before use.

Extinguish and discard pillar and taper candles when they get within 2 inches of the holder. Extinguish votives and container candles before the last ½ inch of wax is melted. When the flame burns too close to the bottom of the container, it can get hot enough to burn you if you touch it or damage the furniture it sits upon.

If at all possible, do not carry lit candles during power outages. Use flashlights when moving around instead.

Cooking During Disasters

In many cases, cooking during disaster situations requires the use of an open flame. The best way to avoid cooking is to eat packaged food, but for postdisaster periods longer than 3 days, that probably isn't practical.

Whether or not you're able to cook in your house in the aftermath of a disaster depends on whether you have an electric or gas range and whether you can use that utility. If you have an electric range and have power, you're in great shape. Electric ranges are the safest option in disaster situations. However, it's very likely that power won't be available.

Gas ranges are fine to use as long as the stove hasn't been damaged. However, if gas lines in your area are compromised, the utility company might turn off the gas, leaving you without the capability to cook. In Chapter 12, you did a damage assessment on your home to determine if you could stay or not. If you found *any* leaks in your gas lines, you *must* turn off the gas. This will leave you without a range—and with the need for a backup plan for cooking.

If you lose the ability to cook on an indoor range, you must cook outside. You might be tempted to bring your gas grill into the house or onto the enclosed porch; *do not do this*. Only a properly vented and professionally installed indoor range can be used inside the house for cooking.

Outside, you have more options for cooking. Obvious choices are barbecue grills and open fire pits. If you have a grill, it's probably a good bet you've used it a time or two. Cooking in the backyard following a disaster isn't any different from cooking in the backyard on a lazy Sunday afternoon.

Still, be extremely vigilant with any sort of flame. The fire department is not likely to respond very quickly, if at all.

FIREPLACE COOKING

Cooking over an open fire in your fireplace or woodstove is an option during a disaster—but only if you have the proper equipment and only if it's something you've done regularly in nondisaster situations. Cooking in your fireplace can change the airflow and interrupt the draft, causing smoke to push into your house instead of up the chimney. Plus, having the fireplace doors or screens open risks stray embers alighting on the carpet, your clothing, or other flammable items. It's best to take your cooking needs outside..

Fire Extinguishers

You should have at least one fire extinguisher in your home—and preferably one in the kitchen, another one in the garage, and another one in the laundry room. The fire extinguisher is an essential tool, during disasters or otherwise.

Different types of fire extinguishers spray different types of material on the fire. Several agents can be used, but the most common are water, dry chemical, carbon dioxide (CO_2), or halon. Each has different strengths and weaknesses. Water isn't safe to use on electrical components, except in special cases. Dry chemical extinguishers leave a powder residue that can damage delicate electrical devices like computers. Carbon dioxide and halon don't leave residues, but they can be dangerous in areas that aren't properly ventilated. For most homes, dry chemical is the best type of extinguisher to use.

When choosing the right fire extinguisher, think about the kind of fires you'll use it to put out. Each extinguisher is rated for a certain type of fire, and the rating helps determine where in the home, office, or car it should be placed:

- **Class A fires:** Ordinary combustible solids like paper, wood, and plastic; good for general use if you're not sure which type to get

- **Class B fires:** Flammable or combustible liquid fires such as gasoline or kerosene; good for the garage or car

- **Class C fires:** Energized electrical components; good for the media room or office

Other, specialized fire extinguishers are used in other types of fires. For example, class D extinguishers are used for combustible metals, and class K extinguishers are designed for use in commercial kitchens.

Fire extinguishers must be readily available, and you must know how to use them correctly. No matter which type of fire extinguisher you have, the basic technique for putting out the fire is the same:

- Only fight fires that are small and contained.

- Do not fight a fire between you and the exit unless you can't get by it.

- Tell others to get out of the building immediately, whether you choose to fight the fire or not.

- Tell another person to call 911. Specifically point to someone and order that person to call; don't just shout "Somebody call 911!" because "nobody" might.

- Use the acronym *PASS* to remember what to do when extinguishing a fire:

    P: Pull the extinguisher's pin.

    A: Aim the nozzle at the base of the fire, and at the item that's burning, not the flames, while standing back several feet.

    S: Squeeze the trigger to spray the extinguishing agent on the fire.

    S: Sweep the nozzle side to side as you spray the fire. Remember to spray the base of the flames.

Fire extinguishers are immensely helpful, but they do have limitations. They're only really useful for putting out small fires. And choosing to put out a fire delays your evacuation from the house, so the decision to use a fire extinguisher must be made and acted on quickly. Either grab it and use it to extinguish the flame, or skip the fire extinguisher and immediately evacuate the house.

The Dangers of Carbon Monoxide

Carbon monoxide (CO) is an odorless, colorless gas produced when something burns. It doesn't really matter what's burning. CO can come from a fire in the fireplace, from a barbecue grill, or from an engine like the one in your car or on your gas-powered generator.

Carbon monoxide is dangerous because your bloodstream likes it but your brain doesn't. Red blood cells—the ones that carry oxygen—will ditch the oxygen and bind to CO given the chance, leading to carbon monoxide poisoning.

Carbon monoxide poisoning results from exposure to too much of the gas for too long. Because the gas has no color or smell, it's extremely dangerous—and extremely sneaky, earning it the nickname the "silent killer." In fact, authorities believe more people are exposed to carbon monoxide every year than what's reported. Carbon monoxide poisoning is a serious concern during disaster situations when folks are cooking with outdoor grills and using generators for power.

Symptoms of Carbon Monoxide Poisoning

The symptoms of carbon monoxide poisoning mimic problems in the brain, like strokes and headaches. Here are some symptoms to look for:

- Headache
- Confusion
- Weakness or fatigue
- Dizziness
- Unstable gait/stumbling around
- Nausea and vomiting
- Unconsciousness

Most of the time, interruptions in the amount of oxygen in the bloodstream turn a person blue or purple. Carbon monoxide poisoning is an exception to that rule. Blood saturated with carbon monoxide is bright red, which makes people look flushed—sometimes even very brightly red flushed—rather than blue. Those affected exhibit confusion and headaches, and even become unconscious, long before any bright redness appears, so do not ignore the symptoms of carbon monoxide poisoning just because someone isn't bright red. If you wait that long, it could be too late.

Treating Carbon Monoxide Poisoning

The only definitive way to treat carbon monoxide poisoning is to breathe pure oxygen for hours. In some cases, the person will have to be taken to a hyperbaric chamber where doctors can force oxygen into the red blood cells and force out the carbon monoxide.

BEWARE THE SILENT KILLER

It can be very hard to identify carbon monoxide poisoning in one isolated case. However, you should highly suspect carbon monoxide poisoning if more than one person in the home is complaining of headaches, fatigue, and dizziness or more than one person is confused.

Treating carbon monoxide poisoning on your own is really all about getting professional help. When you suspect carbon monoxide poisoning, get into fresh air or a well-ventilated area immediately. Fresh air will stop the poisoning from getting worse, but it won't reverse the damage that's already done.

Call 911 if it's available. If 911 isn't available—which it might not be after a disaster—take the victim to emergency medical providers (see Part 4).

If you can, locate and remove the source of the carbon monoxide. Sometimes, carbon monoxide can come from a faulty furnace, or it can leak into the house from the garage if a car therein is left running. Here are some potential carbon monoxide producers to investigate: wood stoves, fireplaces, or fire pits; gas stoves, water heaters, clothes dryers; gas or charcoal barbecues; gas or oil space heaters; smudge pots; gas or diesel generators, cars, or trucks; motorcycles; motorboats; or gas-powered lawn equipment. Never leave any of these items running for long periods of time, and never try to heat your house using an oven or range.

Carbon Monoxide Detectors

Carbon monoxide detectors help identify when CO levels get too high and stay there for too long. Many CO detectors require AC power, but some also have a battery backup.

You should have a carbon monoxide detector for each level of your house. Be sure the type you buy comes with a battery backup.

If you hear an alarm from your carbon monoxide detector, *get out of the house immediately.* Carbon monoxide detectors are designed to alarm before the levels get high enough to make you sick. Far too many stories exist of folks getting annoyed with their CO detectors "beeping for no reason" and then getting sick or dying of carbon monoxide poisoning.

When you're out of the house, call the fire department and explain that your carbon monoxide alarm is beeping. The fire department will respond and test the levels of carbon monoxide in your home. It will also determine the source.

We humans have a long, bittersweet relationship with fire and the smoke that goes with it. For the most part, that relationship has been beneficial. Using fire to help you through a disaster and its aftermath is usually easy and economical—and low-tech enough to not be affected by the disaster. As long as you work with fire with the respect it demands, follow basic fire safety rules, and be sure you know what to do in the event that something goes wrong, fire can be one resource that's nearly always available, even when others are limited or unavailable.

14

Safety and Security

In the Gulf Coast after Hurricane Katrina, police officers, firefighters, and paramedics were left just as homeless as the population they protect and serve. Many evacuated alongside their neighbors, victims of the storm just like everyone else.

When authorities are affected as much as the rest of the population, what feels like a power vacuum can develop. The very people we turn to for guidance and assistance are struggling with their own survival. Our uncertainties can bring us perilously close to panic, as we feel like no one can keep us safe from the predators. In extreme situations, such as Hurricane Katrina, it might seem as though the predators are the only people left, as we hear reports of looting, rioting, and other unscrupulous behavior—much of which is actually caused by feelings of panic in others.

In this chapter, we examine what you should do to keep your family safe and secure in the aftermath of a disaster when safety and security resources are far from operating at full strength. We also look at how society changes and what those changes mean for you.

You're on Your Own

For the first 72 hours of a disaster, plan on taking care of yourself and your family. In early chapters, we taught you how to stock your emergency supply shelves and make plans. You should have water, food, and shelter to last through the next 3 days. You have things for the kids to do and supplies for your medical needs. You have a process for communicating with family and reuniting with the rest of your clan. While you're safe inside, what's going on outside?

You've no doubt heard the stories of looting and riots that often follow in the wake of a disaster. Perhaps you saw news reports of looters cleaning out businesses in New Orleans after Hurricane Katrina or on Coney Island after Superstorm Sandy. What about personal security? How can you protect yourself, your family, and your home from these dangers while you're dealing with everything else?

Looting

Looting is almost always expected after a disaster—so much so that journalists report with surprise after nearly every disaster that looting has been at a minimum. They surmise how this is due to variety of uncommon factors like rapid police presence or extraordinary community bonds. Elected officials are equally confounded by the lack of lawlessness following most natural disasters.

DEFINITION

Looting is stealing property during a state of emergency or crisis. Most of the time, looting happens during behavioral emergencies, such as riots or uprisings. However, looting sometimes occurs after catastrophic natural disasters when law enforcement resources are absent for long periods of time, especially in areas wrought with poverty prior to the disaster.

Just because looting is expected doesn't mean it has to happen or that it will be pure chaos. Instead, evidence suggests that looting and lawlessness are rare in most cases while cooperation and compassion are much more common in disasters. Researchers have documented this trend for decades, but the power of the media is hard to overcome. Twenty seconds of video footage showing a man leaving a store with a bag full of goods is enough to convince the world that anarchy is afoot. It doesn't matter what the man took or if he's even the owner of the store.

Without a doubt, some theft—call it looting—happens after disasters, and those incidents serve to reinforce the media's expectations. Reports of crimes are usually treated as routine while accounts of cooperation are considered extraordinary. If you're living in the middle of a disaster situation and hearing stories of mass hysteria, it's natural to assume you could be a victim as well.

The media documented the looting of New Orleans after Katrina, and some researchers believe it was made worse by the catastrophic size of the storm and the number of residents living under the poverty level. By contrast, nearly a month after Superstorm Sandy tore through New York and New Jersey, the *New York Daily News* reported that over half of the looting cases—only 37—in Brooklyn and Queens were being thrown out.

Frank (not his real name) worked as an EMT in the Gulfport area. His home was still standing after Katrina, but the water damage was extensive. Between shifts on the ambulance, Frank removed all the appliances in his home and placed them on his front lawn to dry out. Sitting on his tailgate after a shift, he told the story of an encounter in his driveway.

"These guys showed up the other night after I got home from work," Frank said in his slow Mississippi drawl. "I just finished up takin' the stove out and was standing on the porch. I s'pose they didn't see me standing there. One of them got out of their pickup and was nosin' around my refrigerator.

"I watched him lookin' it over, and I took a seat in my rocker. He didn't hear nothing until I picked up the 12 gauge leaning on the porch railing." Frank smiled. "Soon as he saw me, he hopped back in the truck, and they left."

Frank had no idea what the stranger was up to, but he was conditioned by popular belief and by news reports coming out of New Orleans to assume the man wanted to take his refrigerator. It's possible, but Frank's presence—and possibly his shotgun—easily deterred any attempts to rob him.

This is the most important thing to realize about looting: it's almost never directed at your house. Looting, when it does happen, is concentrated on stores—particularly big box chain stores—rather than people's homes. Plus, looting is a crime of convenience, and in Frank's case, his presence was enough to prevent it.

Rioting

Yes, people riot on occasion. Generally speaking, the rioting is more often a result of political and civil unrest than actions of fear and panic after a disaster.

In her book *The Unthinkable: Who Survives When Disaster Strikes and Why,* Amanda Ripley differentiates between panic the emotion and panic the behavior. Panic the emotion causes people to run for their lives; it's a "rippling kind of terror that robs us of self-control," she writes. Then there's panic the behavior, which is more "the irrational shrieking and clamoring and shoving that can jeopardize the survival of ourselves and those around us," Ripley reports.

Both types of panic happen—but not nearly as often as people expect. Most people in disasters do nothing. A few can think clearly, show great presence of mind, and work to get everyone out safely, while a few lose their control and cave in to their fears, to the detriment of everyone else. Because their panic can endanger the rest of the group, most groups generally have little patience for it and work to dispel it quickly.

We see panic the behavior in stampedes, but not in riots. Riots are a completely different behavior, stemming from anger more than fear.

Politicians and law enforcement may make decisions based on an expectation or fear of public panic, but as Ripley points out, the history of disasters proves the opposite. In her extensive interviews with survivors of the September 2011 attacks and other major disasters, she shows how time and again, the majority of the time, panic and rioting does not happen. People in evacuations not only tend to be orderly and respectful, but kind and considerate toward others.

WHEN PANIC DOESN'T HAPPEN

History shows that despite people's fears of panic, it happens less than we believe it does. In most disasters, people tend to be orderly and helpful, feeling a sense of unity, a "we are all in this together" mentality. In 1954, the American Journal of Sociology published a paper written by Enrico Quarantelli outlining a history of when panic occurred following a disaster and when it didn't. Quarantelli found that panic only happens when three factors are present: people believe they're trapped, they feel powerless, and they feel alone. If all three factors are not present, if one or more is missing, panic and its offspring—rioting, looting, and violence—do not occur.

Should You Have Weapons?

When thinking about disaster preparedness, there's a tendency to imagine the end of life as we know it coming through several different scenarios, from complete power grid collapse, to worldwide riots. To some, weapons are a reasonable expectation—some would say a requirement.

But in real-world disaster scenarios like hurricanes, wildfires, or tornadoes, weapons have very limited use. In fact, being armed could lead to disastrous consequences.

An adult brother and sister fought over a bag of ice in Hattiesburg, Mississippi, after Hurricane Katrina. It was reportedly the last bag of ice left on a pallet in the middle of the street. The brother allegedly shot his sister in the head for the ice. Admittedly, we don't know what kind of relationship they had before the storm, but if he hadn't been armed in the first place, he couldn't have shot her.

What's more, carrying a weapon is only a legitimate deterrent if you are willing and able to use it. As any law enforcement officer can tell you, there's a huge difference between brandishing a gun and pulling the trigger. Without the training and mind-set necessary to put a gun to use, it won't help you at all.

Safety in Numbers

One of the best ways to stay safe and secure after a disaster is to stay in groups. Whether it's with your family, your church, a shelter, or another organization, staying together is the best option for security and survival. The more pairs of eyes there are watching over homes, businesses, and supplies, the less likely someone will choose to violate them.

Staying in groups is also helpful for basic survival. It's easier to get things done if there are more of you. People naturally group together in times of stress, so don't be afraid of it. If you have a plan in place before the flood, tornado, or other disaster, you'll know who to turn to when the time comes.

ISOLATION OR NO?

Preppers—the more hardcore disaster preparedness folks—often suggest isolation during and after a disaster to prevent others from looting your ample supply stores. On the surface, it seems like a solid concept, but only if your neighbors are untrustworthy. Oftentimes, most neighborhoods band together for survival rather than ransack each other's storm cellars.

The Rumor Mill

As the room filled, it was clear that responders had come from all corners of the United States. Paramedic and EMT patches indicated help had come from as far away as San Francisco, Connecticut, and Seattle. Many of these folks had helped out during disasters at home, but the gigantic scope of Katrina was more than most could imagine. They were excited to be able to help out but scared of what to expect. The news coverage—mostly of New Orleans—suggested a level of lawlessness and anarchy far beyond a typical day on the ambulance.

The briefing started with a welcome and heartfelt thanks from the local authorities. The new arrivals were told where to find food and beds, and credentials were collected and photocopied. It was announced that GPS receivers in the ambulances weren't loading correctly, so hardcopy maps were provided. One of the physicians explained where to go to be vaccinated, a requirement before staffing an ambulance.

At the end came the safety briefing. Be careful, the newcomers were told. A crew was held up at gunpoint in a rural part of Hancock County. Apparently, the bandits wanted narcotics and emergency supplies. Of course, the joke was on them because no narcotics were carried in the disaster zone. No details were provided about the time or exact location of the holdup, but the story was relayed as a factual account and a cautionary tale for the new arrivals: keep your eyes open.

An ambulance crew getting held up for drugs is a perfectly plausible situation that does happen occasionally. It usually makes news in a community precisely because it happens so rarely. In this case, the idea may very well have morphed from possibility to virtual reality without ever coming true. Such a story would grant undeniable bragging rights to the folks who lived through it. The crew who were held at gunpoint would be minor celebrities, notorious in camp at least.

Safety is a big part of emergency services. Whether in law enforcement, the fire service, or on an ambulance, personal security is on first responders' minds every time they step onto the scene of an emergency. Their jobs require them to consider all possible scenarios. During a disaster, the rumor mill serves a purpose—it helps cultivate situational awareness.

Even though there may never have been a real holdup, the new folks were still acutely aware of the number of citizens roaming the streets with weapons clearly visible on their hips and slung over their shoulders. No doubt some of those guns and owners might have been just a few harsh words away from shooting someone over a bag of ice.

DON'T BELIEVE EVERYTHING

Benjamin Franklin said, "Believe none of what you hear and half of what you see." That's good advice for disaster situations. Franklin didn't have television, so figure today he'd probably lower that percentage for believing what you see a bit.

Put your biggest trust in official sources first. If it comes from a press conference and you are listening to an official standing at a podium, chances are what's coming out of that official's mouth are the best facts known at that time. Despite myriad spy novels and conspiracy theories to the contrary, be assured that government officials are trying hard to provide as much accurate information as possible to the public in times of crisis.

Aside from official sources, listen to the mainstream media for useful information about shelters, evacuations, and where to get aid. You'll also hear complete coverage of the negative—that's what sells—but be skeptical of any doom and gloom you hear from nongovernment sources, especially neighbors and reporters.

What to Expect from Authorities

You'll interact with three levels of government in any disaster: local (city and county), state, and federal. The members of your local government have the same problem you do—they live and work in a disaster area. Your police, paramedics, and firefighters finish taking care of the population only to go home and take care of their own damaged houses. Local authorities will quickly turn to their state and federal partners for help.

Theoretically, for a state to qualify for federal aid, it has to follow the National Incident Management System (NIMS) and use the Incident Command System (ICS). ICS is pretty straightforward, but NIMS is one of the most complicated organizational charts ever developed. Rather than a clear chain of command, the dotted lines to indicate communication channels are so numerous they make the chart an almost unreadable jumbled mess. With so much information flowing in so many directions, there's plenty of room for interpretation and mistakes.

All the little details of the NIMS organizational chart do serve a purpose, and the minutia keeps the government in check. There are certain odd uses of terminology in emergencies and disasters. For instance, local authorities and state governors can *proclaim* an emergency but only the president can *declare* one. The point of this particular distinction is lost on most people, including many of us in emergency management. It's these types of minute details, however, that keep the feds and the state authorities under control in situations that have a tendency to evolve quickly and dangerously.

WITHOUT AUTHORIZATION

In his book, *Decision Points,* former President George W. Bush wrote that Louisiana's governor, Kathleen Blanco, was not willing to authorize armed federal troops to come into the state for several days after Hurricane Katrina, delaying federal aid to the state. Without that authorization, said Bush, the federal government was powerless to intervene and provide assistance. To make matters worse, the reason troops couldn't come in was because the military wanted them to be armed in the face of civil unrest in New Orleans—civil unrest that was seriously overstated.

What does this mean for you? Simply put, it means government sources are there to help, but you must be patient as you navigate the complicated process. Knowing how authorities will respond is important as things progress.

First, as the disaster first strikes, local authorities are in charge of the response. This is typical, even in disasters with lots of warning, such as hurricanes. Local law enforcement officials, fire departments, and ambulance agencies respond to 911 calls. Depending on how quickly the disaster evolves, this first phase lasts an hour or two. During this time, officials might not be able to respond to all requests for service and may not even realize a disaster is forming.

When regional resources are overwhelmed, the state moves in. State response might be enough to handle some disasters, depending on how large the disaster is and how large your state is. California, New York, and Texas, for example, can handle much larger disasters than, say, Delaware can.

The final stage of a disaster is when the feds show up. Several federal agencies help, or coordinate help, during an incident. The Federal Emergency Management Agency (FEMA) is responsible for coordinating all the help once federal resources are deployed.

The bigger the incident, the more responders you'll see. As the rain fell and the winds blew during Superstorm Sandy, paramedics and emergency medical technicians from Modesto, California, began evacuating sick newborn babies from NYU Langone Hospital in Manhattan.

Any emergency responder can help guide you to someone who can help with your needs. Not all the responders will know where to turn, but they'll all have someone in charge they can ask. If you know you need something from authorities but don't know who to turn to, ask the first emergency worker you see.

Bringing in the Troops

The National Guard has a long and storied history in the United States and has a split mission: part state and part federal. In disaster situations, the National Guard can be called upon to provide aid and protection to the citizens of their state.

When the National Guard arrives, they serve several different roles. Typically, they offer security and law enforcement assistance or help distribute food, water, and ice. The most important thing about military troops is that they're easily identified and are able to help, or obtain help, if approached.

When talking about the military showing up and a lack of law enforcement during times of disaster, the question of martial law arises. Martial law is a broad term related to the use of the military for all types of law enforcement, including trials and punishment. The U.S. Supreme Court explained it during Abraham Lincoln's presidency in response to him declaring martial law in the United States. The Court declared Lincoln's version of martial law unconstitutional and laid the foundation for the proper use of it in the future. One very important aspect of the Court's definition required martial law to be limited to an "area of actual war."

Despite the terminology, the reality of military law enforcement looks more like martial law than the courts might be comfortable with. It has been widely reported that after Katrina, police in New Orleans were ordered to "shoot looters" and that the city was placed under martial law. Officials have denied both allegations, but the police did shoot 11 people in the aftermath of the storm.

The massive destruction on the beaches of Gulfport, Mississippi, after Katrina led to local authorities putting up razor-wire fences along the railroad tracks. Two checkpoints allowed residents and officials to enter or leave the area during daylight only. At night, nobody got in or out, including emergency vehicles.

Despite these severe responses, military units providing security after a disaster should not be an issue. However, unless the military personnel are specifically trained in law enforcement techniques, they likely will not follow all the same procedures you'd expect from your local police or deputies.

Mandatory Evacuation

At some point in a disaster, either before or immediately after, there might be an order from some level of government to evacuate. Evacuation orders are generally issued from state or local officials rather than federal. These are the folks on the ground going through the same things you are, and they understand the complications that will come with both the disaster at hand and the logistics of trying to get people out of the way.

As discussed in Chapter 8, sometimes an order to evacuate is labeled as *mandatory,* but that's really not true. It's highly unlikely that anyone of authority will *force* you to leave. For one thing, there aren't enough resources to arrest everyone who fails to comply with the evacuation order. Where would they put the violators?

Because so few resources are available, you can't count on help if you get in trouble after a mandatory evacuation. Search and rescue may only come after the disaster is over, and getting ambulances to respond to falls or cardiac arrest, for example, is extremely unlikely. Law enforcement in areas ordered to evacuate will be spotty or nonexistent.

Only you can make the decision on whether or not to comply with an evacuation order. However, it's best to heed any order to evacuate and make use of whatever assistance authorities can provide. If you choose to ignore an evacuation order, do so with your eyes wide open.

Your personal security and that of your family is as important as your food, water, and shelter during and after a disaster. Having a plan makes a difference and helps you have peace of mind. Interacting with authorities should be a positive experience and can be as long as you cooperate and act in good faith. And remember, information is the most important commodity during or after a disaster. Listen to authority figures first and then the media, and don't believe rumors.

15

Shelter Safety

Lesley got checked in to her hotel and had just settled into her room when she was startled by the sound of a bullhorn and a loud siren. An announcement soon followed, saying that, if necessary, the hotel would be evacuating the guests to the first-floor lobby. This would be a mandatory evacuation, and no one, not even pets, would be allowed to stay in their room.

At 10:45 that night, the orders came to evacuate.

The lobby could have loosely been called a "shelter" because it provided physical protection from the storm, and from people trying to break in afterward, but any resemblance ended there.

For 4 nights, the hotel guests slept on the floor. All they had been permitted to bring with them was a pillow, a sheet, a blanket, and a couple of personal items.

"I tried to go back up to my room to get a toothbrush, jeans, and pajamas," Lesley recalls, "but the hotel management stood by the doorways and said 'nobody's going anywhere.'"

"I remember there was a guest who tried to get back up to her room. She was bipolar, and her medication was up there. I felt so bad for her because she was begging the hotel staff, 'Please, I have to get my medication,' and they refused to allow her to go to her room."

"The power went out at 5:30 Monday morning," Lesley remembers, and "you could hear a collective gasp." The lack of electricity and, therefore, ventilation combined with heat, humidity, body odor, and pet dander in the cramped lobby. Multiple times Lesley slipped and fell on the floor—which was covered with animal waste. Toilets weren't working, and bathroom trash from both men and women was piling up, creating extremely unsanitary conditions.

New Orleans heat and humidity are at their worst in August and September. No ventilation, days and days of sweat, and no showers lead to unsightly conditions, to say the least. "It was pretty rank in there," Lesley recalls.

Tempers began to flare—not among the guests, but among the hotel management and city officials. "They were blaming the guests for asking them questions," says Lesley. "I know everybody was under stress at the time, but I think they should have been given some sort of instructions about how to handle these sorts of disasters."

To pass the time, Lesley bonded with a doctor from South Carolina. He had come to New Orleans 2 weeks earlier to bury his mother and had returned to the city just before the storm hit to care for his ailing father, who was diabetic, incontinent, and had many other health issues. "The treatment I saw toward the elderly was appalling," Lesley recalls. "They wouldn't accommodate them for any of their medicines, [and] the lack of medical care was just so startling to me."

After 6 days in the lobby, when she finally boarded the bus to the airport, Lesley was covered with bruises on her legs, hips, arms, elbows, and back from constant falls on the excrement-covered floor. But she was better off than many others. The stories coming out of the Superdome, where thousands had evacuated to, told of horrors much worse.

The Need for Shelter

It's possible that after a disaster such as flood, fire, or tornado, your home won't be habitable and you'll need an alternate place to stay. A community shelter isn't the first choice when looking for an alternate place to stay; hotels, family, and friends are often tried first. But if none of these options are available—as will probably be the case after a widespread disaster—you might find yourself at the nearest community shelter with many other similarly displaced people. It's more than likely, however, that your shelter experience will be much better than Lesley's.

Shelters exist for the purpose of providing temporary relief to disaster victims. They range in size and function from community evacuation centers to basic-care facilities. Some may include tented areas, or they may be residential sites such as dormitories or hotels. They also might be nonresidential sites such as schools, churches, sports centers, or large auditoriums.

RED CROSS SHELTERS

If you find yourself in a shelter operated by an established organization such as the American Red Cross, most likely a range of services will be provided for you and your family, including a place to sleep, food, health care, and mental-health support.

Not all shelters are created equal. But hopefully, with a bit of planning, you won't find yourself in Lesley's position in a hotel lobby-turned-unplanned makeshift shelter.

Finding Shelter

Each state sets its own requirements for emergency care and shelter at the local level. If you and your family are in need of shelter, you'll most likely look to your local government agencies first. Many local governments have partnerships with the American Red Cross; the Salvation Army, the United Way, and local neighborhood organizations, churches, and nonprofits might offer shelter during or after disasters, too. Within hours and days after an event, multiple shelters should be open. Local emergency management usually shares lists of these locations through media outlets.

Hotels sometimes provide coordinated, monitored shelter through FEMA's Transitional Shelter Assistance (TSA) program. FEMA provides a per diem for each stay to these hotels based on their locations. To find a list of participating hotels in your state, go to femaevachotels.com, select your state in the "Participating Hotels" area, and click Find Hotels. The results page provides a list of participating hotels (sorted by city), with addresses and information on whether pets are allowed, if rooms come with a kitchen, and how many rooms with ADA accommodations are available. Use the "Worksheet: Shelter Checklist" at the end of this chapter to help organize this information.

When creating your disaster preparedness plan, add this list of hotels to it, along with the page instructions so you know in advance where you can go to get information about hotel shelters.

And remember, FEMA only pays for the cost of lodging. All other costs are your responsibility.

Plan Ahead

You are responsible for your own and your family's welfare. To that end, there are some things you can do or learn ahead of time that will make your time in a shelter a better experience for you, your family, the shelter provider, and your fellow shelter guests.

If possible, research ahead of time who might be providing shelters in your area, and speak with them about what you can expect in the way of provisions for your physical and emotional well-being. Some shelters might have counselors on hand to help alleviate the anxiety that often accompanies being displaced, while others might not have those resources. Some shelters might have prepackaged nonperishable food to offer, while others might provide home-cooking. Some may have emergency medical staff on hand to help treat injuries, while others may have to rely on first-aid kits. Find out what to expect, as well as what you're allowed to bring in from the outside, and pack your preparedness kit accordingly.

Be sure to ask about basic bathroom facilities and hygiene maintenance, access to phones and computers so you can communicate with other family members, and whether or not smoking is permitted. If you're a smoker, you'll want to know there's a designated smoking area for you. If you're not a smoker, and/or have a family member who is allergic to smoke, you'll want to know that they won't come in contact with cigarette smoke in the facility.

Be sure to ask about their pet policy, if you intend to bring your pets with you. It's important to plan for your animal family members as well as the humans. It is also important to understand that not all shelters may accept animals due to health reasons (many people are allergic to dogs and cats), and not all shelters are equipped to handle the hygienic issues that would arise.

Ask what kind of security will be on hand. Some shelters have volunteers from the local police department, county sheriff's office, or uniformed court officers. This may be important in a large shelter, where people might reside for an ongoing period of time.

Also ask about any special accommodations or provisions you or a family member might need. In some shelters, for example, one family member with special needs might need to be moved to a separate facility at a different location. That separation could result in anxiety for that person, as well as tracking difficulties later on for shelter staff and reunification problems for the family. Avoid separation if at all possible. If not possible, insist that at least one other family member can accompany the separated member, and insist that the shelter staff develop and implement a reunification plan for your family.

GET INVOLVED

You can help make your local shelter friendlier to special needs populations by getting involved in advance and helping plan the shelter. Time spent volunteering before a disaster could save you and many others headaches later.

Some emergency shelters aren't compliant with the Americans with Disabilities Act Accessibility Guidelines (ADAAG), making them inaccessible to those who have mobility impairments, for example. Respiratory issues or sensitivities to chemicals or other properties could be an issue for some people as well. Ask the shelter where you're looking to ride out the storm how it accommodates people with disabilities. Does it have a patient lift or wheelchair-accessible shower facilities?

Inquire about the shelter's access to power via generator. This might be especially important if you have a family member who needs power for specialized medical equipment such as respiratory equipment or to charge battery-powered wheelchairs.

Some shelters have plans in place to retrieve certain medical equipment such as oxygen tanks, sleep-aid machines, or other specialty equipment from residences when possible. If it looks like you're going to be in a shelter for some time, you can help the shelter in this effort by including in your family preparedness plan that family member's medical equipment information. Then you'll have that information readily accessible and easy to share.

Medical and mental health provisions are sometimes available. Some shelters have emergency medical staff or Medical Reserve Corps volunteers on hand. You might want to inquire about what kind of mental health counseling and/or spiritual counseling is offered.

If you or a member of your family has a service animal, ask how those animals are accommodated. This is a different issue from pets because service animals are often necessary for the welfare of an individual with special needs.

Ask about the shelter's building, too. Is it susceptible to mold? Does it have carpet? Embedded dust, dust mites, cleaning agents, and other agents could irritate and exacerbate some respiratory health issues.

Come Prepared

The goal of any shelter is to provide basic emergency assistance for anyone who needs it. The shelter provider could be a TSA-participating hotel, it may be a Red Cross endeavor, or perhaps it's a small church auditorium—whatever the situation, you should go in realizing that the shelter may not accommodate as many emergency needs as the organization might like.

If it's a small local nonprofit, for example, you might encounter shortages of some basic items. Therefore, it's a good idea to have your preparedness kit packed and ready to take with you to the shelter.

Assume only the basics—food and water—will be supplied, so pack everything else you might want or need in your kit. That includes snacks, toys and books for the kids, and prescription medications. Also take your family's preparedness plan, disaster kit, copies of critical cards you usually carry with you (driver's license, insurance, credit, etc.), and the medical history for each member of your family. The later "Worksheet: Shelter Checklist" helps you organize what to bring.

BE CAREFUL WHAT YOU BRING

Don't bring to a shelter anything expensive that you wouldn't want to lose, such as MP3 players, electronic games, etc.

Depending on the shelter, different rules may apply. Some shelters have restrictions on what you can and cannot bring in from the outside. Find out ahead of time, if possible, what those rules include.

Mind Your Manners

When stuck for long periods of time in cramped quarters with people you don't know, when you're unsure about the condition of your home, your job, and possibly some friends and family members, it's easy to become impatient, irritable, and even combative. Crowded conditions accompanied with anxiety, lack of certainty, as well as lack of privacy can lead to conflict and even spread of illnesses. You can avoid these unnecessary unpleasantries by adhering to the basics rules of a polite society.

IF YOU FEEL ILL

If you do contract a cold, virus, or other illness while at the shelter, let shelter staff know immediately so you can be isolated from the others as much as is possible.

Treat others with the same respect with which you wish to be treated. Just making people feel respected and heard can go a long way. And remember that people are often scared in these situations. It's okay to let them know you're scared, too. You're all in the same boat together.

Realize that even if your family has no members with special needs, others might. So if you see someone who has a little more space than you do, it might very well be because they have accessibility issues and need the space to be able to better access their cot.

Keep your personal space neat and clean. A tidy area goes a long way toward creating a sense of calm. The shelter staff will appreciate it, too.

Remember that some people have allergies and are sensitive to certain chemicals. So although to you it might only be a candy bar, to someone with peanut allergies, that candy bar could be fatal. Find out if anyone around you has allergies you could unknowingly trigger. Some allergies can be quite serious, with symptoms ranging from itching and hives to anaphylactic shock, but can be prevented with a little forethought and consideration. Use the appropriate well-sealed containers for any outside nonperishable food you bring in with your kit to avoid others' possible contact with allergens and also to reduce the chances of attracting ants or other insects.

It's also a good idea to remain fragrance free while you're confined in a small area together. Some perfumes can cause respiratory reactions, headaches, and nausea, and people with these ailments will be grateful to not have to deal with that added anxiety on top of everything else.

To help prevent the possible spread of infection, wash your hands frequently. Keeping your hands clean is recommended whenever significant hand contamination is possible, such as in a place of close quarters with many strangers, and after touching potentially contaminated items such as toys, blankets, money, and used dishes and utensils, just to name a few.

To avoid potential contamination, wash your hands thoroughly …

- Before and after food preparation.
- Before and after eating and drinking.
- Before and after touching your face and mouth.
- After using the toilet.
- After sneezing, coughing, or blowing your nose.
- Before and after contact with wounds.
- After cleaning up from any bodily fluid accidents.
- After cleaning bathrooms and kitchens.
- After handling dirty laundry.
- Before and after spending time in a children's play area or around small children and their toys.
- After handling pets.
- After any activity that causes you to become dirty or sweaty.
- After taking out or handling garbage.
- After changing diapers.
- After caring for someone who is sick.

Here's the best, and safest, method of washing your hands:

1. Run your hands under clean running warm water and lather with soap.
2. Scrub your hands thoroughly, front and back, under your nails, and between your fingers for 20 seconds or as long as it takes for you to sing "Happy Birthday" twice in your head.
3. Rinse your hands well under the warm water.
4. Use an air dryer or paper towel to dry your hands. If you use a cloth towel, be sure it's clean and hasn't been used by anyone else in the shelter.

Washing your hands is the best way to get rid of germs and prevent illness by contamination, but soap and water might not always be available. Although not as effective as hand washing if you're dealing with obvious dirt, hand sanitizers can be a decent substitute. Opt for alcohol-based sanitizers with at least 60 percent alcohol. Simply apply a bit to your hands, and rub your hands together until your hands are dry. Be thorough.

Carefully monitor the use of hand sanitizer by small children, who may try to put it in their mouths, especially if it smells good. The alcohol and essential oils could cause problems for those with allergies or chemical sensitivities, and they're flammable. And finally, remember that hand sanitizers do not get rid of all germs, so consider them a second choice to washing with soap and water.

If you are in a place that has no running water, or the water isn't safe due to contamination, use water that has been boiled or disinfected.

If you're staying for several days in a shelter that has working bathrooms and showers, do your part by cleaning up after yourself. Wipe down sinks and toilets after you use them, and continue to wash your hands and use hand sanitizer. If you can't shower, but you do have access to a sink and some privacy, use the opportunity just to do some basic cleaning. Remember to use deodorant, too. Your neighbors will be grateful, and being clean will increase your personal sense of well-being.

DEALING WITH SAFETY RISKS

If you notice someone who appears to be a safety risk, notify shelter personnel immediately. A safety risk might be a person carrying some kind of weapon such as a knife, or it might be someone who is showing signs of drug use. Or it might simply be someone who is having a difficult time handling his or her anxiety and keeping him- or herself under control. Not all shelters will have security personnel, but some will have people trained to deal with possible safety risks. Most of the time, this won't be an issue, but it's an important thing to be aware of.

Making Your Shelter Stay More Bearable

Staying in a shelter during a disaster when things seem a bit uncertain can be emotionally draining, especially if you have nothing to do but worry. If you see that the shelter is short-staffed, volunteer to take on some tasks. You'll help the shelter operate better, distract yourself from your own problems, and boost your sense of well-being. Helping others has a tendency to alleviate anxiety, so if you have the opportunity, get involved. You'll help yourself as you help others.

Look at staying in a shelter as though you're staying as a guest in a friend's home. Pick up after yourself, offer to lend a hand with dinner and cleanup, and make your bed. Be a grateful and gracious guest. If you treat your shelter stay in much the same way, the experience will be more pleasant for you, for the staff (many of whom are volunteers), and for the other anxious evacuees.

If you or someone in your family is having difficulty dealing with anxiety, ask to speak to a mental health counselor. Many shelters have trained counselors on hand to help evacuees deal with what can be overwhelming emotions after a disaster.

Disasters can be stressful, even if you and your family are uninjured, and even if your loss is minimal compared to what others might have lost. Don't discount the emotional impact evacuating to a shelter may have on you or your loved ones. Even temporary displacement can be hard on adults, and especially on children, who may suddenly feel much less secure and haven't developed the skills to talk about their fears and feelings of insecurity.

Shelters not only provide a roof over your head when you need it, but also help you and your family transition your way through an extremely stressful time by providing food, water, medical assistance, security, and emotional support. Allow the shelter staff to help you. That's why they're there.

Worksheet: Shelter Checklist

Shelters are a significant piece of the disaster response and recovery puzzle, and it's important to make a potential shelter stay a part of your preparedness plan. The following checklist gives you the steps to take to ensure you're as well informed about area shelters as possible—and well-prepared for a possible stay.

❑ When making your preparedness plan, call your county emergency management to find out where shelters will be located during a disaster.

❑ Check FEMA's Transitional Shelter Assistance program (femaevachotels.com) to find out which hotels in your community participate:

Hotel	*Address*	*Phone*
_____	_____	_____
_____	_____	_____
_____	_____	_____
_____	_____	_____
_____	_____	_____

❑ Call shelters ahead of time to find out what to expect in the way of accommodations, special needs, counselors, medical staff, ADA accommodations, backup power for respirators and other medical equipment, computer and internet access, security, hygiene, and service animal accommodations. Also ask how you can help:

_____

_____

_____

_____

_____

What to bring to the shelter:

- ❑ Your disaster preparedness plan
- ❑ Your disaster kit
- ❑ Copies of critical cards such as credit cards, driver's license, insurance cards, etc.
- ❑ Medical histories for each member of your family
- ❑ Snacks
- ❑ Toys and games for your kids
- ❑ Any prescriptions you need
- ❑ Anything else you can think of that will make your stay more comfortable.

16

City Mouse, Country Mouse

The differences between urban and rural living are numerous and profound. In the city, noise can be constant and unpleasant. Yet the quiet of a country night, broken up only by the chirping of crickets or the sound of night birds, can keep a visiting city-dweller, who's used to the sounds of traffic and people, awake all night.

In Beatrix Potter's version of *The Tale of Johnny Town-Mouse,* Potter tells the ancient tale of the city mouse and the country mouse, giving it her own particular spin where the moral is that tastes differ. Everyone has his or her own living preference—city versus country—and each lifestyle has its pros and cons, including its own distinct set of challenges when preparing for likely disasters.

The following sections, along with the "Worksheet: City and Country Mouse Checklists," can help you ready yourself, no matter where you live.

Special Challenges in Urban Settings

While Lesley Smiley was hunkered down in a hotel lobby in New Orleans preparing for the oncoming storm, co-author Crystal was evacuating from Pensacola Island, Florida, where she had been staying while responding to Hurricane Dennis. She headed to a hotel in Pensacola proper, where she remained under orders to be ready to evacuate at a moment's notice.

As Katrina made landfall on August 29, Crystal's anxiety levels were high. She watched through her hotel room windows as the tail end of the storm grazed Pensacola, bringing rain in sheets, sometimes horizontally, while palm trees whipped in the wind. Crystal had never been in a hurricane, and she found herself wishing for a good, old-fashioned Oklahoma tornado she was more familiar with.

The next morning, Pensacola was nonfunctional. The 50-plus-mile-per-hour winds had done some damage, and power was out throughout the city. Gas stations were closed, grocery stores and restaurants were shuttered, the post office wasn't open, and banks remained locked with ATMs offline. Then Crystal saw a blinking red "Open" sign. The tattoo parlor next to her hotel was open and operating. Bored, and with nothing else to do, Crystal went inside.

It's true that people living in the city depend on an infrastructure that provides freeways, rails, waterways, seaports, airports, and mass transportation. If any of these are down for a day or more, it can throw our lives a bit off kilter. And in a disaster, it can throw things far off kilter. But that doesn't mean our dependence on these things renders us helpless and without resources. A well-prepared person—urban or rural—can figure out how to find workarounds to these problems and make the most of their situation.

SOFT? NO WAY

Some view urban dwellers as soft, without resourcefulness, dependent on city infrastructure and technology, completely untrained and unable to survive in a situation without these amenities. On the contrary, urbanites are highly resourceful. It's simply that their resources are different from those of their rural counterparts.

Challenge: Shortage of Supplies

In the hours leading up to a hurricane or a winter storm, the public often makes a run on grocery stores, as well as home improvement stores, for bread, water, canned meat, flashlights, batteries, and generators. And gasoline—for the car and for generators.

In the days after Hurricane Katrina, gas stations in Pensacola reopened to long lines of people waiting in lines that ran down the street and around the block to fill up not only their cars' gas tanks, but also the many gas cans people brought with them. Crystal waited an hour and 15 minutes to get to the pumps one day, only to find them empty when she finally got there.

Solution: Prepare in Advance

Be sure you plan for and include gasoline, food and water, and other emergency supplies in your preparedness kit. With the exception of bread, everything else people usually make a run for as a storm approaches can be purchased and stockpiled ahead of time, helping you avoid the last-minute rush.

Always keep your gas tank at least half full. If you want to have some extra fuel on hand, buy the large-capacity containers in advance so you don't have to worry about finding them later.

Challenge: Power Blackouts

On December 10, 2007, Tulsa, Oklahoma, was hit with a massive ice storm. Freezing rain, tree limbs crashing down under the weight of the ice, and exploding transformers resulted in a city without power and coated in ice up to 3 inches thick in spots. Neighborhood streets were impassible as trees fell and blocked roadways. More than 80 percent of residents had no electricity— some for up to 11 days. The few families who still had power graciously opened their homes to friends and family without.

Supplies at American Red Cross shelters ran low. Restocking meant a trip that should have taken 40 minutes, but instead took 6 hours due to the treacherous ice. More than once the shelters ran out of urgent supplies.

Solution: Prepare for All Outcomes

You never know when your electricity will go out and for how long you'll be without power. To prepare for prolonged power outages, purchase a generator and practice using it. Be sure you have enough gasoline on hand to operate it. Keep your car's gas tank at least half full, too. Gas station pumps require electricity to dispense fuel.

Speaking of your car, you can use it to charge your phone during a power outage. If you have a phone charging cord for your car, you can turn on the engine (or just the battery) long enough to make some calls, check email or social media, or get news updates if your phone is so equipped. Be sure not to run your car inside a closed garage.

If you usually keep your car in the garage, know where the manual release lever is on your garage door. Practice disengaging the electric lift and opening the garage door by hand as part of your preparedness measures.

When the lights go out, flashlights come in handy, as do those extra batteries you packed in your emergency preparedness kit. And although many people don't like or recommend the use of candles due to the risk of fire, responsible candle use can help you extend the life of your flashlight batteries. But be smart when using candles: carefully monitor all burning candles, don't go to sleep without extinguishing any lit candles, and don't leave the house with candles burning.

COOL IT

Make room in your refrigerator and freezer for extra plastic containers. Fill the containers with water, leaving about 1 inch headroom in each to allow for the water to expand as it freezes. When the electricity goes out, the chilled or frozen water keeps your refrigerator and freezer colder for longer. Remember to keep the refrigerator and freezer doors closed to retain the cool inside as much as possible.

If you have a gas stove, cooking on it might still be an option, even if your electricity is out. If you find yourself in a position of having to cook a great deal of food before it goes bad, cook what's likely to go bad first. If there's too much for your family to consume, consider sharing with your neighbors or other family members. Your neighbors may be in a similar situation, and a communal dinner of all the food needing to be cooked can be a wonderful bonding opportunity.

Challenge: Responders Can't Reach You Right Away

During a disaster, first responders are often spread thin. FEMA recommends you be prepared to be on your own for the first 72 hours. During that time, what do you do if you need the lifesaving services only first responders can give?

Solution: Learn to Become Your Own First Responder

Community Emergency Response Teams (CERTs) operate all over the United States. These neighborhood groups of volunteers are trained to respond to a disaster in their neighborhood. In the case of a widespread disaster when there aren't enough police, fire, and emergency medical to go around, CERTs are trained to be the first responders until the professional responders arrive.

CERT teams are trained in light search and rescue. They learn to assess a damaged building for safety before going in; turn off utilities; remove heavy debris from injured people; move injured people; and triage people into groups of minor injuries, severe injuries, and deceased. They also learn firefighting techniques and how to assess and treat injuries. Find out if your community has a CERT team by visiting citizencorps.gov/cc/CertIndex. do?submitByState.

STARTING A CERT TEAM

If your community doesn't have a CERT team you can join, consider starting your own in your area. Find more information for starting a CERT team at fema.gov/ start-and-maintain-cert-program.

Challenge: Cultural or Language Barriers

Language barriers can present another problem after a disaster in a city, especially among larger immigrant populations.

In the communities surrounding Biloxi and Gulfport, Mississippi, one particular group found themselves at a distinct disadvantage following the British Petroleum (BP) Deepwater Horizon oil spill. After the spill, the Vietnamese fishermen who made their living off the abundant seafood in the Gulf Coast were no longer allowed to bring in fish from the waters suspected of being impacted by the oil. That combined with a decreased demand for seafood due to people's fears of contamination.

The state and BP worked together to provide assistance for the fishermen who lost their livelihoods, but the fishermen weren't coming forward for the help.. It was discovered that the language barrier prevented them from being notified that they could ask for assistance.

Solution: Community Outreach in Advance

Many communities are home to multiple ethnic groups and contain multiple spoken languages. If this describes your family, or you know of a family this applies to, check with your municipal and county emergency management ahead of time to find out what safeguards are in place to ensure non-English-speaking people receive all communications related to any warnings and, later, to any assistance programs they may need to utilize. Include this information in your family preparedness kit so you don't have to hunt for it later.

Challenge: Lack of Internet Access

When you find yourself without the power to keep your laptop or tablet charged, you're also without one of the fastest ways to get information that could be vital, or at the very least, useful: the internet.

Solution: Wi-Fi Tethering

If you have a smartphone, it (charged in your car) can act as a Wi-Fi hotspot. Your cell phone carrier may provide this service for a fee or as part of your monthly plan. And if it doesn't, you can purchase apps for your phone to give it that capability.

Special Challenges in Rural Settings

Billy Bass, whom we met in Chapter 1, is now a retired sheriff's deputy for the Tulsa County Sheriff's Department. The large, soft-spoken man with kind eyes shares similarities with Dan Blocker, who played "Hoss" on the hit TV series *Bonanza*.

Billy has never feared tornadoes but has been fascinated by them his whole life—since seeing that F-5 tornado in April 1964 outside his Wichita Falls home. He has witnessed quite a few others since then, yet he never tires of the dangerous beauty and power tornadoes unleash.

Rural living, with its pastoral beauty and dazzling, star-studded night skies, has great appeal for a great many people. And although many urban dwellers can't imagine living where there's so much peace and quiet and few friends or neighbors nearby with whom to chat and gossip, that's exactly the appeal to many who live a country existence.

However, many of the things that make urban centers a better place to be in a disaster—proximity to responders, hospitals, emergency medical, etc.— provide unique challenges for rural dwellers.

Challenge: Farming/Livestock Concerns

Many people who live in rural areas are farmers who raise livestock and grow crops for commercial use. This is their livelihood, and these resources must be protected.

Solution: Plan and Prepare Ahead

You might not be able to do much to preserve your crops in a disaster, but by including your livestock in your family's preparedness plan, you may be able to save them—or at least lessen your losses a bit.

If you raise horses, cattle, sheep, goats, or pigs, make plans for their transportation in an evacuation. Map out your route in advance, and have a place ready for their relocation. Be sure the vehicles you need are available, along with the necessary drivers and handlers. Be sure your animals are tagged and identified to avoid any problems retrieving them later.

If evacuation isn't a possibility, you have to decide in advance whether or not to get them into some kind of shelter. The alternative is to turn them outside.

For more detailed information on pets and livestock in a disaster, see Chapter 8.

Challenge: Compromised Communications

Limited cell phone reception, cable television, and internet access in some very rural areas can make it difficult to get important information, or to let people know you are okay. In a disaster, cell phone reception can be further limited or even unavailable.

Solution: Go Low-Tech

One easy solution is to have a land-line telephone hooked up the old-fashioned way—with wires and cords. Don't rely on a cordless phone because if the power goes out, the phone won't work.

Even if you lose your cell phone reception and your electricity, your land-line phone should still work and enable you to call 911, if necessary, or anyone whose phone is still working.

Challenge: Distance from Responders and Hospitals

Rapid emergency response, particularly medical response, depends on hospitals and emergency medical service providers. Firefighters are also called into action in the role of EMTs. The health department that serves rural areas might work with less money and manpower than their city counterparts. For example, you're more likely to find mental-health professionals, who are very important in helping disaster survivors overcome post-traumatic stress disorder, in the city than in the country.

And although many rural communities have hospitals, they often have to deal with the same lack of resources. They often don't have surge capacity, meaning that in a large, widespread disaster that results in many, many injuries, the hospital probably won't have enough beds or staff to handle them all. They also might not have the best or most up-to-date equipment due to a lack of funding.

If you or a family member suffers a major injury during a disaster, and there's no room for you at the local hospital, you might be diverted to a distant metropolitan hospital—maybe even transported by a medical helicopter service. Or you may have to wait for hours for a responder, depending on the breadth of the disaster and the available manpower.

RURAL CARE

According to a 2005 National Rural Health Association policy paper, volunteer emergency personnel respond to medical emergencies in more than half the country. Rural medical facilities are usually smaller, farther apart, and less technically capable than those in more urban areas. Most responses and transports involve long travel distances, which translates to high operating expenses. EMS personnel, many of whom are volunteers, may be the only healthcare providers around and must seek medical direction from physicians who are far away—sometimes by hundreds of miles.

Solution: CERT Training

Treatment during the first hour after trauma is critical to recovery, so it's important to know what you can do while waiting for emergency medical services to respond, especially if they're not able to get to you right away.

CERT training can be useful here. CERT teams learn more than simple first aid. They learn how to stop bleeding, move wounded people, assess for shock, and set broken bones—simpler things you can do to help while waiting for the professionals who may not get there for hours or even days.

Challenge: Limited Transportation During an Evacuation

If you live in a rural area that's rather isolated, chances are you don't have access to public transportation. You probably have a car or other vehicle, but during an emergency or when you need to evacuate, the roads in your area might not be easy to access or travel.

Disasters such as wildfires, floods, or landslides may require an evacuation. Limited transportation could make that more of a challenge in the country than in more urban areas, where more people own cars, public transportation is more available, and access to car rental companies is easier. If you live in a rural area that's rather isolated, chances are you have less access to these transportation resources.

Solution: Preplanned Transportation

Pay attention to who in your surrounding area might need your assistance during an evacuation. Make plans in advance to ride together. This means you'll have to account ahead of time for any luggage they might bring as well as any pets. Be sure they know ahead of time just what you have room for, and what you won't be able to transport so there are no surprises, and precious time isn't wasted in trying to negotiate.

Challenge: Lack of Emergency Shelters Nearby

Emergency shelters, food distribution centers, and FEMA Disaster Recovery Centers may not be located close to you, or you don't know where they're located.

Solution: Plan Ahead

Locate shelters ahead of time by calling your emergency management director. Be sure to plan for your transportation to the shelter if that could be a problem later.

If you don't know where your closest FEMA Disaster Recovery Center is, that's okay. You don't actually have to go there in person to apply for Individual Assistance. Just call 800-621-3362. (This is where your old-school land-line comes in handy.) You can apply over the phone and also check the status of your application.

Add this number to your disaster preparedness kit so you don't have to search for it when you need it.

Challenge: Caring for Elderly Neighbors

Your elderly neighbors might have special needs other than transportation but no one to check on them after a disaster and be sure they're safe and uninjured.

Solution: Adopt a Neighbor

You can adopt an elderly couple or an elderly man or woman you know who lives alone or doesn't have children or friends to care for them should a hazard hit. Find out what medications they must have and what medical equipment they regularly use, such as an oxygen tank. Talk to your local hospitals and medical clinics to ensure they can accommodate your neighbor in an emergency. If electricity is necessary to operate your neighbor's medical equipment, ask the medical professionals how you can care for your neighbor during a loss of electricity.

If your neighbor has family members who frequently look in on them, share with them your plan to help if necessary, and work together with them. Be sure someone outside the home has a key to your neighbor's home in case you need to get in during an emergency and your neighbor can't reach the door.

Also be sure to include your neighbor in your family preparedness plan.

CERT TEAM CAREGIVERS

If you belong to a CERT team, challenge your team members to each adopt an elderly neighbor to look in on and care for during a disaster in the absence of his or her own family members.

Looking in on your neighbors is a good idea whether you're a country mouse or a city mouse. Remember, no amount of planning can prevent disasters, but we can control how we respond to them, and by so doing, better control our losses.

We all live with unique challenges during a disaster, regardless of our geographical location. Through some simple preplanning, we can make those challenges easier to face.

Worksheet: City and Country Mouse Checklists

Whether you live in the city or in a more rural area, it's important to prepare for situations and events specific to your surrounds.

If you're a city mouse:

- ❑ Call your municipal/county emergency management to find out what safeguards are in place to ensure non-English-speaking people receive all warning communications, and afterward, all information related to receiving assistance.

- ❑ Set up your cell phone for Wi-Fi tethering. Call your phone provider for assistance.

- ❑ Join a CERT team. Find your community's CERT team at citizencorps.gov/cc/CertIndex.do?submitByState.

- ❑ If no CERT teams are in your area, start one. Find out how at fema.gov/start-and-maintain-cert-program.

- ❑ Call emergency management to find out where shelters and food distribution centers will be if a disaster strikes.

- ❑ Keep this number on hand to locate FEMA Disaster Recovery Centers where you can apply for Individual Assistance in a presidentially declared disaster: 800-621-3362.

If you're a country mouse:

- ❑ Plan for livestock evacuation and transportation. Have all the necessary trucks, drivers, and handlers in place before you need them.

- ❑ Tag and identify your animals for quick retrieval after a disaster.

- ❑ If evacuation of animals is not possible, plan for their shelter or for turning them outside.

- ❑ Pre-plan transportation during an evacuation.

- ❑ Join a CERT team. Find your community's CERT team at citizencorps.gov/cc/CertIndex.do?submitByState.

- ❑ Start a CERT team if none exists near you. Find out how at fema.gov/start-and-maintain-cert-program.

❑ Call emergency management to find out where shelters and food distribution centers will be in a disaster.

❑ Keep this number on hand to locate FEMA Disaster Recovery Centers where you can apply for Individual Assistance in a presidentially declared disaster: 800-621-3362.

❑ Adopt an elderly person in your area to care for during a disaster. Know ahead of time what medications they take, what their particular needs are, and the contact information for their family members.

4

First Aid During a Disaster

In all our coverage of planning, preparing, practicing, drilling, and those first few hours and days, one of the things we haven't touched on a lot is the potential for injuries and what to do if you or someone in your family is burned, suffers a broken bone or other injury. What if no emergency medical service is available for possibly days?

In Part 4, we talk about what to do when faced with some of the more immediate threats such as cardiac arrest, choking, and anaphylactic shock. We also look at how to control bleeding, treat burns, and care for broken bones. Heat and cold exposure get some attention here, too, as do other illnesses and their symptoms.

Even if you don't anticipate needing any first-aid information, read these chapters anyway. You never know. And absorbing this information makes you that much more equipped to handle these scenarios if faced with them.

Note: The first-aid information within these chapters is intended to be a basic guide for dealing with injuries and illnesses in a disaster situation. For more information, see the American College of Emergency Physicians First Aid Manual, 4th Edition.

17

Immediate Life Threats

Rod's first patient in Mississippi after Hurricane Katrina lived in a nursing home. She had called 911 herself, against the wishes of the nursing home staff. The woman was in her mid-50s and dependent upon dialysis due to severe kidney disease. Like most dialysis patients, she usually had treatment three times a week. But because the storm knocked out all the dialysis centers for miles in every direction, she hadn't received dialysis for 5 days and she didn't know how much longer she could live without it.

Once public health authorities pulled together enough machines and technicians to open an emergency center, Rod's patient and dozens of others were transported there. Each patient was given minimum time on the dialysis machine to keep them going until more machines would be available. Although it was enough for Rod's patient to survive, it wasn't nearly enough to completely detoxify her body.

Unfortunately, the center was running 24 hours a day and was swamped with patients. The situation was dire; there simply wasn't room, manpower, or resources to care for everyone as thoroughly as everyone would have liked.

After a disaster like Katrina, there's not always enough to go around.

Lack of Resources

One thing that can turn a significant event into a true disaster is the lack of resources, and nowhere is this more relevant than during medical emergencies. After a disaster, you or a family member might be injured or otherwise in need of an ambulance, emergency room, or physician, but those resources are likely either missing or helping others. Remember, disasters are as overwhelming for responders as they are for everyone else.

When it comes to postdisaster medical care, knowledge is power. Try to be as self-sufficient as you can be. Plan ahead and take a first-aid and CPR (cardiopulmonary resuscitation) class if you can, and definitely put together a first-aid kit like the one discussed in Chapter 3. Life-threatening emergencies will still require professional help, and that help will no doubt be harder to summon in a disaster than on any typical day, but in the meantime, you can help treat the smaller issues.

NO MORE DANGER

Life-threatening emergencies will be as rare after a disaster as they are any other time. There's no evidence to suggest you'll be in more danger of having a heart attack or a stroke after a disaster than before. If you've gone your whole life without needing an emergency room, you probably won't need one now—unless, of course, you're injured as a result of the disaster.

In this chapter, we also offer guidance on when 911 is necessary and when you can try to handle things yourself.

Cardiac Arrest

Cardiac arrest is the ultimate medical emergency. There's no worst-case scenario than when one's heart stops pumping blood. No oxygen can get to the brain or to the heart.

To completely reverse cardiac arrest—to get the heart started so it's supporting life again—requires a team of health-care providers all working together. You must summon responders to get that ball rolling. In the meantime, the *only* thing that will help is to do CPR.

Symptoms of Cardiac Arrest

When the heart stops moving blood around the body, fresh blood no longer flows through the brain, which causes the brain to stop working. This leads to loss of consciousness, no regaining consiousness, and a cessation of breathing. You might hear some gasps or snores, but they'll be several seconds apart and not effective.

The only way to treat cardiac arrest is with immediate CPR. *Do not wait!*

Treating Cardiac Arrest

Here's how to treat cardiac arrest:

1. Try to wake the patient. Be forceful. If tapping, yelling, and some gentle shaking don't do the trick, go to the next step.

2. Call 911. Have someone else make the call if possible.

3. Push hard and fast in the middle of the person's chest, at least 2 inches deep, right on the breastbone. Push about twice per second.

4. Don't stop pushing on the chest until help arrives.

If you or another person is able to call 911, the dispatcher should be able to give you directions on what to do next. If so, follow what the dispatcher tells you.

If someone else is available to help you perform CPR, switch with that person every 2 minutes. If you're doing CPR vigorously enough, you should be pretty winded after about 2 minutes of pushing on the patient's chest, so let the other person push for 2 minutes and switch back. Keep doing that until help arrives.

When you switch, be fast. Don't allow more than 5 to 10 seconds to pass without someone pushing on the patient's chest.

If 911 is not available, send someone to get help. *Do not stop CPR until help arrives or you become physically exhausted and cannot continue.* If you are alone with the patient, try CPR for 2 minutes and then go get help. As soon as you find another person, send that person for help and return to the patient to continue CPR until help arrives or you become too exhausted to continue.

If the patient begins breathing again, roll her on her left side. You may put a pillow under her head but only if she's lying on her left side. Keep an eye on the patient until help arrives. If she stops breathing, begin CPR again.

Performing CPR on an Infant

Babies are built differently than adults. They're smaller, obviously, but they're also much more pliable. It doesn't take as much pressure to compress their little chests as an adult's, and you only need to use two fingers to do CPR. There are a couple of ways to do it.

In the first way, you can lay the baby along your forearm, on her back with her head in your hand and her legs straddling your bicep. Using two fingers on your other hand, push on her chest, on her breastbone, right between her nipples.

The other option is to lay the baby on a flat surface and wrap your hands around her body. Place your thumbs together on her breastbone, between her nipples, and use your thumbs to compress her chest.

Either way you do it, push about twice a second, and be sure you push about a third of the way into her chest. Push hard, and push fast.

SIZE MATTERS

For the purposes of this chapter, we're considering children 12 months or younger as infants. But if you think a baby is small enough to be an infant or needs gentler care, that's fine. It doesn't really matter if the child is a few months older than a year.

Choking

Rod's wife, Melanie, is an EMT, and they occasionally have opportunities to staff an ambulance together. On one of those days, they were standing near the doors to the emergency department at their local hospital, chatting with another crew between patients, when a woman approached with a girl maybe 2 years old. "I think my daughter is choking," she said.

Rod took a step forward, and one of the other paramedics grabbed his stethoscope to assess the girl's condition. But they never got the chance.

Melanie swept in, lifted the girl, and turned her face down with her head low. She gave the girl several quick blows on her back between her shoulder blades. The girl gagged, coughed, and spat out a bit of food. Melanie flipped her back over and handed her to Mom.

Quick action like Melanie's, especially when someone is choking, makes all the difference.

HEROES

For almost every disaster, there is a hero.

—Amanda Ripley

Choking is caused by something stuck in the windpipe (or trachea). This airway obstruction can be anything from a toy a baby was chewing on to a piece of food swallowed too quickly.

Airway obstructions block the lungs from getting fresh air and oxygen. Airway obstructions must be cleared immediately and really can't wait for help to arrive.

Helping Someone Who's Choking

When treating a choking patient, don't put anything in her mouth to pry out the airway obstruction. You can cause a lot of damage to the patient's throat and windpipe that way. Other than prying it out, anything you can do to loosen the airway obstruction and persuade it to come out is fair game, even slapping the patient on the back.

If she's able to cough and speak even a little, she can also breathe a little. Any air movement is better than no air movement. As long as she's awake, encourage her to cough. She could dislodge the obstruction on her own.

When the patient stops coughing and talking, she isn't breathing anymore, and very soon, she'll pass out from lack of air. Time is critical at this point. You must get the airway obstruction out immediately.

Here's how to remove an airway obstruction from adults who can't speak or cough:

1. Stand behind the patient and wrap your arms around her, as if to give her a hug.

2. Make a fist with one hand, and place it just above the patient's belly button.

3. Cover your fist with your other hand, and forcefully thrust inward and upward.

4. Repeat the thrusts until the patient is able to breathe again or passes out.

5. If she loses consciousness (passes out), call 911 and start CPR.

If 911 isn't available, send someone for help while you keep doing CPR. If you're alone with the patient, do CPR for 2 minutes before leaving to find help.

When an Infant's Choking

Babies are flexible and inquisitive, and they love to put things in their mouth. When a baby has an airway obstruction, you have only moments to get it out.

If an infant is choking, unable to cough or breathe, but is awake, follow these steps:

1. Hold the baby on your knee, face down, with her head lower than her body. Strike the baby five times on the back, right between her shoulder blades with the heel of your hand.

2. If she's still unable to breathe, roll her face up, keeping her head low. With two fingers on her breastbone between her nipples, give her five chest thrusts, pushing her chest about a third of the way down.

3. Keep rolling the baby face up and face down, repeating steps 1 and 2 until she starts breathing again (and probably starts crying) or until she passes out. If she passes out, start CPR.

If you have someone with you, have them call 911 or go get help while you help the baby. If not, help the baby *before* calling 911.

As long as the baby isn't awake, continue to do CPR. After 2 minutes, call 911 if nobody else has called already. If you must go find help because 911 isn't available, take the baby with you and keep doing CPR.

Unconsciousness or Confusion

Unless the patient has a medical condition that leads to either on a regular basis, confusion and unconsciousness are true emergencies. These are signs the brain is malfunctioning for some reason. Any problem that leads to brain malfunction could possibly cause permanent brain damage or death. Even if a known medical problem exists, unless the confusion or unconsciousness can be treated and reversed easily, it's still an emergency.

Assuming you aren't familiar with any cause explaining why a patient is unconscious or confused—and assuming you aren't able to treat it—call 911 or get help immediately. If the patient is also not breathing, start CPR (see the earlier "Cardiac Arrest" section).

Getting help might take a while in a disaster situation, which makes it that much more important to try to figure out the cause of the confusion or the unconsciousness. There are more causes than we have room to cover here, but let's look at those you might be able to treat.

Diabetes

Diabetic patients under treatment with medication are prone to developing low blood sugar, or hypoglycemia, which can lead to confusion and eventually unconsciousness. If not treated, hypoglycemia can cause death.

If a glucose meter (called a glucometer) is available, you can use it to check the patient's blood sugar level to determine if that's the cause. Any result below 60 should be treated.

The easiest treatment for low blood sugar is to give the patient something to eat or drink that contains sugar. The only way to do this at home without medical assistance is if the patient is awake enough to follow instructions and swallow food. She could be confused, but she must be able to follow instructions enough to eat.

IF SHE'S UNCONSCIOUS

Never put anything in the mouth of an unconscious patient.

The best food for treating hypoglycemia is juice, especially orange juice. Some people sweeten the OJ with a few spoonfuls of sugar, but that's not necessary. If you have frozen juice concentrate, try feeding it to the hypoglycemic patient with a spoon. It tastes like a smoothie, and the sugar absorbs quickly into the patient's blood.

If juice isn't available, a candy bar will do. Stay away from hard candies, though, because they can be a choking hazard for a confused patient.

Seizures

Seizures are uncontrollable muscle contractions that can take many forms. For the purposes of this book, we're concerned with muscle contractions that involve most of the body and the patient is unconscious. In cases where the patient is awake, treatment isn't as critical.

If a patient is known to suffer from seizures—if she has been diagnosed with epilepsy, for example—it might not be an emergency. On the other hand, you should treat the presence of seizures exactly like you would any unconscious patient. Call 911 or get help immediately, and if she's not breathing, start CPR (see the previous "Cardiac Arrest" section).

For patients with a known seizure disorder, the situation might only be an emergency if her seizures are prolonged. It's best to discuss with the patient how she'd like to be handled if she has a seizure. If you never got around to that discussion and now she's seizing, call 911 or get help if the seizing lasts more than 10 minutes. You should also get help if she has multiple seizures in a row without waking up.

During a seizure, do your best to move furniture and heavy items away from the patient—or move her away from the furniture. Do not put anything in her mouth while she's having a seizure.

SEIZING PATIENTS

It's a myth that seizing patients can swallow their tongues. Patients might bite their tongues during a seizure, but the damage is usually very minor.

Heart Attack

Heart attacks can be deadly on any given day, but health-care providers are pretty adept at handling them when the sun is shining and the freeways are clear. During and after a disaster, however, when resources are limited and roads could be blocked, heart attacks might not be treated as quickly or aggressively as they would be otherwise.

In everyday situations, always call 911 for a suspected heart attack. As a backup plan, you could take the patient to the emergency department. Your primary-care physician probably isn't prepared to aggressively and definitively treat heart attacks in the office. If you go to the doctor's office with symptoms of a heart attack, the doctor will redirect you to the emergency room.

Symptoms of a Heart Attack

Each person is unique, and there are several different types of heart attacks. Most people experience some sort of chest pain or discomfort, but there's no one way to describe the symptoms of a heart attack.

Health-care providers use a mnemonic to evaluate chest pain and determine if it might be a heart attack: OPQRST. This stands for *onset, provocation, quality, radiation, severity,* and *time.* The following table explains more.

Is It a Heart Attack?

Evaluation Criteria	More Likely	Less Likely
Onset	Comes on suddenly without exertion	Comes on gradually or only after exertion or stress
Provocation	Nothing makes the discomfort better or worse	Moving or pressing on the chest worsens or alleviates the pain
Quality	The discomfort feels like pressure or squeezing	The discomfort is sharp or stabbing
Radiation	The discomfort travels from the chest to the arm or neck	The discomfort is isolated to one part of the chest
Severity	The discomfort is severe	The discomfort is mild

Time, you might note, is not on the table. That's because we don't use time to decide if it's a heart attack; we use time to determine how much heart damage might have occurred. The longer the heart attack goes untreated, the more damage is done and the greater the chance of death.

A few other signs and symptoms should make you more concerned that it might be a heart attack:

- Shortness of breath

- Cold sweats or clammy skin

- Pale skin

One thing from the table or this list is enough to be concerned. The more symptoms a patient is experiencing from the "More Likely" column, the more likely she's experiencing a heart attack.

CARDIAC ARREST VERSUS HEART ATTACK

A heart attack isn't the same thing as cardiac arrest. As you learned earlier, cardiac arrest is the medical term for a stopped heart, or when the heart fails to adequately pump blood to all parts of the body, including the brain. Without treatment and without exception, cardiac arrest results in death. A heart attack, on the other hand, refers to heart muscle death. In the vast majority of cases, heart attacks are caused by a blockage in one of the major arteries feeding blood to the heart muscle. Heart attacks are often survivable with proper treatment and, in rare cases, even without treatment.

Treating a Heart Attack

Once you determine that chest discomfort is potentially a heart attack, the clock is ticking. You must find a way to get the patient to a health-care provider immediately.

Call 911. If someone answers, follow the directions the dispatcher gives you. If the system is down or there's no answer at 911, take the patient to any health-care provider or emergency responder—doctor, paramedic, nurse, firefighter, or police officer—as soon as you can. You can also reach out to the Red Cross or the National Guard. The patient should not drive unless you are the patient and absolutely no one else is around to drive you.

In a disaster, the rule about not going to a physician with chest pain is out the window. Get the patient to *any* health-care provider you can. Eventually, there will be a process for getting help out to you in a medical emergency, but in the first few hours after a disaster, and maybe even the first few days, the network of health-care providers and emergency responders develops organically. They talk and exchange phone numbers or radio channels. Anyone in the medical field or a position of authority is the best place to start to get the right care.

We can't stress enough that you should get the patient to medical assistance or call an ambulance to you. That comes before any other type of home treatment. Anything else you do is simply buying a little more time for caregivers to provide definitive treatment.

While you're on your way to get help, or waiting for help to arrive, do these things:

1. Make the patient rest. The more she exerts herself, the more stress she places on her heart and the more damage may be done.

2. If she's not allergic to aspirin, have her take some. If it's the usual buffered white 325 milligram pill, have her chew and swallow one pill. If it's the chewable style—a small, typically pink, 81 milligram pill—have her chew and swallow 4 pills.

3. Loosen her collar, belt, pants, and other restrictive articles of clothing. Make it as easy as possible for blood to flow through her body.

If the patient has a prescription for nitroglycerin, have her take one. If she has the small white tablets, place one under her tongue.

IMPORTANT

If you're treating a male patient, before having him take nitroglycerin, be sure he has not taken Viagra or Levitra in the last 24 hours. Don't let him take nitroglycerin if he's taken Cialis in the last 48 hours either. The interaction between these drugs and nitroglycerin is potentially lethal.

Anaphylaxis

Nearly everyone has an allergy to something. Allergies can be as simple as hay fever or as dangerous as anaphylaxis. Simple allergic reactions are no big deal and most of us manage our seasonal allergies without issue on a daily basis.

When an allergic reaction worsens and becomes anaphylaxis, however, it must be treated immediately or the patient is at risk of dying.

Symptoms of Anaphylaxis

There are four ways a patient can come in contact with an allergen:

- Injection (a shot of medication or an insect sting)
- Ingestion (eating)
- Inhalation (breathing it in)
- Topical (absorption through the skin)

With simple allergies, the result can be symptoms such as cough, watery eyes, sneezing, itching, swelling, hives (raised red bumps), and wheezing. Anaphylaxis symptoms are the same as any allergy, but they develop more severely. Consider it anaphylaxis if a patient with any of the preceding symptoms also experiences shortness of breath, difficulty swallowing, dizziness, fatigue, confusion, or unconsciousness.

Simple allergic reactions can often be tied to a single allergen. For instance, poison ivy is a topical allergen and causes an itchy rash on the skin. Likewise, pollen is a common seasonal allergen that, when inhaled, causes coughing, sneezing, and wheezing. Consider the possibility of anaphylaxis whenever a different part of the body develops symptoms away from the allergen. You'd expect a bee sting to cause a raised, red bump at the site of the sting, for example, but it's anaphylaxis if it also causes an itchy throat or trouble breathing.

As soon as you recognize an allergy is getting worse and beginning to affect other areas of the body, or any time a patient has trouble swallowing or breathing after coming in contact with a possible allergen, consider it anaphylaxis.

Treating Anaphylaxis

The first step in treating anaphylaxis is to remove the allergen if you can. If a bee stinger is left in the skin, pull it out. If it's a topical allergen, wash it off. If the patient began to eat something and it made her mouth tingly or itchy, instruct her to spit out whatever's left. If she already swallowed something and you suspect she's allergic, don't attempt to induce vomiting.

As soon as you recognize the potential for anaphylaxis, call 911. If 911 service isn't available, take the patient to a health-care provider. Like a heart attack, the patient should not drive unless you are the patient and no one else can do it.

If the patient has an epinephrine autoinjector pen, use it now. Follow the instructions on the pen.

If you suspect anaphylaxis is developing, you can give the patient diphenhydramine (Benadryl) to stop the allergy. Don't use other allergy medicines unless that's all you have. Follow the directions on the bottle; the usual adult dose is 50 milligrams. Diphenhydramine might make the patient drowsy. Some people complain of feeling anxious, whether they become drowsy or not.

Strokes

Much like heart attacks, *strokes* need immediate treatment—beyond what a primary-care physician can provide. If you suspect someone of having a stroke, get her to the emergency room quickly. Strokes require specialized diagnostic equipment, and the time when treatment is most effective for strokes is extremely short.

DEFINITION

There are two basic types of **strokes:** blockages and bleeding. Strokes caused by blockages in arteries of the brain can often be treated with a variety of tools or medications to remove the blockage. Strokes from bleeding in the brain are less treatable.

Treating strokes the wrong way could be disastrous, but the only way for doctors to know which type of stroke a patient has is by doing a CT scan. In disaster situations, CT scanners are often not available or the patient has to be transported several hours away to get to one. However, you should still seek help as soon as you suspect a patient is experiencing a stroke.

Look for these telltale signs to determine if someone is having a stroke:

- Weakness or numbness on one side of the body
- Facial "droop," which looks like one side of the face isn't working
- Trouble speaking or understanding speech
- Sudden confusion
- Sudden trouble seeing in one or both eyes
- Sudden trouble walking, loss of coordination, or dizziness
- Sudden, severe headache

You don't have to see all the symptoms on this list, but the more things you see on this list, the more concerned you should be. If you suspect a stroke, call 911 or get help immediately.

Trust Your Gut

There's absolutely no way to cover all the potentially life-threatening situations you could encounter in the pages of this book. Sometimes, recognizing a developing medical emergency requires years of training and experience.

Trust your instincts. Your gut will tell you when something isn't right. In a disaster, you'll encounter many things "not right," and they'll all be competing for your gut instinct. When a medical issue wins your attention, it's likely to be very serious. When in doubt, call for help.

Remember that whenever we tell you to call 911 or get help, it means you might have to take the patient with you. You could be the only way for the patient to get to a doctor. Be assertive, and don't be afraid to approach authorities. It might be the difference between life and death.

18

Treating Injuries

Superstorm Sandy was approaching fast. At first, the strike team was assigned to an EMS fire station on the Lower East Side of Manhattan. The fire captain there told Pete this station had flooded during Hurricane Irene in 2011, and the storm surge for Sandy was predicted to be even bigger. The waves of the East River were cresting over the sea wall already.

The team filled hundreds of sandbags and put them around the station to protect it from the rising water. Then, as the storm grew stronger and closer, the team followed the locals out of the neighborhood, leaving it without emergency services.

After a disaster, medical and other emergency staff will be overwhelmed or maybe even completely unavailable. Many minor injuries will need to be handled without medical help. In this chapter, we walk you through how to care for smaller bleeding injuries, concussions, burns, broken bones, and more. Armed with a little advance information, you'll be more comfortable treating injuries such as these until you can get professional help.

Controlling Bleeding

Your body has a limited supply of blood. You can make more if you need it, but it takes time and energy. A cut or other type of injury that bleeds is basically a leak, and in most people, the blood will eventually clot and stop "leaking." Just like a river is harder to stop when it's flowing fast, so it is with blood. The trick is to slow the flow of blood from an injury to allow clots to form.

There are three ways to control bleeding and eventually stop it: direct pressure, elevation, or by using a tourniquet. Putting pressure directly on the cut or injury essentially plugs the hole and keeps blood from spilling out.

Elevating the injury above the level of the heart makes it harder for blood to get there and, therefore, slows the bleeding. Only injuries to the arms and legs can be elevated. To elevate injuries to the legs, have the patient lie down first.

For severe bleeding that could be life-threatening, a tourniquet may be the only way to control bleeding. Only use a tourniquet if you believe the injury is severe enough to cause death. Typically, only use a tourniquet after multiple attempts to control bleeding are unsuccessful or if the bleeding is bright red and spurting.

NOT ALWAYS THE ANSWER

Putting on a tourniquet is not an easy decision and might lead to permanent damage or loss of a limb later on. Don't treat with a tourniquet without very careful thought first.

Here's how to put on a tourniquet, if the situation warrants it:

1. Use nonstretchy material such as terrycloth or a tie or scarf. Fold it lengthwise until it's between 1 and 2 inches wide and long enough to wrap around the limb.

2. Tie the tourniquet around the limb several inches above the injury. If the injury is below the elbow or the knee, you might need to go above the joint. Tie it in a square knot (like tying your shoes, but don't make a bow).

3. Using something strong enough to handle twisting the tourniquet, such as a wooden spoon, tie it on top of the knot with the loose ends of the cloth. This is called a windlass.

4. Twist the windlass repeatedly to tighten the tourniquet until bleeding stops. Tie the windlass in place with another piece of cloth, and note the time.

If you're dealing with significant bleeding and you think there's a chance the patient's life could be at stake, call 911. If 911 is unavailable, take the patient to medical help immediately. If you had to put a tourniquet on to stop the bleeding, *you must get professional help immediately.* Once a tourniquet is in place, the patient runs the risk of losing the limb.

If a bleeding patient becomes pale, sweaty, dizzy, or lightheaded, have him lie down flat on a bed, a couch, or on the floor. If the bleeding has stopped, prop the patient's legs up with a few pillows.

Cuts and Scrapes

Not all open wounds are deadly bleeders. Most cuts and scrapes are very minor injuries that need little more than some tender loving care. The most important thing to remember about minor cuts and scrapes is to keep them as clean as possible.

Here's how to treat minor cuts and scrapes:

1. Rinse the injury thoroughly with clean water. If tap water has been deemed safe to drink by authorities, you can use it to rinse an injury. If not, use purified water or bottled water.

2. Cover the injury with a sterile bandage. If it's small enough, an adhesive bandage will work.

3. Change the bandage at least once a day, and keep the injury covered to help it stay clean.

There's no evidence antibiotic ointments actually help avoid infections in minor cuts, but some people like to use them. If you do use antibiotic ointments, squeeze the ointment out of the tube onto a clean piece of gauze or cotton swab to dab onto the cut. Never squeeze the ointment directly from the tube onto the cut; you run the risk of contaminating the tube for future use.

Bloody Noses

Bloody noses are common in kids and some adults. For people taking blood thinners, bleeding from the nose can be deadly if it's not stopped. Also, for people with no history of nosebleeds and no history of taking blood thinners, a nose that suddenly starts bleeding without an injury can be a sign of dangerously high blood pressure.

The most common cause of nosebleeds is what medical professionals call *digital trauma,* or "picking your nose." It's relatively harmless.

Stopping a nosebleed might take as long as 30 minutes, and you have to be diligent when treating it:

1. Have the patient lean forward. Most people want to lean back with a bloody nose because they don't want to see the blood or get any on themselves. But having the patient lean forward is the only way to see when the bleeding has stopped. Plus, swallowing the blood that drains to the back of the throat can irritate the stomach and lead to vomiting.

2. Press firmly on the bridge of the nose. The bridge is the hard part where eyeglasses often rest. Pressing on this part pinches off the blood vessels that feed blood to the soft insides of the nostrils. If you're pressing on the right spot, the blood should stop flowing but the patient should still be able to breathe through his nose. Keep adjusting where you press until you're able to stop the blood flow and the patient can still breathe.

3. Hold the pressure for at least 20 minutes. If you let go before the 20 minutes is up, the clock starts over. Resist the urge to check before 20 minutes has passed.

4. Don't allow the patient to blow his nose. When the bleeding has stopped, the patient will likely complain of a stuffed nose. This is because there's likely to be clots in the nostrils following treatment. Don't let the patient blow out the clots or the bleeding will start again, which means you'll have to start the entire treatment process again.

Caring for Concussions and Brain Injuries

A growing body of evidence suggests that concussions and minor brain injuries are much more common than once thought. Boxers and football players are exhibiting long-term brain damage from multiple hits on the head, even when no obvious injuries were present at the time of the hits. Experts say this is an example of cumulative minor brain injuries and concussions.

In a disaster, we don't have the luxury to have ourselves or our children evaluated for every knock on the noggin. However, there are times when a patient should be evaluated for a possible concussion, even if it'll be difficult to reach medical help. Call 911 or take the patient to medical help if you see these signs or symptoms after a blow to the head:

- Loss of consciousness (getting knocked out)
- Confusion
- Inability to pay attention
- Memory loss
- Loss of balance or coordination
- Headache
- Nausea
- Dizziness or vertigo
- Ringing in the ears

Remember to treat any patient who is unconscious as having a potentially life-threatening injury or illness and act quickly.

"IF"

... If you can meet with Triumph and Disaster
And treat those two impostors just the same; ...
Yours is the Earth and everything that's in it ....

—Rudyard Kipling

Treating Burns

Burns destroy the skin and leave victims prone to infection and hypothermia (cold exposure; see Chapter 19).

If someone has just been burned, cool the burn with running water for 20 minutes. If authorities have deemed tap water unsafe to use for showering, you should use bottled water. Do not skip this step unless you simply don't have water.

If the skin is charred or missing, call 911 or get help. If the burn is on your face or genitals, call 911 or get help.

Never use ice or chemical cold packs to cool a burn. The damage burns cause the skin leaves the victim highly susceptible to frostbite and hypothermia. Besides being susceptible to hypothermia, burn patients are also at risk for dehydration because fluid can seep from the damaged skin. Burns of more significant depth need might need professional care, depending on the location, depth, and size of the burn.

After the initial treatment, treating a burn depends on how deep the burn goes into the skin. If the burn is superficial (first degree), use a burn ointment such as aloe vera to soothe the discomfort. Many aloe vera products include lidocaine, which helps with the pain.

Partial-thickness burns (second degree) are identified by a separation of the skin (blisters, weeping, or *sloughing* skin). Any partial-thickness burns of the face or genitals, or any partial-thickness burns that reach all the way around an arm or leg, need to be treated by a professional. Likewise, any partial-thickness burns that cover an area larger than your chest (not including the belly) should be seen by a professional.

DEFINITION

Skin is **sloughing** when it's coming off in layers while weeping fluid. In burns, the smallest sloughing looks very similar to blisters from friction like those you get while hiking. In large partial-thickness burns, the sloughing sometimes comes in large sheets.

Full-thickness burns are characterized by charring or complete removal of skin. Any full-thickness burns should be treated by a professional.

Dealing with Fractures and Dislocations

Broken bones, or fractures, need to be evaluated by a physician. However, most of the time you can take a patient with a broken bone to a physician without needing an ambulance. In most cases, fractures will be treated by immobilization in a cast. Sometimes surgery is necessary.

Ruling Out Sprains and Strains

It can be impossible to tell some broken bones from *sprains* or *strains* without an x-ray. The two injuries have some very common signs and symptoms:

- Pain

- Bruising

- Swelling

- Reduced function (the injured arm or leg doesn't work as well)

DEFINITION

A **sprain** is a stretched ligament or tendon—the connective tissue that holds together joints like the elbow and hip. Ligaments ensure the joints don't bend in the wrong direction, and tendons connect bone to muscle, allowing the muscles to pull the bones. Sprains can be minor or severe. A **strain** is an injured muscle, also known as a pulled muscle. The bones, tendons, and ligaments often aren't injured.

Broken Bones

Many people think you can't use a limb at all if it's broken. That's not true. Plenty of folks have walked on broken feet and lifted things with broken arms. Whether or not "he can walk on it" doesn't have anything to do with whether or not it is broken.

It does have to do with the urgency, however. If the patient can use his injured limb, he probably can wait a day or two for treatment if help isn't immediately available.

But if you see either of these signs of serious fractures, seek professional attention as soon as possible:

- *Crepitus* is a grinding under the skin that's usually felt rather than heard. It comes from the ends of broken bones rubbing together.

- *Deformity* is the medical term that means "this doesn't look right."

Either deformity or crepitus at the site of an injury is a harbinger of very bad news. It's quite rare that a bone is not broken if either of these is present.

Dislocations

Dislocations can come with fractures or not. A dislocation is when bones no longer line up in the proper anatomical position. Basically, a dislocated shoulder means the humerus (the upper arm bone) is no longer seated correctly against the shoulder blade.

Because the bones are actually in the wrong spots, dislocations definitely have deformity. They also have loss of function because all the tendons (the pull wires that move bones around) aren't lined up correctly.

Dislocations need professional medical treatment as soon as possible because the bones need to be put back in place quickly. The longer a dislocation goes without treatment, the more damage is done.

RICE

Treating a sprain, strain, or fracture at home is all the same; dislocations cannot be treated at home. Use RICE:

1. *Rest* the injured limb. Avoid using it as much as possible for the first 3 days after an injury.

2. *Ice* the injury to reduce swelling. Do not put ice directly on the skin; keep a layer of cloth between the ice and the skin. Leave ice on the injury for no more than 15 minutes and then remove it for at least 15 minutes.

3. *Compress* the injured limb by wrapping it with an elastic bandage. Wrap it firmly but so you can still get a couple fingers under the wrap after it's in place.

4. *Elevate* the injury.

If an injury doesn't seem to be getting better after about 3 days, get medical help. By that time, the services disrupted by the disaster will most likely be starting to come back online.

You might encounter plenty of other injuries in a disaster situation. Remember to keep it simple: if a patient is unconscious, get help immediately. If you are unsure, get help immediately.

19

Heat and Cold Exposure

Bill was a fine pilot, but he struggled with his weight. At more than 300 pounds, he had trouble fitting into his Cessna AG Truck crop duster. Still, he would squeeze into the cockpit every day and deliver his payloads on fields all over northern California.

Summers in the Central Valley are always hot, but rarely do triple digits come more than 3 days in a row.

One Friday night after a short day of him flying in unseasonably high temperatures, Bill's family noticed he wasn't feeling well. He complained of being tired and nauseated, so he went to bed early.

Bill never woke up.

During extremes in temperature like those you're likely to experience in a weather disaster, you must be aware of the potential complications that come with exposure to the elements. In this chapter, we explain the symptoms of heat illness or hypothermia and show you the steps to treat it.

Severe cases of exposure need to be treated by medical professionals, but you can do some things on your own. You should always seek help, regardless of the cause, when the patient is confused or fatigued to the point of exhaustion. Energy and the ability to think clearly are the hallmarks of health during a disaster.

Dealing with Dehydration

Dehydration is common with heat illness. It's also common when people are experiencing vomiting and diarrhea, which are symptoms of "food poisoning" and can be the result of contaminated water. One of the worst combinations you can experience is to develop a food-borne illness in severe heat or humidity. It's hard to keep up with fluid intake if the fluid won't stay in you.

Look for these signs and symptoms of dehydration, especially if you're really hot or you have vomiting or diarrhea:

- Dizziness

- Headache

- Nausea

- Weakness

- Dry mouth and nose

- Inability to urinate

If dehydration gets to the point of dizziness or weakness, medical intervention might be necessary. In cases of vomiting or diarrhea, it's likely that drinking fluids won't be enough, and your body might not even tolerate it.

If you can drink something and hold it down, that's the best treatment. It might take several hours to a day to fully recover from dehydration, but the best way is by drinking fluids.

MEDICALLY INDUCED DEHYDRATION

Certain medications can make dehydration worse, especially diuretics (medications that make you urinate) and medications for blood pressure. When your doctor prescribes you a new medication, ask if it will affect hydration.

Heat Illnesses

Exposure to high heat and humidity is difficult to treat when the power is out. Without air-conditioning or even fans helping move the air around, it can be difficult to cool your body, leading to heat stroke, heat exhaustion, and other heat illnesses.

Heat illnesses start slowly but progresses quickly if left untreated.

IT HAPPENS GRADUALLY

Medical conditions aren't always easy to identify, especially when they come on gradually. Even though we describe two heat-related illnesses in this section, they're not either/or situations. The body doesn't develop heat exhaustion suddenly and then switch to heat stroke. It happens gradually. In fact, it's typical to see symptoms of both conditions at the same time.

Heat Stroke

Heat stroke is the worst-case scenario arising from exposure to the severe heat and humidity of summer storms. It results when heat exhaustion (more on this coming up) is left untreated and the core body temperature rises to dangerously high levels. Heat stroke is a serious medical emergency that can lead to brain damage, coma, seizures, and even death.

According to the Centers for Disease Control and Prevention (CDC), here are the signs and symptoms of heat stroke:

- High body temperature (above 103°F or 39.5°C)
- Red, hot, dry skin (no sweating)
- Throbbing headache
- Dizziness
- Nausea

If you suspect heat stroke, get help! Either call 911 or find an emergency responder. Until you can get the patient to medical professionals, do the following:

1. Put her in the coolest place you can find. Air-conditioning indoors is best. If you don't have air-conditioning or can't get inside, outside in the shade is better than in the sun.

2. Remove as much of her clothing as possible. Naked is best.

3. Put ice packs under her armpits, on her groin, and on her neck. The blood flows closer to the surface of the skin in these areas, and the benefits of cooling will spread quickly.

4. Don't let her eat or drink anything. Not even water. She won't be able to process fluids and will likely vomit, creating the possibility of aspiration.

If the patient has the ability to follow commands, she might not be suffering from heat stroke … yet.

Heat Exhaustion

Heat exhaustion is the precursor to heat stroke. It's more common and actually can happen during *lower* temperatures. Maybe you've heard reports of sports fans developing heat exhaustion while sitting in the stands on cold days because they're bundled up. Heat exhaustion is just easier to get as it gets hotter outside. Untreated, heat exhaustion leads to heat stroke. Unlike heat stroke, you can try to treat heat exhaustion at home.

During a disaster, it's imperative to recognize and treat heat exhaustion before it gets to heat stroke. Watch for these signs of heat exhaustion from the CDC:

- Sweating although the skin might not feel hot—it might be cool and clammy from all the moisture

- Pale skin color

- Muscle cramps

- Fatigue or drowsiness

- Weakness

- Dizziness

- Headache

- Nausea or vomiting

- Fainting

- Fast, shallow breathing

Treat heat exhaustion just like you'd treat heat stroke. Have the patient sit inside an air-conditioned room (or vehicle) in as little clothing (even just her underwear) as possible to cool off.

The biggest difference between heat stroke and heat exhaustion is the ability to think clearly. If the patient is able to do that, have her drink water or an electrolyte replacement such as Gatorade. Even if your water supply is getting low, don't ration it. Give the patient what she needs now; you can find more later.

Keeping Cool

When the power is out and you don't have the option of air-conditioning, or you just don't have it, you can still keep yourself cool.

A GALLON A DAY?

The CDC recommends drinking at least 1 gallon of water on hot days. A whole gallon per person per day—even on hot days—is a lot. The most important thing to remember is to drink when you're thirsty, and do not ration your emergency water supply.

To stay as cool as possible during and after a disaster, conserve your energy and work during cooler hours of the day when possible. Otherwise, distribute the workload evenly throughout the day. When you do have to be outside, wear light-colored, loose-fitting clothing.

Look for signs of heat illness in yourself and others, especially heat stroke. Get help or call 911 if you see any signs of heat stroke.

Probably the best way to stay cool when air-conditioning isn't available is with water. A dip in the pool or a cool bath is a great idea, but that's not always possible after a disaster. Do *not* swim in a pool after a disaster until the pool can be decontaminated and treated.

Hypothermia

Hypothermia is when the body is too cold, when it's unable to produce as much heat as it loses.

Your body produces heat naturally all the time by burning oxygen and fuel and by doing work in your cells and body tissues (metabolism). Some of this heat is released through your skin and some through your breath. Your body also regulates heat loss by how much blood it allows to flow near the surface of your skin, where the blood expels some of its heat into the air and then recirculates cooler throughout your body.

Temperatures don't have to be below freezing for you to run the risk of developing hypothermia. It just needs to be cold enough that your body loses heat too fast and you can't burn enough calories or do enough work to replace that heat. During a disaster, relatively mild temperatures can lead to hypothermia when enough food is available and there's no way to start a fire or create heat.

Normal body temperature is about 98.6°F (37°C), plus or minus 1 degree. When your temperature drops below 95°F (35°C), you are suffering from hypothermia.

Hypothermia is a dangerous curve. As soon as the core body temperature falls into hypothermia range, the body has to work even harder to maintain while trying to recover at the same time.

COLD WATER AND MOVING AIR

Water conducts heat about 25 times better than air does, which means submersion in cold water results in hypothermia much faster than exposure to cold air. If someone falls into cold or icy water, get her out of the water, and out of her wet clothes, immediately. Submersion in water could lead to hypothermia in a couple minutes. Likewise, wind is colder than still air. Developing hypothermia from exposure to cold, still air might take hours; the same temperature in breezy or windy conditions could shorten the time it takes to a fraction of that time.

The symptoms of hypothermia aren't always obvious to the person who is experiencing it, so it's important to pay attention when you're in the cold, especially to others who are in the cold with you.

The first sign of hypothermia is shivering. Shivering is a mechanism your body uses to warm itself. Your body burns calories to create heat, and burning calories (fuel) to make heat creates energy. Your body gets rid of that energy by funneling it to your muscles, causing them to shiver.

Shivering is a costly and inefficient way to get warm, and your body will only do it for a few minutes. When you no longer have the energy or the fuel to spare, the shivering will stop. Rather than being a sign that the patient is getting better, especially if nothing else has been done to warm her, the absence of shivering is a sign hypothermia is getting worse.

Look for these other signs and symptoms when exposed to cold temperatures:

- Exhaustion
- Confusion
- Fumbling fingers (loss of fine motor control)
- Memory loss (or having trouble concentrating)

As hypothermia gets worse, it gets more difficult to recognize the symptoms in yourself. That's why it's so important to watch others for signs of hypothermia when exposed to the cold.

Fixing hypothermia is simple: get warm. Cover all of the patient's bare skin, including her hands, feet, neck, face, and head. Any area of bare skin is a potential for losing heat. Using a *space blanket* will slow the heat loss considerably.

DEFINITION

Space blankets are reflective blankets, usually made of Mylar, that redirect heat to the person using them.

Call 911 or find help if someone is cold enough to have trouble speaking or is confused. As the patient gets colder and develops more symptoms, the possibility of getting her warm enough to survive without medical intervention gets very slim.

In very severe cases of hypothermia, the heart can slow and the blood pressure can drop so low the patient appears dead. Luckily, it's possible for patients with such severe hypothermia to be revived. Follow the directions in Chapter 17, and start CPR on any patient who isn't breathing. Start CPR even if you think it's too late, especially if you suspect she might have hypothermia.

Frostbite

Hypothermia doesn't take extremely cold temperatures to set in, but frostbite does require freezing temperatures. However, you don't have to be outside in the snow to get frostbite.

Frostbite is frozen skin and muscle tissue. It can look like a burn, and the damage to the skin is very similar. Sometimes it's even called *freezer burn* or a *cold burn*. Like a burn, how well frostbite heals depends on how deep the damage is.

Frostbite is most common on the parts of the body farthest from the heart, where the blood doesn't flow as well. The nose, earlobes, fingers, and toes are the most common places to get frostbite.

Usually, exposure is the key. When tissues are exposed to freezing temperatures for too long, damage is caused. The less blood that flows through the tissues, the less heat is transferred and the easier it is to get damage.

Frostbite doesn't always come from outside. Putting ice on an injury is a frequent cause of frostbite, especially if the ice is placed directly on the skin and left there for more than 20 minutes.

To identify frostbite, look for the following signs:

- Redness and swelling (similar to a burn)
- Blisters
- White or waxy appearance to the skin
- Numbness or tingling
- Extreme pain
- Inability to move injured areas

Treatment depends on whether medical care is available. If 911 is available, call for help. If not, get assistance as quickly as you can. The longer frostbite is left untreated, the more permanent the damage.

FREEZING AND THAWING

Do not thaw frostbitten body parts unless you are completely out of danger of the body parts freezing again. Thawing and refreezing body tissues causes more damage than leaving it frozen.

To thaw frostbitten tissues—only when you're completely out of the cold and only if medical care isn't readily available:

1. Protect the patient from the freezing temperatures. Don't thaw frost-bitten tissues if it's possible they could freeze again.

2. Cover the frostbitten body part in water that's about 98ºF to 105ºF (37ºC to 41ºC)—a little warmer than normal body temperature.

3. When the water cools, add more. Keep the water temperature as consistent as possible, and maintain water coverage until you get help or the feeling and movement comes back.

As soon as you can, get medical care for frostbite, even if it's already thawed. The damage to body tissues is often hard to see early on. Physicians even have a hard time identifying tissue damage until much later, after frostbite heals.

With a little awareness, you can avoid the consequences of extreme heat or cold exposure. Always be sure you have plenty of water during the heat and you wear layers during the cold. Stay with others as often as you can; in many cases, the only way to know if the extreme temperatures are getting to your family is to watch them carefully. Likewise, they need to keep an eye on you.

20

Other Signs and Symptoms of Illness

Rod and his partner, a young paramedic from Washington State, followed the quick-response paramedic through the rural parts of Hancock County, Mississippi. Far from the water, this countryside was mostly intact after Hurricane Katrina. Fallen trees and debris showed evidence of Katrina's wrath but, unlike the coastal areas, the roads were passable and street signs still marked the way. Still, it took the paramedics more than 30 minutes to reach the home.

They found their patient in a rural farmhouse near the county line between Hancock and Pearl River. Sarah (not her real name) was a young mother of three. Her kids and husband were there, waiting near the door as Rod and his partner evaluated Sarah, who was doubled over with severe abdominal pain. She said she's had pancreatitis before, and this was the same kind of discomfort.

Sarah was out of medication and couldn't bear the pain any longer. Normally she would call her doctor in Poplarville, but the phones didn't always work and she was afraid he had evacuated before the storm. So she'd finally called 911.

Because of short supply and the difficulty of accounting for it, out-of-town responders like Rod weren't carrying the narcotic pain relievers that would help her, so they loaded Sarah into the ambulance. After almost an hour drive, during which Sarah was in severe pain, they arrived at the parking lot in Bay St. Louis where the Disaster Medical Assistance Team (DMAT) had set up shop in a semi truck trailer. A nurse gave Sarah some pain medication, and an hour later, Sarah was in another ambulance, on her way to a Florida hospital 300 miles away.

During and after a disaster, going to the doctor won't be easy. Even if you aren't directly affected by the event that led to the disaster, you might not be able to contact your primary-care physician or even reach basic medical services.

Plenty of illnesses are treatable at home, whether you're in the middle of a disaster situation or not. Physicians regularly address some of these illnesses on an everyday basis, even though it might not always be necessary. In a disaster, it's a good idea to tough it out when you can. Getting to a doctor will be difficult and might take you farther than you planned. In Sarah's case, the pain was too bad to wait it out, and the distance was a small price to pay.

In this chapter we discuss different types of aches, pains, and general complaints that don't readily fit into specific, life-threatening conditions. In many cases, whether or not you seek medical care is a difficult decision with several variables, including how uncomfortable you are and how far medical care might take you.

Nausea, Vomiting, and Diarrhea

Some say nausea, or the urge to vomit, is more uncomfortable than pain. Not only is it a miserable feeling, but it's also often harder to control than pain.

Understanding the cause of nausea is key to figuring out whether to control it, live with it, or seek medical help for it. Nausea can be the result of a number of things, such as motion sickness, vertigo, carbon monoxide poisoning, and digestive disorders.

Motion Sickness and Vertigo

Motion sickness is the most common cause of nausea. If, after a disaster, you evacuate by bus or other mass transit, the extra stress of evacuation can make motion sickness worse. If you know you'll experience motion sickness, it's best to take medication ahead of time to control it.

You can treat motion sickness–induced nausea with several medications, many of which you can get over the counter. The following table lists some common medications available to treat nausea brought on by motion sickness. If you know this is something that affects you, it's a good idea to stock these in your preparedness kit well ahead of any disaster so you have them when you need them.

Nausea Medications

Brand Name (Generic Name)	Who Can Use It	Potential Side Effects
Antivert (meclizine)	Adults and kids 12 and over	Drowsiness, but not as bad as the others
Benadryl (diphenhydramine)	Anyone older than 6	Drowsiness
Dramamine (dimenhydrinate)	Adults and kids as young as 2	Drowsiness
Scopace (scopolamine)	Anyone 12 and older by prescription	Used as a patch; might cause irritation and drowsiness
Zofran (odansetron)	Anyone 4 and older by prescription	May cause anxiety and blurred vision

Vertigo is a form of dizziness that comes on without any motion. In everyday situations, sudden dizziness is often caused by problems with the inner ear or with conditions that affect the brain. In a disaster, dizziness is more often related to dehydration or a blow to the head (see Chapter 17 for concussions and brain injuries).

If you experience vertigo on a regular basis, you should treat it exactly the same way after a disaster as you would any other time.

On the other hand, if a disaster is the first time you've experienced sudden dizziness, check for symptoms of dehydration (Chapter 19) or get medical help.

LOOK FOR THE GOOD

My mom once told me that when I see tragic disasters and accidents, to look for the good. People are always helping each other out. There's still some good left in this world.

—Marisa Stein

Carbon Monoxide Poisoning

Nausea can be a symptom of carbon monoxide poisoning. As you learned in Chapter 13, carbon monoxide poisoning is a common problem in and after disaster situations, often caused by gas-powered generators or cooking on an open flame in poorly ventilated areas.

Without special equipment, it can be difficult to identify carbon monoxide poisoning. Headaches, nausea, and drowsiness are the most common symptoms. You should suspect carbon monoxide poisoning in these cases:

- Several people in the home or shelter experience nausea, headaches, dizziness, or drowsiness.

- Barbecues, outdoor grills or camp stoves, gas lanterns, or open flames are being used in the vicinity.

- Gas appliances that are still working after a disaster incident, especially those that use a pilot light, are in use.

Treatment for carbon monoxide poisoning is fresh air or medical oxygen administered by a health-care provider. If you suspect you or someone in the house or shelter with you is suffering from carbon monoxide poisoning, get everyone out, including yourself, and seek medical help immediately.

Digestive Disorders

In a disaster, contaminated food or water can result in gastroenteritis, an inflammation of the stomach and intestines. In cases where the patient is both vomiting and has diarrhea, it's a good bet he has an infection of some sort in his digestive system.

When contaminated food or water is ingested, the organism or its toxins irritate the lining of the digestive system. This results in vomiting, diarrhea, or both. In severe or prolonged cases, the vomiting or diarrhea can include a small amount of blood.

FOOD POISONING

The term *food poisoning* is commonly used to describe an irritation to the digestive system from food or water contaminated by organisms or toxins. Because it's not really *poisoning* per se, the correct term is *food-borne illness*. In this book, we refer to water or food as being *contaminated* because the culprit (bacteria, virus, or toxin) doesn't matter as much as the effect.

Unlike nausea from motion sickness or dizziness, vomiting as a result of an infection in the digestive system is difficult or impossible to control. In this case, your body is expelling toxic substances, a process that should be allowed to happen.

Vomiting and diarrhea interfere with your ability to absorb water from the food and fluids you consume. Instead of being absorbed, the water in your gut is expelled. Losing fluid from vomiting and diarrhea can result in dehydration, especially in hot and humid weather.

It's important to remain hydrated, but the vomiting might limit or restrict fluid intake and lead to more serious fluid loss. If vomiting and diarrhea last for more than 12 hours in an adult, it's time to get medical help. In kids, seek help after 6 hours.

Consuming contaminated food or water is a serious concern in a disaster. If you suspect your food or water supply is the culprit, throw it out and seek additional supplies elsewhere.

If your food or water supply is contaminated and you don't have more, you might need to seek shelter elsewhere. If you chose to shelter in place instead of evacuating, contaminated supplies mean you either have to find new, clean supplies or evacuate.

In Chapter 2, we explain how to purify water. If you or someone in your party gets sick after drinking water you attempted to purify, throw out that water—do not try to purify it a second time. If you're unable to purify water, either the method you're trying is insufficient or the water is too contaminated to be potable.

Fever

Fever is a sign of an infection in the body. Mild fevers between 99°F and 100.4°F (37.2°C and 38°C) can be left alone for up to 24 hours.

Fevers ranging from 100.4°F to 103°F (38°C and 39.5°C) that aren't from exposure to heat or the sun can be treated with fever reducers such as acetaminophen (Tylenol) or ibuprofen (Advil, Motrin). Follow the directions when taking these medications and be careful not to take too much. Be extra careful if combining these with other medications. Some brands add acetaminophen or ibuprofen to other drugs and you can accidentally overdose.

Get medical help for the following fevers:

- Any fever lasting more than 48 hours
- Any fever accompanied by headache, neck stiffness, and vomiting (This is an emergency, so call 911 if possible.)
- Any fever brought on by exposure to heat or sun that can't be reduced (This is an emergency, so call 911 if possible.)
- Any fever that comes and goes, especially if it's accompanied by night sweats, swollen lymph nodes, or trouble breathing

Besides using drugs, you can treat fevers by using cooling measures such as taking a cool bath, stripping down to underwear or a diaper only, sipping ice water and eating ice chips, or using cool compresses on the forehead and underarms.

STUBBORN FEVERS

If you have or encounter a fever that can't be brought lower than 103°F (39.5°C) using cooling methods and medications, get professional medical help.

Shortness of Breath

Cyrus (not his real name) had emphysema long before Hurricane Katrina came to town. When the ambulance crew arrived at his rural home, they found Cyrus sitting on the sofa working hard to breathe. Family members in the room told the first responders Cyrus was running low on his albuterol, the medication he used to open his lungs when he was having a hard time breathing. He only had one inhaler left, and it was almost gone. They feared there was no way to get more.

The ambulance crew didn't have inhalers, but they did carry albuterol and a nebulizer and showed Cyrus how to use the nebulizer by hooking it up to his oxygen tanks. Once he'd demonstrated to their satisfaction that he could administer the albuterol through the device, they left him at home with enough albuterol to get him through the next week.

Trouble breathing can be caused by a variety of things, whether there's a disaster or not. In many cases, folks who suffer from shortness of breath are well acquainted with how to handle it. Those diagnosed with asthma or emphysema often have the tools and the knowledge to address their breathing trouble.

In a disaster, supplies can run low and even the most well-prepared people can run out of important medications. This is true of anything, but serious cases of respiratory illness come with complicated machinery and tanks of compressed oxygen. It's important to know what you have and how long it will last so you can get help before you run out.

Not all shortness of breath is chronic. Any cases of sudden trouble breathing in someone who doesn't have a respiratory disease should be treated as an emergency. There are too many potential causes of sudden shortness of breath to list, and the worst are life-threatening conditions. Call 911 or get medical help if you or someone you're with begins experiencing shortness of breath.

Abdominal Pain

Pain in the abdomen is the hardest type of pain to diagnose. It's just too complicated in there, and even with fancy diagnostic tools, doctors often can't figure it out.

Like shortness of breath, some folks experience abdominal pain regularly and are familiar with their conditions. If you're in that category, be sure to stock any medications or supplies you might need in your disaster preparedness kit so you're sure to have enough when the time comes.

New abdominal pain, on the other hand, can be caused by relatively minor issues or severe, life-threatening conditions. If you or someone you're with experiences abdominal pain combined with the following symptoms, seek medical assistance or call 911 if it's available:

- Fever

- Abdominal pain above the belly button (Treat this like chest pain, and consider the possibility of a heart attack; see Chapter 17.)

- Constipation for more than 24 hours

- Bloody diarrhea or vomiting

- Blood in the urine

- Distended (bloated) belly

- Tender belly (hurts when you touch it)

- Rigid (hard) belly

- Dizziness or weakness

- Pain in the neck, shoulder, chest, or back

SEVERE ABDOMINAL PAIN

Have a medical professional treat any sudden and severe abdominal pain, whether there's currently a disaster or not.

Knowing when you need to seek medical help versus when you might be able to wait is invaluable when emergency services are stretched thin. You're sure to have many other things on your mind during and after a disaster, so if you have a medical complaint that's bad enough to distract you, pay attention to it. If, after you read this chapter, you're concerned enough to seek medical attention, don't hesitate to do so.

5

After the Dust Settles

Living through a disaster is physically, mentally, and emotionally stressful. But you're not out of the woods yet.

It's time to recover. To rebuild—hopefully to rebuild better, smarter, and stronger so the next time you're hit with the same disaster, its impact is far less than it was before.

In this last part, we address the question, "To stay and rebuild, or move on?" We navigate the bureaucratic red tape that is federal disaster assistance and learn how to get help from nonprofit relief agencies such as the Red Cross, the Salvation Army, and others.

21

———◆———

Coping with the Aftermath

Rodney Ballance was sleeping in his Escalon, California, home when he woke to a loud gurgling sound. He got up and saw dirty water pouring out of the toilet in the master bathroom. Within minutes, the same was coming out of the sinks and the shower drains.

Rodney raced down the hallway to find more brown water coming out of his other bathroom. Raw sewage, complete with the smell, was filling up his small-town, tranquil home. What he didn't know yet was that to a lesser degree, five other homes were going through the same ordeal.

The sewage flowed through the house, pouring into anything floor level. Carpets and laundry were soaked. Floor air vents were filled with sewage. It spilled through cracks in the floor to the dirt under the raised foundation below. It even came up through the return pipes attached to the washing machine in the garage.

A worker using a machine in the street—a man not qualified to run the machine according to Rodney—pumped too much pressure into the sewer line while trying to clear a blockage. The resulting pressure—and, therefore, raw sewage—backed up into neighborhood houses.

Furniture, clothing, and bedding were destroyed. The dollar amount of the loss was incredible. "We were out almost nineteen thousand," Rodney said. "None of it was covered by homeowners insurance because it originated outside our property line." He said his insurance agent told him after the fact about a rider he could have attached to his insurance to cover that sort of damage.

Rodney and his wife and their two kids were forced to move out of their house. They couldn't live in their sewage-tainted house during the restoration. For 3 months, the city covered living expenses, food, and lodging. The city disagreed with the amount of the losses, however, and only reimbursed Rodney and his family about $2,000 toward their damaged property.

Rodney said it was difficult to change his whole life for that 3-month period. The hotel where they stayed was outside of town and outside his kids' school district, leaving them no option for walking to school or taking the bus. The hotel catered to youth sports teams, which meant each weekend another busload of kids arrived … and kept Rodney and his family awake as they ran up and down the halls.

What's Next?

It's been a few days now, and you probably find yourself feeling shell-shocked and uncomfortable. You might long for life before this disaster, with all your old routines and surrounded by your familiar home and family.

Many issues will surface in the next weeks and months, with plenty of questions to be answered. Where will you live? Will you have a job? Where will the kids go to school? Can you rebuild? What services are still available, and what's missing?

The answers will come in time. Overwhelmingly, people recover from disasters and either rebuild their lives where they were or start over in a new home. It can take a while. In a 2009 study of people displaced by Hurricane Katrina, a small percentage still didn't feel they were in a permanent home 4 years after the storm.

Getting Used to New Routines

There's no trick to snap you out of the feelings that come after a disaster. You'll have to establish a new routine for your life. Routines are important to help get life back on track. Humans are creatures of habit, and we respond well to doing relatively the same thing every day.

That might mean a new home, at least until you can return to yours, or other things that depart from your old normal. Even if your new routine involves going to your damaged home and working on recovery, it's important to have a starting time and ending time for that work. Follow a typical workday schedule. Recovery from major disaster damage will likely take weeks if not months. This is more of a marathon than a sprint. Be reasonable and pace yourself.

FEMA offers these insights into what feelings to expect after a disaster:

- Everyone who sees or experiences a disaster is affected by it in some way.
- It's normal to feel anxious about your own safety and that of your family and close friends.
- Profound sadness, grief, and anger are normal reactions to an abnormal event.
- Acknowledging your feelings helps you recover.
- Focusing on your strengths and abilities helps you heal.
- Accepting help from community programs and resources is healthy.
- Everyone has different needs and different ways of coping.
- It's common to want to strike back at people who have caused great pain.

Not everything that happens in a disaster is a bad experience. Many survivors talk about the amazing folks who offered them assistance in some way. Churches and lodges often step up in a disaster to help feed survivors. Organizations like the American Red Cross help with coordinated responses. Paramedics, firefighters, police officers, and other emergency workers often come from all over the country to help out in a major disaster.

DISASTERS AND BLESSINGS

There's no disaster that can't become a blessing, and no blessing that can't become a disaster.

—Richard Bach

As you and your family work through the complex thoughts and feelings that come with the stress of a major disaster, look for signs you or a loved one might need help:

- Trouble concentrating or articulating thoughts
- Trouble sleeping
- Easily frustrated
- Headaches
- Stomach upset

- Colds or flulike symptoms

- Confusion

- Not wanting to leave home

- Feeling depressed, sad, or hopeless

- Mood swings

- Crying easily

- Feeling guilty

- Drinking too much alcohol

- Using illegal drugs

- Trouble at work

- Afraid of being alone

- Afraid of crowds

Luckily, there are several things you can try to help you or your loved ones deal with the stressful feelings that result from disasters. One of the easiest is to talk it out. Share the feelings you're having with someone you trust, and be honest. If you need it, ask for help from professional counselors. You can often get in touch with them by asking at churches or talking to disaster responders.

Spend time with your family. Family and friends help you relax, listen to you, and share their thoughts and perspectives with you. What's more, they're often going through the same experiences. Understanding that you're not alone can be very helpful.

Establish and maintain a routine to help lessen your and your family's stress. Limit your responsibilities each day to a manageable level. Go to work in the morning, and allow yourself to be off at night.

Eat healthfully, and exercise. It sounds like a cliché, but being smart with your activities and diet really makes a difference in how you feel. Don't forget to get plenty of rest and drink plenty of clean water.

ACCOUNTABILITY

Don't hold yourself accountable. Feeling responsible or even frustrated because you can't assist with rescue activities is normal, but try not to feel at fault. You didn't create the disaster, and you're only trying to survive it like everyone else.

Participate in memorials, if they're available. The military often demands that soldiers and sailors participate in memorial services when one of their own is killed. Participating helps put things in perspective and allows you to connect with other survivors.

Dealing with feelings of anxiety or stress related to the disaster is much more likely to be a problem as the reality of the situation sinks in, but the immediate need to make decisions and respond to the crisis wanes. Part of nearly every disaster response around the country includes counseling for the feelings and anxiety that accompany disasters.

Helping Children Cope

Everyone reacts differently to stress, and some people cope better than others. Children are particularly prone to stress, even though they don't always express it the same way adults do.

It doesn't matter if kids are in the disaster, watch it on TV, or just hear their parents or teachers talking about it and develop anxiety from what they've overheard. Kids are often confused about what's happening and whether or not it will happen to them or their families. They can feel afraid or insecure.

Typical Behavior

Children can show different responses to stress. Depending on the age of the child, some behaviors are typical.

Younger children often re-exhibit behaviors they might have had at a younger age but seem to have grown out of, such as bedwetting, disrupted sleep, and separation anxiety. Older children may show behaviors they haven't shown before, such as trouble at school, anger or aggression, or being withdrawn and moody. These behaviors are normal reactions to abnormal events.

However, some kids can develop more severe distress that lasts for longer periods. FEMA pinpoints three major risk factors for this more enduring level of psychological stress. The first is direct exposure to the disaster, such as being evacuated, observing injuries or death of others, or experiencing injury along with fearing one's life is in danger. Loss or grief is another, especially in relation to the death or serious injury of family or friends. The third is ongoing stress from the secondary effects of disaster, such as temporarily living elsewhere, loss of friends and social networks, loss of personal property, parental unemployment, and costs incurred during recovery to return the family to predisaster life and living conditions.

If the child was exposed directly to the disaster rather than watching it on television or hearing about it third-hand, he or she could have recurring stress triggered by reminders of the event, such as sirens, smoke, lightning or thunder, high winds, or debris. Kids with other history of stress or traumatic events besides the disaster incident are even more likely to experience these symptoms.

How Adults Cope Matters

How well parents cope is often directly related to how well kids cope. Children know when adults are scared or upset. They read those clues well and constantly. Parents who maintain their composure during a crisis help their children do the same.

GET THEM INVOLVED

Helping your children participate in the planning process before a disaster can empower them to respond appropriately. After a disaster, kids can assist with developing a recovery plan for the family.

Children mimic the way adults cope with stress. If adults talk it out in a meaningful and open way, children will, too. Adults should encourage kids to talk about how they're feeling. Be sure to listen to the children's fears and alleviate them as much as possible by addressing any misunderstandings. Often, kids think things are more dire than they really are.

Kids know when you're not being straight with them, so it's as important to validate kids' fears when they're warranted as it is to clarify when they're more worried than they should be.

Answer all the questions your kids have, but understand that some kids like more information than others. It's a delicate balance, because a kid who likes to know everything will feel anxious if he or she doesn't have all the information. On the other hand, kids who get by on fewer details might develop some stress by knowing too much. Start small and add details if it seems like they're necessary.

According to FEMA, kids most fear the event happening again, someone close to them being killed or injured, or that they'll be left alone or separated from the family. Not sure how your kids are feeling? Have them draw a picture of what's going on. Often the picture gives you clues as to what's most troubling them.

Helping Your Child

In addition to answering questions and getting your kids involved, here are some more suggestions to help your kids cope with disasters:

- Spend more time with them.

- Hug them. Kids like personal contact.

- Let them in on the plan—calmly.

- Let them know you're there to listen, and encourage them to share their feelings.

- Get back on a routine. We can't emphasize this enough.

- Give your kids work to do to keep them involved.

- Praise good behavior, but don't allow bad. Set boundaries.

- Be patient.

Limit kids' TV time during disasters, especially the news. Repeated images of a disaster might lead them to think it's happening over and over again. The bigger the disaster—or more violent—the worse it is. If the child was involved in the disaster, it can complicate things even more.

If you do allow your children to watch news reports covering the incident, watch with them. Discuss what you see on the screen and how that makes them feel, and alleviate any concerns they might have about the disaster happening again.

If none of this seems to be working, or if your child's stress seems to be getting worse, reach out to a pediatrician or school counselor.

Above all, know that kids are resilient and often recover relatively quickly without any problems.

Dealing with Insurance

Nearly all disaster survivors have stories about insurance claims and the adjusters they deal with. In disaster situations, claims adjusters are often deployed to the area from all over the country to handle the massive influx of claims. They're under strong pressure to handle claims quickly, and mistakes are unavoidable. However, there are things you can do to avoid mistakes on your property.

Make the Call

Especially if you've just lived through it, it might seem obvious a disaster just hit and your insurance company is going to know. But you still need to call and issue a claim if you have damage.

Although there's likely a huge range of destruction and loss around you— some homes and businesses probably are barely touched, while others are completely devastated—it's your job to let your insurance company know you've got a claim. After calling your out-of-town contact to let him or her know you're safe, make one of your next calls to your insurance company.

Document Your Damage

It might take some time for the claims adjuster to get to you, and the insurance company isn't going to be happy with further damage or something that's gotten worse since the disaster. So after you've documented all your damage using Chapter 12's "Worksheet: Evaluating Your Home" and taken lots of evidentiary photographs, cover any holes and try to dry your property as best you can.

REIMBURSEMENTS

Keep track of any repairs you do so you can be reimbursed for those costs. The insurance company expects you to stop the damage from getting worse, but if the claim is covered, it will most likely pay for the repairs.

When things settle down a little, go through your documentation, especially the pictures you took, and write down or clarify all the damage you can find. Be very thorough, and know that nothing is too minor to make note of until the insurance adjuster has an opportunity to go through it. If you can document any damage or cleanup with video, even better.

In Chapter 5, we discussed taking an inventory of your entire home and its contents. This is especially important if your insurance plan covers replacement costs of the contents of your home. If you have that video, sit down with it now, and go frame by frame, room by room to make a list of everything that's now missing or destroyed. If you don't have that video or a list of your home's contents, have the whole family do a walkthrough of your house. Have each person try to remember what was in each room, and make your list that way.

Be Patient

It's unfortunate but true: getting an adjuster to see your home might take a while. With the multitude of other claims after a disaster situation, claims processing seems to move very slowly.

Be patient, and know that in reality, insurance companies often process the claims extremely quickly, but right now they're overwhelmed with the number of claims and can't keep up.

Most policies contain a provision to help with living expenses if you cannot live in your home because of its condition or because the government has ordered you out of it. If this applies to you, be sure to keep receipts for everything: meals, lodging, laundry, etc.

When You Want to Help

If you were lucky enough not to be affected by this particular disaster, you can still help others who were. Maybe your house was spared and others were much more damaged. Maybe you'll just feel better if you could help out your neighbors.

Helping out is a natural reaction to a disaster event. Rather than panicking and adopting an every-man-for-himself attitude, people are much more prone to helping one another in and after a disaster. Volunteerism and heroism are hallmarks of disasters around the world.

You can help in a few ways:

- Donating cash
- Donating goods
- Volunteering

However, there's a right way and a wrong way to do each of these.

Making Donations

Donating cash so others can help those affected by a disaster is the easiest for everyone. Money helps volunteer organizations like the American Red Cross and the United Way fund their response efforts. Plenty of other organizations—both faith based and secular—help, too. However, scams are a serious problem during large-scale disasters.

BEWARE SCAMS

Never donate to an organization that calls you without you reaching out to it first. Even if the organization sounds like something you'd want to support, look it up on your own first and then find a way to donate other than over the phone to the representative who called you. FEMA maintains a list of reputable organizations at ready.gov.

Donating goods is another way to get supplies to folks in disaster areas. However, please don't simply start shipping your extra cans of beef stew to the disaster area. Check with the organization of your choice to find out what types of goods are needed.

If you send unsolicited items to a disaster area, volunteers are pulled from what they're doing to help the response effort to sort and repackage your donations. If it turns out the item isn't needed, the organization has to warehouse it until a later date, which costs money and time.

If you are a business owner with a large supply of one type of item—let's say you're a flashlight manufacturer and you want to donate 1,000 flashlights—call your favorite organization and arrange to have the items shipped to wherever they'll do the most good.

Often, several disasters are occurring at the same time and the organization you're offering to donate goods or cash to is responding to all of them. You can request that your donation be used on a specific disaster incident if you like. But by allowing the charity to handle the finances or donations in whatever way best suits its needs means the supplies or funds are used more efficiently. Anything that increases efficiency leads to more money and supplies making it into the hands of survivors at all disasters.

Volunteering Your Time

Volunteering is the stickiest of all three. There was a time when it was fine to simply hop in the car and head to a disaster scene to help out. Nowadays, it's not so easy.

Volunteer organizations are responsible for ensuring that anyone who comes in contact with vulnerable disaster survivors has been adequately vetted and is safe to be there. Usually, this means the volunteer has gone through some sort of background check and has been fingerprinted.

Depending on the disaster and the organization, volunteers might also have to be given vaccinations and be fitted for personal protective gear.

There are ways to volunteer, even in last-minute situations after a disaster has occurred. Last-minute volunteers might not get to work directly with disaster survivors, but you can still help. Contact one of the volunteer disaster response organizations if you're interested. These organizations have fast-track processing when disasters are big enough and high numbers of volunteers are needed.

One of the most useful ways to volunteer is to join a Community Emergency Response Team (CERT) in your area. As a CERT member, you participate in training and become part of the deployment plan for disasters. CERT teams are sometimes used outside their immediate area when neighboring communities need help.

The most important thing to remember about volunteering is not to self-deploy. If you find yourself in an area and want to help, move out of the way. Believe it or not, that's the best way to assist during complicated responses like those in the midst of a disaster.

22

Navigating the Red Tape

When Lesley Smiley arrived in Dallas, her friend from Oklahoma City and his sister, who lived in Dallas, were waiting for her. They offered her the option of going home with them or checking into a hotel. Grateful for the choice, Lesley opted for the hotel. Considering she had just lived in filth for nearly a week with no air-conditioning or showers, she felt the need to take the longest shower in the history of mankind.

Also staying in Lesley's Dallas hotel were FEMA staff, in town to work in Disaster Recovery Centers (DRC) processing Katrina evacuees through the Individual Assistance Program. They helped Lesley get set up to receive assistance in relocating. In addition to an initial payout of several thousand dollars, Lesley received help getting new eyeglasses, food stamps, rental assistance while she looked for a job, and a $300 voucher for a new work wardrobe from Walmart. In her mid-50s, Lesley was starting her life over.

During the week following the Joplin tornado, Jim Lane attended six funerals. Unable to stay at his own home, he rented a room from a friend whose house was still intact. It took some time, but his homeowners insurance paid out, and he eventually bought a new home, a lovely ranch-style house. He can often be found there, hosting his many friends who picked him up, and for whom he was there to provide support. Jim and his friends formed a sort of survivor's club, sharing memories and bonds forged by their losses of property, loved ones, and way of life.

For 4 days, Debi Gade and her family slept in the second-floor master bedroom of their Long Beach home. During that time, they were fed by Red Cross crews and other agencies who came by to check on them and be sure everyone had food. They also brought other much-needed items for which Debi and her family were grateful: winter coats, shovels, bleach, and socks. And more food. "Some people were barbecuing in parking lots," Debi recalls. "Everybody was helping everybody. It was a beautiful thing."

Debi's home had been in her husband's family for four generations, and at the time of Sandy, Debi and her family had lived in it for more than 20 years. Even though they were family, Debi and her husband were not on the deed. His parents in Florida were the owners, so they applied for hazard mitigation funds to elevate and flood-proof the home as they rebuilt. As a result, FEMA considered Debi and her family renters and provided rental assistance, which helped them get into a townhouse. They had no furniture, but they were all together in a house that had electricity, heat, and a clean slate upon which they could build new memories.

After the Disaster Comes Recovery

When a community is broken, it takes the efforts of everyone to arrive at a place that even remotely resembles normal. But that's the goal—to restore the community and everyone in it to normal.

The disaster declaration process and FEMA's role in providing disaster assistance is widely misunderstood. In this chapter, we examine FEMA's role in providing federal assistance programs and how you can access them after a disaster. We also look at what help is offered by nongovernmental organizations such as the Red Cross and other nonprofits.

AT YOUR FINGERTIPS

Use the "Worksheet: Postdisaster Assistance Checklist" at the end of this chapter to organize the necessary recovery numbers and addresses you need after a disaster so they're at your fingertips when you need them.

Government Programs

Whether a small town, a large city, or a county/parish, a community's resources are finite. They can be very quickly consumed in what can be an unimaginably expensive recovery process. When a community has gone through its resources, or sees that it won't have the necessary resources to fully recover after a disaster, it asks the state for help.

The state may be facing similar requests for assistance from many other communities ravaged by the same event. Knowing that the scope of assistance required is beyond its capacity, the state requests a presidential disaster declaration so it can receive government resources. That's where FEMA comes in.

FEMA

When the president declares an area a disaster, FEMA can begin to step into those areas with several federal disaster assistance programs, including the Hazard Mitigation Grant Program (HMGP), Public Assistance (PA), and Individual Assistance (IA).

HMGP and PA are grant programs designed to help local and state governments repair critical facilities such as utilities, hospitals, government buildings, and infrastructure. HMGP funds specifically help communities rebuild smarter and stronger, in a way that's more resistant to future damages in a similar disaster. In this chapter, we focus on Individual Assistance because that is the program you and your family will interact with the most after a presidentially declared disaster.

Presidential disaster declarations are made based on a combination of factors used to determine a disaster's magnitude and impact. One major factor is whether the state and communities have the resources required to meet the needs of your family and many, many others.

Not all requests for a presidential declaration are signed. It's possible that your community might be declared a disaster and eligible for Public Assistance funds but not eligible for Individual Assistance funds. The state has the option to appeal, but it's important to realize that your community might not receive federal disaster aid. In that case, you'll have to rely on other alternatives.

RECOMMENDATION FACTORS

FEMA considers several factors when putting together a recommendation for a presidential disaster declaration, including the amount and type of damage (number of homes destroyed or with major damage), the impact on the infrastructure of affected areas or critical facilities, any imminent threats to public health and safety, any impacts to essential government services and functions, the unique capability of the federal government, the dispersion or concentration of damage, the level of insurance coverage in place for homeowners and public facilities, any assistance available from other sources (federal, state, local, voluntary organizations), any state and local resource commitments from previous undeclared events, and the frequency of disaster events over a recent time period.

Sometimes, counties and parishes are immediately designated as disaster areas, but because it takes time to evaluate the extent of the damage, other counties and parishes may be added later. So although your area might not be immediately designated a disaster, that doesn't mean it won't be at some point.

When your state has requested and received a presidential disaster declaration, Disaster Recovery Centers (DRCs) are immediately established in multiple locations throughout your area. The DRC is where you go to register and apply for assistance through the federal Individual Assistance program.

To find out where your local DRC is, or to apply for assistance by phone, call 800-621-FEMA (800-621-3362). You also can register online by web-enabled mobile device at m.fema.gov. If you have computer access, log on to disasterassistance.gov. If you don't have phone or computer access, look for FEMA's Community Relations teams. These groups fan out throughout an impacted community, search for people who need help, and offer them the information they need to apply for assistance.

Individual Assistance includes the following:

- Mass Care and Emergency Assistance
- Individuals and Households Program
- Small Business Administration (SBA) loans
- Disaster Unemployment Assistance
- Disaster Legal Services
- Crisis Counseling Assistance

To ensure you're able to take advantage of the assistance available after a declared disaster where Individual Assistance has been approved, let's look at what's offered under the Individual Assistance Program.

Mass Care and Emergency Assistance

For an area to receive a presidential disaster declaration that includes Individual Assistance, the damage would have to be widespread and severe and too great for the resources of the community and the state. Many families, perhaps yours included, will be in great need.

This is where FEMA's Mass Care and Emergency Assistance Program kicks in. Designed to provide life-sustaining resources, the program offers food, shelter, emergency supplies, emergency first aid, care for household pets, disaster welfare, evacuation support, and family reunification assistance.

Individuals and Households Program

The goal of the Individuals and Households Program (IHP) is to help you and your family into a permanent home while also assisting with your other immediate needs. The IHP is divided into two groups: Housing Assistance and Other Needs Assistance. These groups most commonly help disaster survivors with home repair, rental assistance, and replacement of essential personal property.

AVAILABLE TO EVERYONE

Housing Assistance doesn't depend on your income; it's available to everyone, regardless of economic status. Disasters can be amazing equalizers.

When you register with FEMA and complete a disaster assistance application, you'll be asked if your home was damaged. If it was, FEMA will send an inspector to your home to assess it and determine if it's inhabitable—if it's safe and if it's clean. If not, and if you're uninsured, the application moves forward. You may be eligible for repairs, rental assistance, or lodging expense reimbursement.

If you have insurance, you go first through your insurance. If your insurance doesn't cover all or a portion of the damage, you have to be able to prove that with documentation of your insurance settlement or denial in order to qualify for housing assistance since of course FEMA is not going to pay out for something your insurance covers. For example, if your insurance is going to cover your roof repairs, FEMA is not going to provide money to repair the same roof.

If your insurance coverage is delayed, it is possible that FEMA may provide advance assistance which may or may not need to be repaid depending on whether the insurance provides full or just partial coverage.

Other Needs Assistance comes in two forms, Non-SBA Dependent and SBA-Dependent. Non-SBA Dependent Assistance includes medical, dental, funeral, and other costs. You won't need to fill out an SBA loan packet to get this kind of assistance, but you might have to provide proof that the expenses are disaster related. "Other costs" include miscellaneous eligible items purchased because of the disaster, such as a chainsaw used to clear out trees blocking access to your house.

SBA-Dependent Assistance includes personal property, transportation, and moving or storage. If you're denied an SBA loan or only receive a partial amount of the requested loan, FEMA is notified and you are referred to Other Needs Assistance.

The Small Business Administration

Whereas the IHP covers immediate needs and helps those who lost their homes get into a permanent housing solution, the SBA offers assistance in the form of low-interest loans homeowners and renters can use to replace or repair uninsured property damaged by the disaster.

The SBA offers home (real property) and personal property loans that include up to $200,000 for repair or replacement of real estate, up to $40,000 for repair or replacement of personal property, and an additional 20 percent of the eligible loan amount for mitigation. Business, physical, and economic disaster loans include up to $2 million for physical damage repair to businesses, economic injury disaster loans, and an additional 20 percent for mitigation.

When you register for FEMA Disaster Assistance, you'll be asked to report your annual income. Depending on the amount of income reported, you may be referred to the SBA, which automatically sends you a packet to fill out. If you need help repairing or replacing personal property, complete the SBA application. If that application is turned down, FEMA forwards it to Other Needs Assistance for consideration.

It's possible that you might receive a larger amount of assistance through the SBA loans than through grant awards.

REPAYMENT REQUIRED

Remember, unlike other federal disaster assistance, SBA loans must be repaid.

Disaster Unemployment Assistance

Depending on which study you read, somewhere between 25 and 40 percent of businesses that close their doors after a disaster never reopen. That means all the people who staffed those businesses are left without a job as a result of the disaster. Disaster Unemployment Assistance (DUA) is funded by FEMA, through the U.S. Department of Labor, and is administered by your state's unemployment agency.

To be eligible for DUA, you must have lost your job as a direct result of the disaster, and you must be ineligible for regular unemployment benefits. You also might be eligible for DUA funds if you're self-employed, own a farm or ranch, work on a farm, or are otherwise not eligible for regular unemployment.

If you suddenly become the head of your household due to the loss of your spouse in the disaster, you are eligible for DUA coverage. Naturally, that will be the last thing you'll be thinking about in such sad and tragic circumstances, but it's information you will need, nonetheless.

To find out how you can access your DUA benefits, contact someone at your state unemployment agency. He or she can walk you through the process.

The Crisis Counseling Program

Lesley, Debi, and Jim have all had to grapple with post-traumatic stress disorder (PTSD).

Lesley couldn't be in large crowds for months after moving to Oklahoma.

Debi couldn't socialize at all and could only be comfortable with people who had gone through the same thing she went through or those who had come to help. She separated people into those who got it and those who didn't get it. "And if you didn't get it, I had no use for you."

The loss of Jim's Joplin home was nothing compared to the unexpected accident that took his daughter Mandy only weeks after the tornado. Already exhausted, fatigued, frustrated, and confused about where to live, this sudden loss sent him off the deep end. Jim's happy-go-lucky nature failed him in the face of such a terrible personal tragedy, and for a brief time, he found himself self-medicating at a local bar.

PTSD can show itself in a variety of ways. As a survivor, you might not realize for quite some time the toll the disaster has taken on you physically, mentally, and emotionally. If you've suffered any kind of loss in a disaster, you might well be in need of counseling.

The Crisis Counseling Program (CCP) is available to help you and your family recover from the impacts of the disaster through individual and group crisis counseling. It's funded through the state, using FEMA grant money.

Two counseling programs are available. The Immediate Services Program provides funds for up to 60 days of services immediately following a disaster declaration. The Regular Services Program provides funds for up to 9 months of services following a disaster declaration.

Getting counseling is not a sign of weakness. Many people see it as a matter of pride to get through traumatic events without counseling. That's an unnecessary signpost. People who have experienced a traumatic event sometimes just need to tell their story. The simple act of talking about what you've been through helps you process what's happened to you and come to terms with it so you can heal and move forward in your life. That's nothing to be ashamed about.

If you'd like more information on CCP, ask your FEMA application representative for a referral in your area.

Disaster Legal Services

It seems unfair, like you're being kicked when you're down, but too often it's true: disasters often beget more disasters. Perhaps you're struggling with a landlord who refuses to waive your lease, even though the house you're renting isn't safe to live in. Or perhaps you were fired from your job because you couldn't get to work due to the destruction of your car or damaged roads and bridges.

Disaster Legal Services (DLS) offers free legal assistance for low-income disaster survivors on issues such as insurance claims, landlord-tenant disputes, power of attorney setup, and home repair contracts. You can access this assistance through your DRC. Often a hotline will be set up. Your DRC should have more information.

WHAT DLS WON'T DO

If you feel you need to sue someone or take them to court to recover money you feel they owe you, you'll need to find another resource for legal representation. Disaster Legal Services can't be used for lawsuits.

FEMA won't duplicate insurance benefits. So when applying for federal disaster assistance, you're required to submit documentation of your insurance settlement or denial.

If you only received partial or no insurance coverage, your application will go forward. If you received full coverage from your insurance company, you might not receive any federal assistance for the insured item.

State Disaster Assistance Programs

Your community has experienced a disaster, and your state's governor has declared many counties, including yours, disaster areas. However, as is often the case, your county didn't meet the criteria required for a *presidential* disaster declaration, meaning no federal assistance is available. Or maybe your county met the criteria for a presidential disaster declaration where Public Assistance was approved but Individual Assistance wasn't. Because one of the criteria for federal disaster assistance is the state's inability to provide the necessary resources, it may be that the federal government considers the state able to meet the needs for disaster assistance, even if the state says otherwise.

Whatever the reason, you're not eligible for federal disaster assistance.

Each state is a little different in what kind of disaster assistance it provides and how that help is accessed.

Ohio, for example, offers a State Individual Assistance program for "disaster-related unmet needs to individuals and families that have uninsured essential private property damages or losses." Part of Ohio's criteria is that the disaster must be declared by local government, the governor, and the U.S. Small Business Administration, but not by the president or the federal government. According to Ohio's website, the program exists to fill a gap for those who have serious and essential unmet needs or losses not addressed by anyone else, including insurance, government, and nongovernmental organizations. The state requires that the applicant first be denied a loan from the SBA before he or she can register for the state assistance program.

The Iowa Individual Assistance Program is slightly different. It's activated at the request of local officials after a governor's disaster proclamation is issued. It provides up to $5,000 in damage reimbursements for families whose income is at or below twice the federal poverty level. If a presidential disaster declaration for Individual Assistance is issued for the same event, the state program is automatically canceled.

If no federal disaster has been declared, how the state approaches Individual Assistance can vary. As part of your emergency preparedness plan, find out from your state's emergency management agency how it approaches Individual Assistance in this case.

Nongovernmental Organizations

Volunteer organizations such as the American Red Cross, the Salvation Army, and charities tied to a variety of church denominations are often the first on the scene to offer assistance and the last to leave the disaster area. They also often catch applicants who fall through the cracks of federal and state disaster assistance.

Many organizations offer assistance after a disaster. Some are well-established organizations, and others may be small local churches that offer home-cooked meals and little else to displaced persons. But the goal of each is helping survivors in whatever way they can. It's good to understand what some of these organizations offer and how they can help you and your family after a disaster.

FEMA works with many of these voluntary agencies and even helps coordinate their assistance. Volunteer agencies work together at the state and federal level through Voluntary Organizations Active in Disaster (VOAD).

The American Red Cross

With more than 650 chapters throughout the country and volunteers in 187 countries around the world, the American Red Cross (redcross.org) is the largest and probably most well-established nongovernmental organization. Each year, the American Red Cross responds to more than 70,000 natural and man-made disasters to provide humanitarian relief in the form of food, water, shelter, health services, emotional health services, and other immediate needs. The organization also provides food for responders, engages in family reunification efforts, and provides blood to injured disaster survivors.

After catastrophic events such as the Moore, Oklahoma, tornadoes on May 20, 2013, the Red Cross may work with other relief organizations. In Oklahoma, for example, it combined efforts in Multi-Agency Resource Centers (MARC).

If you and your family have been devastated by a hurricane or earthquake, you might visit a MARC, where you can load up on supplies such as personal hygiene items, diapers, rakes, shovels, gloves, and much more. You might talk to caseworkers from the Red Cross, the United Way, and the Salvation Army. MARCs offer insurance representatives and internet cafés where you can go online to let friends and family know where you are, as well as to fill out your insurance claims.

If you have access to a computer, you can go to the Red Cross Safe and Well site at safeandwell.communityos.org to either list yourself as safe and well or to inquire about loved ones who might have listed themselves. The Safe and Well listings are available 24 hours a day, 365 days a year.

Churches and Charities

Churches and other faith-based charities may offer a narrow or wide range of services, depending on their size and resources. Faith-based organizations may include spiritual services as well as provide for basic needs. There are too many to list them all here, but let's review a few of the more well-established organizations.

These and other faith-based organizations all work together at the state and national level through VOAD.

HELPING HAND

The impersonal hand of government can never replace the helping hand of a neighbor.

—Hubert H. Humphrey

The Salvation Army

Like the Red Cross, the Salvation Army (salvationarmyusa.org) responds to multiple types of disasters and offers relief to responders as well as disaster survivors. It delivers food and drink to disaster survivors as well as emergency responders through both mobile units and nonmobile sites and also may provide shelter either through one of its own sites or through a site owned by your community. (Your local emergency management agency will have information on activated shelter locations.)

In addition, the Salvation Army distributes cleaning tools such as mops, brooms, shovels, buckets, and tarps, and it also provides volunteers to help with cleanup efforts.

In a situation where normal communications are down, the Salvation Army Team Emergency Radio Network (SATERN) provides trained amateur radio operators who work in a network to relay critical information about the disaster and help reunify separated family members.

The Salvation Army also provides help with long-term recovery needs such as restoration and rebuilding, as well as direct financial assistance for immediate needs and disaster-related medical or funeral expenses.

Mennonite Disaster Service

The main focus of the Mennonite Disaster Service (MDS; mds.mennonite. net) is disaster cleanup and repairing and rebuilding homes while touching lives and nurturing hope, faith, and wholeness. The MDS network is divided into five response regions—four in the United States and one in Canada.

Catholic Charities USA

Catholic Charities (catholiccharitiesusa.org) have many offices throughout the United States and serve more than 10 million people every year. The Disaster Response Office addresses both immediate and long-term recovery needs after a disaster. Its mission is to "assist families in developing and implementing a recovery plan to help stabilize their household and achieve economic self-sufficiency."

You don't have to be Catholic to take advantage of the CC's services offered—funds for food, shelter, clothing, and other necessities; vouchers for financial assistance; and counseling, outreach, and referrals. Its services are provided "regardless of religion, race, creed, or socio-economic status."

Southern Baptist Disaster Relief

Southern Baptist Disaster Relief (baptistrelief.org) includes food, water purification, childcare, communication services, shower facilities, laundry facilities, disaster area cleanup, chainsaw and mud-out help, repair/rebuild help, and power generation. Additionally, in some states, the Southern Baptist Disaster

Relief organization includes the Medical Reserve Corps as part of its team. Members of this group must undergo rigorous disaster clinic training, pass a thorough background check, and provide current licensing and certification.

With 82,000 trained volunteers and 1,550 mobile relief units, Southern Baptist Disaster Relief is one of the largest groups of trained disaster relief volunteers in the United States.

Brethren Disaster Ministries

The Church of the Brethren's Brethren Disaster Ministries (brethren.org/bdm) focuses on rebuilding homes, caring for children, and providing volunteers to serve communities impacted by disasters. Its volunteers repair and rebuild damaged homes for disaster survivors who can't afford to hire a contractor.

Its temporary child-care centers use therapeutic activities and toys to stimulate imaginative play and minister to each child's unique emotional needs.

"Such Amazing People"

Debi Gade's Long Beach home remained without water and power for days. Debi and her family had no way to prepare meals, yet they had no shortage of food and water.

"The American Red Cross came by three times a day," Debi remembers. "We had trucks coming in from everywhere to provide food. We had a truck here from Minnesota, a truck from Arizona. They fed us three times a day.

"And then there were the Knights of Columbus," she continued. "They became kind of a central hub where people who wanted to donate food would come. My daughter and I would go there to eat. Some people were barbecuing in the parking lots and everybody was feeding everybody. If you were hungry, and they brought food, they would give it to you.

"I have to say it was the worst time of my life," Debi says. "Yet I saw such hope, such amazing people. It just makes me cry when I think about how people were to us. I can't say enough about the volunteers and the people who came to help us."

Worksheet: Postdisaster Assistance Checklist

Keep the information in this worksheet in your disaster kit so these helpful numbers and addresses are at your fingertips when you need them most.

❑ Apply for individual assistance:

By phone: 800-621-FEMA (800-621-3362)

By web-enabled mobile device: m.fema.gov

Online: disasterassistance.gov

At your local Disaster Recovery Center (DRC): call 800-621-FEMA (800-621-3362) or visit disasterassistance.gov to find your nearest DRC

❑ Call your state emergency management agency (it might also be called the Office of Emergency Services) to find out what kind of disaster assistance it provides.

A

Glossary

adaptability   A person's ability to change to fit his or her altered circumstances.

airway obstruction   A blockage in the throat that interrupts airflow in and out of the lungs. Also known as choking.

anaphylaxis   A potentially life-threatening allergic reaction that affects more than one body system.

biomass fuel   Organic material you can burn to create heat. Examples include small bits of wood, leaves, and pinecones.

black ice   Ice so thin it's completely transparent, allowing the black asphalt underneath to be visible through it.

carbon monoxide poisoning   Exposure to carbon monoxide, a colorless, odorless gas that binds to red blood cells and displaces oxygen. Carbon monoxide poisoning is potentially fatal and common in disaster situations due to undetected gas leaks or misuse of outdoor cooking and heating devices in poorly ventilated areas.

cardiac arrest   When the heart stops pumping blood. Breathing stops shortly after.

catastrophe   An event causing great and often sudden damage or suffering.

Centers for Disease Control and Prevention (CDC)   The U.S. government agency tasked with identifying and preventing the most common causes of injury and illness.

claims adjuster   An insurance company representative in charge of assessing damage and processing insurance claims.

Clinton Global Initiative   An initiative of former President Bill Clinton's Clinton Foundation that convenes global leaders to create and implement innovative solutions to the world's most pressing challenges.

Community Emergency Response Team (CERT)   People trained in disaster preparedness for hazards that may impact their area. CERT members learn basic disaster response skills, such as fire safety, light search and rescue, team organization, and disaster medical operations. Using a combination of theory learned in the classroom and practical hands-on training in exercises and drills, CERT members can assist others in their neighborhood or workplace following an event when professional responders aren't immediately available to help. CERT members also are encouraged to support emergency response agencies by taking a more active role in emergency preparedness projects in their community.

Community Ratings System (CRS)   A voluntary incentive program of the National Flood Insurance Program (NFIP) that recognizes and encourages community floodplain management activities beyond the minimum NFIP requirements. As a result, flood insurance premium rates are discounted to reflect the reduced flood risk resulting from the community actions when they meet the three goals of the CRS: reduce flood damage to insurable property, strengthen and support the insurance aspects of the NFIP, and encourage a comprehensive approach to floodplain management.

concussion   A mild brain injury, often resulting in a sudden, brief loss of consciousness.

constipation   The inability to have a bowel movement.

contamination   The unintended or accidental introduction of infectious material like bacteria, yeast, mould, fungi, virus, prions, protozoa, or their toxins and by-products into food, water, or other resources.

contraflow   An alteration of the normal flow of traffic.

debris   Loose wreckage and sometimes garbage that's often spread around after a disaster strikes. Debris can be hazardous from contamination or have sharp edges.

dehydration   The inadequate intake of fluid. Dehydration can cause loss of consciousness, dizziness, seizures, and even death.

disaster   A sudden event, such as a natural catastrophe, an accident, or an act of man-made destruction that causes great damage or loss of life.

Disaster Recovery Center (DRC)   A readily accessible facility or mobile office where applicants may go for information about FEMA or other disaster assistance programs.

dislocation   When one bone that makes up a joint moves from where it's supposed to be; common in shoulders.

drill   A task or exercise for teaching a skill or procedure by repetition.

dynamo   An electricity generator.

electromagnetic pulse   An intense pulse of electromagnetic radiation, especially one generated by a nuclear explosion and occurring high above the earth's surface.

emergency   As defined in the Stafford Act, any occasion or instance for which, in the determination of the president, federal assistance is needed to supplement state and local efforts and capabilities to save lives and to protect property, public health, and safety.

emergency preparedness kit   A collection of basic items you and your family could need in the event of a disaster.

Enhanced Fujita scale   Abbreviated as the EF-scale; a set of wind estimates, not measurements, based on damage. (It was called the Fujita scale until 2007.)

evacuate   To leave a place of danger and go to a safe place.

exercise   A maneuver, an operation, or a drill carried out for training and discipline; something performed or practiced to develop, improve, or display a specific capability or skill.

family preparedness plan   A plan for how your family will get to a safe place in an emergency. In it, you've noted how you'll communicate, reunify, and respond in different disaster situations.

Federal Emergency Management Agency (FEMA)   The U.S. government agency responsible for mitigation, preparedness, and coordinating response and recovery for federally declared disasters.

fever   An increased body temperature usually occurring as a result of an infection or immune response.

first responder   A person whose job entails being the first on the scene of an emergency; EMTs, firefighters, and police are some first responders.

floodplain   Any land area susceptible to being inundated by flood waters from any source.

flood-proofing   Any combination of structural and nonstructural additions, changes, or adjustments made to structures that reduce or eliminate risk of flood damage to real estate or improved real property, water and sanitation facilities, or structures with their contents.

food poisoning   The common term for foodborne illness; a contamination of food with some sort of organism that can cause medical symptoms. Food poisoning can be mild or severe enough to become debilitating.

fracture   A broken bone. Fractures can be anything from a mild crack to shattered bone.

frostbite   Frozen skin and other body tissues resulting from cold exposure. Frostbite leads to pain and loss of function.

Fujita scale   *See* Enhanced Fujita scale.

hazard   A possible source of danger.

heat cramp   A muscle spasm related to dehydration or electrolyte imbalance, often brought on when the body is too hot.

heat exhaustion   The body's response to being overheated. Can include fatigue, dizziness, confusion, and dehydration.

heat illness   A group of conditions related to the body getting too hot. *See also* heat exhaustion; heat stroke; heat cramp; hyperthermia.

heat stroke   A potentially fatal condition caused by severe overheating and dehydration. Heat stroke causes unconsciousness and possibly seizures.

heart attack   Death of the heart muscle, usually from a blockage in the blood vessel that feeds blood to the heart muscle.

hurricane   A tropical storm with winds that have reached a constant speed of 74 miles per hour or more. The eye, or center, of a hurricane is usually 20 to 30 miles wide and may extend more than 400 miles. Hurricanes produce torrential rains, high winds, and storm surges; can last for 2 weeks or more over open water; and can run a path across the entire length of the Eastern Seaboard.

hurricane category system   The generic wording for the Saffir-Simpson Hurricane Wind Scale, a 1 to 5 rating system based on a hurricane's sustained wind speed that estimates potential property damage. Hurricanes reaching Category 3 and higher are considered major hurricanes because of their potential for significant loss of life and damage. Category 1 and 2 storms are still dangerous, however, and require preventative measures. In the western North Pacific, the term *super typhoon* is used for tropical cyclones with sustained winds exceeding 150 miles per hour.

hyperglycemia   High blood sugar level, found in untreated or uncontrolled diabetic patients.

hyperthermia   Abnormally high body temperature, usually resulting from infection, medication, or head injury.

hypoglycemia   Low blood sugar level, often caused by taking too much diabetic medication or when diabetic patients do not eat an adequate amount of food.

hypothermia   A potentially fatal condition that occurs when the body temperature falls below 95°F (35°C).

Individual Assistance program   Financial or direct assistance provided to individuals and families whose property has been damaged or destroyed as a result of a federally declared disaster and whose losses are not covered by insurance. Individual Assistance helps with critical expenses that cannot be covered in other ways. It's not intended to restore damaged property to its predisaster condition.

insurance claim   A request for reimbursement filed with an insurance company under an active policy.

Incident Command Structure (ICS)   A command-and-control framework developed for wildfire management and now used by responders for incidents involving all hazards.

looting   Stealing property during a state of emergency or crisis.

mandatory evacuation   A lawful order issued by authorities to evacuate ahead of an approaching disaster. Residents are compelled to comply or risk being stranded without emergency or other services.

martial law   A broad term loosely defined as using military resources for all sorts of law enforcement activities, especially after a disaster.

mitigation   The action of reducing the severity, seriousness, or painfulness of something.

National Flood Insurance Program (NFIP)   A U.S. government program Congress created in 1968 to help provide a means for property owners to financially protect themselves. The NFIP offers flood insurance to homeowners, renters, and business owners in participating communities that agree to adopt and enforce ordinances that meet or exceed FEMA requirements to reduce the risk of flooding.

National Incident Management System (NIMS)   A command structure used by responders and agencies during federally declared disasters. *See also* Incident Command Structure (ICS).

National Oceanic and Atmospheric Administration (NOAA)   The U.S. government agency focused on the conditions of the oceans and the atmosphere. It's mission is to understand and predict changes in climate, weather, oceans, and coasts.

potable fluid   Water and other fluids that are safe to consume.

preparedness   A state of readiness.

presidentially declared disaster   A presidential disaster declaration puts into motion long-term federal recovery programs, some of which are matched by state programs and designed to help disaster victims, businesses, and public entities.

Public Assistance program   Provides assistance to state and local governments, tribal governments, and certain types of private nonprofit organizations so communities can quickly respond to and recover from major disasters or presidentially declared emergencies.

recovery   A return to a state of normal.

resilience   The ability to anticipate, sustain, and recover from different kinds of shocks. Also the ability to recover readily from illness, depression, adversity, etc.

response   A reply or reaction.

restoration company   A company that provides property restoration services after a structure suffers damage from fire, water, or wind.

reunification   The act of coming together again, such as the bringing together of family members after a disaster in which they might have been separated.

RICE   The acronym for *rest, ice, compression*, and *elevation*, a treatment for sprains and strains.

risk   A person or thing that's a specified hazard.

rocket stove   A tall, double-walled, very-low-tech cooking device that uses heat to create a draft and push the superheated air toward the food.

safe room   A hardened room within another structure intended to provide a safe place of refuge.

separation anxiety   The fear of being isolated from parents or authority figures. Separation anxiety is more common in children and pets.

shelter in place   During a natural disaster, this means staying inside the building you're in at the time of the emergency or, if you're outside, going into an undamaged building nearby and staying there until it's safe to leave. In the case of a chemical threat, this means to take immediate shelter where you are—at home, work, school, or wherever. It may also mean to seal the room, or take steps to prevent outside air from coming in, as in the case of chemical or radiological contaminants.

shortness of breath   Difficulty breathing caused by a variety of diseases and injuries. Shortness of breath often interferes with a person's ability to speak full sentences without having to pause for a breath.

sloughing skin   Skin that's coming off in layers and weeping fluid, often the result of burns. The smallest sloughing looks similar to blisters; in large partial-thickness burns, the sloughing sometimes comes in large sheets.

space blankets   Reflective blankets, usually made of Mylar, that redirect heat to the person using them.

sprain   A stretched ligament or tendon—the connective tissue that holds together joints like the elbow and hip. Sprains can be minor or severe.

storm shelter   A basement, cellar, or underground chamber for refuge during violent storms.

strain   An injured muscle. Also known as a pulled muscle.

stroke   A blockage in the arteries of the brain or bleeding in the brain caused by a broken vein.

superstorm   A subjective term for any storm that's extremely and unusually destructive.

Tornado Alley   Refers to a zone in the Great Plains region of the central United States, often a north-south-oriented region centered on north Texas, Oklahoma, Kansas, and Nebraska, where tornadoes are most frequent.

tornado warning   A notification that indicates a tornado is either occurring or is imminent based on radar. Take cover immediately.

tornado watch   A notification that indicates conditions are favorable for severe thunderstorms capable of producing a tornado.

tourniquet   A constricting band tied around an arm or leg to stop bleeding.

tropical storm   A localized, very intense low-pressure wind system that forms over tropical oceans and with hurricane-force winds.

tsunami   A large, often destructive sea wave produced by an earthquake, a subsidence, or a volcanic eruption under the water. It's sometimes incorrectly called a tidal wave.

Turn Around Don't Drown   A NOAA National Weather Service campaign to warn people of the hazards of walking or driving a vehicle through flood waters.

vertical evacuation   To move to a higher floor or ground, to get as far above sea level as possible, or to go as far inland and upward as possible, as quickly as possible.

vertigo   A sustained feeling of dizziness.

voluntary evacuation   An advisory by authorities to evacuate ahead of an approaching disaster. Residents are not required to comply.

B

Resources

To learn more about preparing yourself and your family for natural disasters and other hazards, we've compiled the following list of further resources you might want to check out.

Websites

Many websites offer information on disaster preparedness and mitigation. Look to these resources to help you plan for emergencies or any type of hazard:

American Red Cross
redcross.org/prepare

FEMA
ready.gov/make-a-plan

Public Health Emergency
phe.gov/preparedness

Different types of disasters require different types of preparedness. Plus it really helps to understand what to expect during the disasters most likely to occur in your area. The following websites provide specific help for the most common emergencies:

Earthquakes:

San Francisco Department of Emergency Management
72hours.org

County of Los Angeles Fire Department
fire.lacounty.gov/safetypreparedness/safetyprepearthquake.asp

Floods:

CDC
emergency.cdc.gov/disasters/floods/readiness.asp

Just in Case Arizona
justincasearizona.com/be-informed/natural-disasters/flash-flood.asp

Hurricanes:

National Hurricane Center
nhc.noaa.gov/prepare/ready.php

State of Florida
stateofflorida.com/articles/hurricane-preparedness-guide.aspx

Print

In addition to the information in this book, the following books and articles might be of interest to you:

American College of Emergency Physicians First Aid Manual, 4th Edition. New York: DK Publishing, 2011.

Leach, John. "Why People Freeze in an Emergency: Temporal and Cognitive Constraints on Survival Responses." *Aviation, Space and Environmental Medicine.* June 2004. 539–542.

National Rural Health Association. "Recruitment and Retention of a Quality Health Workforce in Rural Areas." Issue paper no. 13, November 2005.

Ripley, Amanda. "How to Get Out Alive." *Time.* April 25, 2005.

———. *The Unthinkable: Who Survives When Disaster Strikes—and Why.* New York: Random House, 2008.

Witt, James Lee, and James Morgan. *Stronger in the Broken Places: Nine Lessons for Turning Crisis into Triumph.* New York: Times Books, 2002.

Index

I–J

T